JAMIE PEACOCK
NO WHITE FLAG

JAMIE PEACOCK
NO WHITE FLAG

WITH **PHIL CAPLAN**

For Faye and Lewis – supporters supreme

First published 2008

STADIA is an imprint of
The History Press Ltd
Cirencester Road, Chalford
Stroud, Gloucestershire, GL6 8PE
www.thehistorypress.co.uk

ISBN 978 0 7524 4612 7

Typesetting and origination by The History Press Ltd
Printed and bound in Great Britain

CONTENTS

	Foreword by Richard Lewis	7
	Acknowledgements and Dedication	9
ONE:	It's Not All Fairytales	11
TWO:	No Pretensions Or Expectations	21
THREE:	Via Wollongong and Featherstone	29
FOUR:	The Bull Begins to Rage	37
FIVE:	On Firmer Footing	49
SIX:	Dirt Tracker to Rolls-Royce	67
SEVEN:	At Last the Aussies	77
EIGHT:	World Champ and in the Depths	103
NINE:	Hand of Fate	123
TEN:	The Best Teams Won	145
ELEVEN:	'Unbreakabull', 'Formidabull', Sensational	165
TWELVE:	Frustration at Home	189
THIRTEEN:	Compensation Abroad	203
FOURTEEN:	Confounding the Doubters	219
FIFTEEN:	A Fitting Climax	243
SIXTEEN:	No End in Sight	251
	Career Statistics	255

'The desire in the boy is phenomenal – he wants to get better. He asks questions, works very hard and will continue to improve. Five years ago, when he came to the club, he couldn't catch a ball.'

– Bradford coach Brian Noble at the end of the 2001 season
as the Bulls take the Super League crown

'I remember sitting on a hillside at Siddal watching his game and thinking: "I don't know how we are going to make a player out of this guy." But he had something and he has made himself a player. He is very determined and very ambitious; he loves a challenge. Nobody will say a bad word about him to me. He's a terrific bloke and a terrific player.'

– Brian Noble's assessment as Jamie Peacock
prepares to leave Bradford in 2005

'He's been enormous for us pretty much all year, the backbone in many ways. On and off the field he has a big influence in the dressing room. We have some great leaders and he is one of them. He can look knackered for long periods of time and still go out and be effective, he's got that ability. You think he's absolutely gone and he gets up swinging. You can't take into account his body language too much; I've learnt that over time.'

– Leeds coach Tony Smith, now the Great Britain supremo,
as the Rhinos qualify for the 2007 Grand Final

'To do what he does for eighty minutes is unbelievable; if ever a player epitomises being a "Man of Steel" it is him. He is massive for us. Every time we need someone to take the ball up, he is there. It can't help but be inspirational.'

– Gareth Ellis, Leeds and Great Britain teammate
and fellow 'Golden Boot' nominee, 2007

FOREWORD

I was delighted and honoured to be asked to write this foreword. Jamie
Peacock is someone I have come to know and admire enormously. He is
one of those people who you sense is a natural leader, from the moment
you first see them play.

Once you meet him away from the pitch and start to get to know him, it
is obvious that the same drive, willingness and enthusiasm he shows in his
profession apply equally to his life. A thoroughly well-rounded individual
and genuine man, he is a great example to everyone within rugby league
and, indeed, outside the sport.

He has shown beyond any doubt that he is a supreme, world-class performer
and an outstanding general in rugby league's most competitive and challeng-
ing environment, the international game. Since assuming the captaincy of
Great Britain in 2005 he has consistently proved himself against the world's
best players and emerged with great personal credit from virtually every contest he has been a part of, even if his team has not always been victorious.

Jamie displays outstanding courage and fortitude in battle and enjoys
widespread appreciation from fellow players who compete alongside him at
Great Britain level, for his club side Leeds Rhinos, and with Bradford Bulls
before that.

However, to his immense credit, he is far more concerned with the team
ethic and earning the respect of those around him, rather than personal
accolades. His primary motivation comes from setting the right example to
teammates, while also maintaining his fierce winning attitude and superb
professional standards.

Jamie is a true gentleman and the perfect ambassador for his club and
code. Despite his elevated status as an international sportsman, he has shown

a strong commitment to the values which ensure that leading rugby league players always remain accessible to their supporters and followers.

The assistance and support he offers to his former amateur club, Stanningley, is clear proof that he retains a strong connection with the community that he grew up in. He is also a devoted family man with a genuine social conscience which, in all, makes him an excellent role model.

Jamie's pathway to his current status as the world's best forward and skipper of his country did not begin in the conventional manner. His transition from academy to first-team player was far from smooth and he was asked to play in the Australian lower leagues in order to prove himself. Since he successfully rose to that challenge and overcame numerous other setbacks along the way, he has gone on to win every domestic trophy available as well as the prestigious individual 'Man of Steel' award.

Jamie looks set to achieve even more in his already distinguished career and players, coaches, match officials and supporters throughout the game will be genuinely delighted to see him enjoy further success. They know he will have truly earned such moments of triumph. I wish him well.

Richard Lewis
Executive Chairman
Rugby Football League

ACKNOWLEDGEMENTS

No man is an island, especially in a team sport and my story has been fashioned on the back of the selfless commitment of others.

Thanks must go to school mate Andy Lightfoot without whom there might have been no tale to tell. If he had not given me a letter to take home about my local rugby club, I may never have found the rugby league family. That introduced me to Stanningley ARLFC and, in particular, Mark Adams, Scott Denevan, Darren Robson and John Darby who all played a massive part in shaping my future. At Wollongong University, I was indebted to Chris Bannerman and David Boyle, while coach Greg Mackey gave me the kick up the backside I needed, although I didn't know it at the time. I have been fortunate to come under some superb coaches who have guided my career and I will be eternally grateful for the patience taken and knowledge imparted by Matthew Elliott, Brian Noble, David Waite, Steve McNamara and Tony Smith. Conditioners Carl Jennings and Martin Clawson made sure that my fitness and strength matched my desire. Everyone who follows a sport needs role models and, if you are a player, mentors. In my early days I had a gang of five who invested a great deal of time on and off the field to guide me in the right direction, whether they knew it or not. To Brian McDermott, James Lowes, Mike Forshaw, Scott Naylor and Bernard Dwyer, thanks for the perfect apprenticeship. Everything I have achieved and experienced has been because of some really special players who I have been privileged to either stand alongside or oppose. Those who have meant the most to me, for a host of different reasons, know who they are but all rugby league players are a breed apart and I respect their bravery and skill. Without the incredible support of the fans of Bradford, Leeds and Great Britain, the deeds would have had little meaning.

When putting pen to paper, Phil Caplan's dedication and ability to pull together the events and anecdotes was invaluable. I am extremely grateful to Richard Lewis for his foreword and his stewardship of the sport during the time I have risen in it. Dave Williams of the excellent rlphotos.com was responsible for the bulk of the pictures. Thanks also to the editorial and marketing staff at Stadia who have been incredibly supportive of the project from proposal to print, especially Rob Sharman, Stevie Holford, Lucy Cheeseman and Reuben Davison. Peter Smith kindly aided with the proof reading.

Grandad and Nana Gray were incredibly supportive and inspirational during the tough early years when I was trying to make it. My sisters, Amie and Sally have sometimes had to live in the shadows but never as far as I am concerned and have shown great fortitude to put up with me being grumpy all the time. Mum and Dad have been constantly there for me in so many ways and I will always been exceptionally appreciative. By their example of honesty, loyalty, diligence and courage, I got the best possible upbringing and life lessons. Two of the most important influences are my immediate family. Faye has continually kept me grounded and made sacrifices for my career. I cannot thank her enough for her love through all the ups and downs of my turbulent journey. Lewis has given my life perspective; he never fails to make me laugh and smile – no matter what the result.

PHOTOGRAPHIC ACKNOWLEDGEMENTS

Plates 8, 10-11, 14-15, 17-18, 19-23, 25-27 and 30-31 supplied by Dave Williams, rlphotos.com; plate 9 courtesy of Ian Beesley, www.ianbeesley.com; plate 29 courtesy of Andrew Varley. All other images are from the author's own collection.

ONE

IT'S NOT ALL FAIRY TALES

I didn't think I'd ever forgive him at the time, but now I can see that Matthew Elliott was right. We trained in the pouring rain near Old Trafford on the day before the 1999 Grand Final and I was desperate to know if I would be playing in the big game the following night. I'd forced my way into the Bradford side that year, mainly off the bench, and had a couple of good games against St Helens, our opponents for the title, in the lead-up. But during that last week of preparation I had the lingering feeling that I was going to be the one to be left out. As the intense, hour-long session ended, I said to former Great Britain international – and one of my dressing-room mentors – Brian McDermott that I really needed to know if I was going to be involved and what he thought my chances were. It was set to be my first major rugby league occasion and I was anxious for some peace of mind. In his typical, honest manner, McDermott blithely said, 'Well go and ask him then.' Matthew looked at me and bluntly confirmed my worst fears; he was a great technical coach but that was poorly handled – communication was not his strong suit, especially with me, probably because I was relatively new to the first-team set-up. During the regular season, I had been about to get on the team bus to go to Saints when he told me not to bother as I wouldn't be playing and that had devastated me. When you are involved in a team sport, especially one where the giving of your all is a prerequisite, being left on the outside is a desolate feeling.

My mood wasn't helped by former teammate Danny Peacock, who I had never really seen eye-to-eye with. There is a dressing room pecking order – even among Peacocks – and there always should be in team sports.

I was abiding to it at Bradford, which went some way towards helping me gain the respect and assistance of the senior players, which I needed. He took the distinction too far, though, and just saw the younger guys as fair targets to be constantly mocked rather than also trying to help them in some way. He was never one to do that so his comments were far from welcome or appreciated. He had flown over from Australia to be a guest at the Grand Final and I travelled back to the hotel in the same car with him after that last training session. He could see that I was fighting to hold back the tears but kept goading me as to what was wrong. I left him in no doubt of my feelings and the atmosphere between us moved from frosty to frozen. Inexperienced and downhearted, I alternated between sulking and fuming which, even at that late stage may have cost me what should have been the most important occasion of my life. Back-rower Steve McNamara went down with a mild dose of food poisoning in the dressing room just before the game. He recovered to play but my reaction to the heartache had ruled me out of possible contention as I was already on my way to the player's lounge to console myself with alcohol. It was a reversion to my old ways, a soft option – the kind I hate now. It also proved why Matt was right; I wasn't ready for that kind of pressure-cooker environment but his decision probably kicked my career on as much as anything else. It put a fire in my belly to train so hard and play so intensely that should the same option ever arise for a coach, he would have no choice but to pick me; it forced me to raise my own personal bar rather than drink it.

It reignited a stubborn streak that has always been within me; not just the desire to prove others wrong but to challenge myself beyond expectations. Even now, I won't even do a training run with an iPod because I feel that the music masks the real reasons for being out there. My mum, Denise, tells me that when I was a very young kid, I never cried like some of the others did when it started to snow, I just went out in it; nothing was going to stop me playing. I can remember my auntie gently mocking me when one of my primary school reports said that I should try not to be too competitive. Then when I was eight and really starting to get into the sport, I dislocated my thumb messing around wrestling in the back garden with a mate, a couple of days before a big seven-a-side tournament. I was desperate to play, which helped take my mind off the pain caused by the nurses in casualty pulling my thumb back out, which was awful, and immediately putting it in plaster. Despite the injury, I could still hold a ball and drove my dad, Darryl, nuts begging him to paint it pink so that no one would know and I could continue to be involved with my team, I was that keen. Without that sort of inner drive and desperation to overcome setbacks, I could not have gone on to captain my country – and by rights I shouldn't have. I was a late developer in the sport; I didn't even come to the attention of a professional club until I was nineteen. Guys like Paul Sculthorpe and Andy Farrell are groomed for the role from an early age, but I did not play any representative football as a junior. The nearest I got was being on the fringes of the Leeds City Boys teams and, as a young teenager – when a firework badly injured my foot – I nearly gave the game up completely.

A few months after that Old Trafford letdown, the same big-game scenario arose at the Bulls. As I'd promised to myself, I had trained my nuts off over the close-season and began the 2000 campaign really confidently as we qualified for the Challenge Cup final at Murrayfield. This time Matthew told me on the Tuesday beforehand that I would be playing, which, conversely, meant that I had plenty of time to feel nervous – especially as the Leeds Rhinos pack we faced contained three of the toughest, meanest, most respected forwards around: Adrian Morley, Anthony Farrell and Darren Fleary. Playing in that cup decider was the culmination of a long-held dream – just as it would be for so many other kids who have grown up with rugby league. I had touched the famous trophy through the fencing at Wembley when Wigan were doing a lap of honour during their phenomenal run of the late 1980s and early '90s but I never imagined – even at the false start of my career – that I would get the chance to contest it. I only played for the first, bruising twenty-six minutes that afternoon in the Scottish capital; I was substituted and, although desperate to get back on, Matthew didn't use me again; but I'd played a part. On the final whistle, my feeling of immense elation was not for me but for my teammate Bernard Dwyer. One of the game's quiet men, yet a natural leader, he had been a huge positive influence on me with his totally professional outlook, utter dedication and willingness to do the unglamorous toil. It is no coincidence that he subsequently became a prison officer. This was his fifth Challenge Cup final and he had lost the previous four – along with five other major deciders – and it meant so much to me, and the rest of the side, that he could finally bask in some deserved glory. I was lucky – this was my first time and I was a winner.

Just over three years after I felt that Matt Elliott had ruined my ambitions, I was slumped in the accident and emergency department of the Bradford Royal Infirmary. It was during the early hours of the morning and I was ruefully contemplating that I had foolishly wrecked all of the hard work and toil undertaken since that first setback, which had seen me establish myself as a first-team player in a top side and play for my country. Having taken the decision over my chosen profession out of the hands of others and put it in my own, I was now once more – and quite literally this time – on the verge of losing everything. To be a professional sportsman in a code like rugby league – especially among the forwards, where physical imposition and controlled aggression are vital components of your armoury – requires an intense dedication and total focus. Because I perform on the edge, I tend to live on it as well and that has meant occasionally letting off steam with as much zeal as when I have the ball in hand or attempting to make that crunching, intimidatory tackle. Inevitably, perhaps, with sport and alcohol so inextricably linked, that has sometimes meant drinking to excess or, more accurately in the current currency, binge drinking. That is not a justification, and with experience comes increasing realisation of the pitfalls and greater control, but in early March 2003, I looked down at the consequences of my actions fearing the worst.

It was all so needless. We had just played a Challenge Cup tie against Second Division Hunslet which had been switched from their base in the south of Leeds to my favourite haunt, Headingley, to accommodate the expected crowd. Even though they had beaten Super League side Huddersfield Giants in the previous round, we were expected to win at a canter. I was looking forward to the game. It was on the home turf I had worshipped as a boy and there were a number of guys in the opposition ranks who I had socialised with but never got to play against. I've been fortunate enough to appear in some huge matches but this wasn't one of them. Bradford romped to their expected success, hammering the minnows 82-0 and, as arranged, a few of us met up to have a drink afterwards. Somehow that snowballed into a session which saw me arrive home in the early hours rather the worse for wear and, following a beer-fuelled argument, I put my right hand through a plate-glass door, severing the tendons of two fingers, slicing open the flesh and breaking the knuckles. Blood was pumping from the wound but I refused an ambulance, so a taxi was called to hastily take me to casualty where all they could do was dress the ineffective limb and make an appointment for me to come back and see the doctor at eight o'clock that morning.

Having returned home to ponder the guilt-laden significance at about five, wait for the painkillers to kick in and then sleep off the effects of the booze, I missed that appointment. I got there about an hour late and by then my hand had badly swollen up; I couldn't move it and it began to dawn on me that my cherished career could be over. The nursing staff said that I had to come back later in the afternoon, no matter how much I pleaded with them that I needed to see a doctor straight away because my job was in jeopardy. I sheepishly called the Bradford coach Brian Noble who, from looking out for me in the reserve team and persuading the club to give me a contract when Matthew Elliott had thought better of it, again came to my rescue. He didn't mince his words about how stupid I had been and then made two decisions which illustrated why he is held in such high regard by the players who work under him. He said he would deal with the Press, releasing a statement from the club that I had broken my hand in the Hunslet game and that I had been sent for an X-ray to cut any speculation that might leak out and take that pressure off. Then he rang his sister, who worked high up in the local NHS and virtually controlled the Bradford hospitals, and she immediately made sure I got to see a specialist straight away. I was incredibly fortunate.

The hand was a complete mess but because the tendons had been severed in a clean and diagonal cut, there was maximum surface area for the surgeon to knit them back together and for them to properly heal. I was booked in for an immediate operation which entailed putting wire rods in my hand to stabilise it. All I kept mulling over was why had I done such a stupid thing. I didn't feel sorry for myself; it was more the thought that I had let myself and so many other people down – including my teammates, who had shown their belief in me and to whom I owed so much. Under the knife, they also discovered a postage-stamp-sized piece of near-century-old glass and several other shards embedded in my hand, which had all become infected.

Having come through the operation successfully, I had to stay in hospital for five days after the surgery to make sure that the antibiotics were working and although some of the Bradford boys came down to visit, being in that room crystallised my frustration and anger as I went stir crazy. My wife Faye was out at work during the day but I wasn't good company to be around any-way and, by the time I was released, I was fuming and disgusted with myself. I vowed to repay those who had shielded and kept faith with me and the 2003 season turned out to be one beyond my wildest expectations. The surgeon did a terrific job but his initial diagnosis – after he had put my mind at rest that it wasn't a career-threatening injury – was that I would be out of action for three months while the tendons repaired. Straight away I decided that it wasn't going to be that long and I used what turned out to be the seven-week lay-off – the longest I have had to endure – to put in an extra pre-season, even though I couldn't do anything for a fortnight. Under the guidance of Bulls' conditioner Martin Clawson, I trained relentlessly with a massive point to prove, put on some weight and came back stronger – defying medical orders to play in the Challenge Cup semi-final and then in the decider in Cardiff, which remains one of my favourite matches of all time.

I'm sure that my mental toughness, above everything else, has enabled me to get to the very top and helped to overcome natural skill deficiencies. It particularly manifested itself during that trying period. Genetically I seem to mend quickly anyway but I also tried to visualise the healing process speeding up and imagined myself to be stronger and fitter, perhaps, than I actually was in a medical sense. I quickly realised in those long, desolate hours of rehab, the ingredients that had been missing from my game and, when I look back, it was that incident that gave me the desire to move up a level again. It has remained a motivation since. The worst thing that could have happened turned into the best over time, and in many ways that is the story of my rugby life.

After that, I played a part in Bradford becoming the first side to achieve a cup and Grand Final double, and while performing with such a sense of purpose and desperation to right my wrong, I ended the campaign with a host of awards, including the highest individual accolade: I was recognised as the coveted 'Man of Steel'. I was also honoured to be named as the 'Professional Players' Player' and the 'Rugby League Writers'' best. There was still one final twist to the saga, however, which proves that in the toughest of arenas, even when you reach the summit, it's never all fairytales. I'd come back early and was playing with a protective plastic shield around the hand – which got me the nickname 'The Claw' – and because I could just about move it, there was an agreement to put off having the metal rods that were keeping my knuckles together removed until the end of the year. After the regular season and our Grand Final triumph, I was included in the Great Britain side to take on the Kangaroos in a three-match Ashes series. Fiercely patriotic, I wasn't going to pass up the chance of playing for my country in the most demanding, highest-profile matches against the very best. That's the stage you aspire to through the long, dark days of gym work and physiotherapy. After each Test, though, the hand swelled to ridiculous proportions, although a regular dose of intravenous antibiotics seemed to do the trick to enable me to take the field. When the dressing was finally taken off at the end of the series, gangrene had set in and it took a quickly administered course of antibiotics from GB doctor Chris Brookes to save my hand – just. They tried to remove the rods under a local anaesthetic but the surgeon could not get them to budge. I could feel him rooting about in there, but initially to no great effect. It was nearly a case of making the ultimate sacrifice.

It's often said that there is a very fine line between madness and genius and in elite professional sport a similar distance divides utter despair and the euphoria of success. The end of the 2007 season marked my tenth anniversary of being a professional rugby league player and I couldn't have wished for a better way to commemorate it, winning the greatest domestic honour with the club I supported and then leading my country to a first series win in fourteen years. On the Super League front, Leeds finished the season in sensational fashion, eclipsing their rivals to confound a number of doubters, not least within the ranks of our own fans. Getting knocked out of the Challenge Cup early hurt us as a team; we had really wanted to be there to christen the new Wembley. It was that setback, though, which probably worked in our favour, allowing us to play in three-week blocks towards the end of the season. We lost, somewhat surprisingly, at home to Wakefield towards the end of July. The Rhinos players were shocked at the outcome, we got booed off and coach Tony Smith suffered some fearful personal abuse walking down the stand afterwards, which was bang out of order. I had an argument with a bloke in the bar who wanted to have a go about Tony. I told the accuser in no uncertain terms not to come to me on the sly and expect me to bag my boss and that he should either keep his opinions to himself or have the balls to confront the man they were directly aimed at. Faye had to hold me back but I felt aggrieved and justified. We were all down, including the boss, which was unlike him, but the massive thing I've learned from our second-rower Jamie Jones-Buchanan – my old mate from Stanningley – is the need to always remain positive. Normally, after a defeat like that, I'd have been incredibly frustrated, annoyed and ranting but, strangely, I was not this time. I went round cajoling the lads, saying: 'Look, let's ignore everyone else, they don't matter. We need to close ranks, concentrate and do this for ourselves because I'm confident we can.' It was the same conversation I had with Smithy, who was in his final few weeks in the job. I stressed to him how we were in this together and could succeed for one another. It was time to stand up for ourselves and disregard the nonsense that was being churned out. He made a couple of speeches over the next few weeks about how fanatics, not true supporters, are the ones that jeer you and that you have to be prepared to go through the bad times to truly appreciate the good.

We improved from that day and it was one of the reasons behind us going on to win the competition; we took our intense desire as a team to a new level. To be fair to that guy in the bar, once we had achieved our goal and I bumped into him again, he apologised for his earlier outburst. Jamie Thackray was important in those intervening weeks, talking up our chances even though he didn't get to play in the Grand Final. He wandered around the dressing room from then on geeing everyone up, saying: 'Are we going to do it, or what?' It was a sense that hadn't been at Leeds the year before and proving doubters wrong again figured largely in my psyche. Twelve weeks after being booed off, those same people couldn't wait to back-slap us.

Super League has become so even that sides can expect to lose one in three of their games now, no matter how good they are, and that trend is set to continue. Supporters need to come to terms with that as the norm and realise that it is the form you get into at the back end of the year that really counts. I've never played as consistently well as I did over the final three weeks of the 2007 campaign that encompassed the play-offs. After that Wakefield defeat we had a two-week break and I set myself a target to give everything I had for the final three regular-season rounds and then into the knockout phase. My form improved each week, getting more carries and making further metres, which is generally a sign that things are going well for me. I felt fit and we had another week off before the final stages kicked in, which helped me refocus into a familiar mindset, and things snowballed from there. It's hard to say if I've ever played better than I did in the Grand Final when we put the favourites, St Helens, to the sword. The amount of work I got through was a massive achievement; the stats were pretty impressive on all fronts. It was my sixth time on that stage and going into the match I knew that I had to lead from the front, taking the ball in when others were tired and doing what I do well. I was really pumped up in the week leading up to Old Trafford and Tony primed us perfectly for the contest.

In 2005, when Leeds had last been there as defending champions but lost to their closest rivals, they didn't take the occasion at Old Trafford seriously enough. I'd witnessed that close up having skippered Bradford to the ultimate triumph that evening, in my final match for them. Tony was smart, he could see what had gone wrong and he changed the routine accordingly.

That included an overnight stay, which proved to be another defining factor in our Grand Final success. You need something extra going into the big games; it's not necessarily greater skill but it's the channelled emotion and determination you take into them that counts at the final whistle. That is helped by building the occasion up a little bit and the night before, in camp, we had a team meeting. I was nearly in tears for most of it, I was holding them back because I didn't want to cry in front of the others but it made me even more desperate to win the most sought-after prize alongside that group. We spoke in turn about who we wanted to win for and veteran centre Keith Senior was one of the first up. He said that he was looking to do it for his daughter who got teased a bit at school because she has a kind of cleft palate but it had made her so proud the last time he collected a winner's ring. Then youngster Carl Ablett told how twelve months before he had been undergoing a full knee reconstruction and was now, after just a handful of games, on the verge of playing in front of over 70,000 fans for the right to be called a champion. Everyone had a compelling reason which we got to share, it was an unbelievable meeting and, with Tony leaving as well, it gave us a massive psychological edge.

Winning the trophy in such a commanding fashion was incredibly important to me, especially after enduring a difficult first season at Leeds when we had underachieved. I had been keyed up to make an early impression with my new club, and did, but threw all my eggs into that basket and then suffered from fatigue towards the end of the 2006 campaign. The fact that I then went on to have a good Tri-Nations tournament skippering Great Britain – culminating in being voted 'International Forward of the Year' – led to some murmurings that I was short-changing the Rhinos. Turning those perceptions around a year later was immensely satisfying because so many of the side were from the city and it meant such a lot to the people closest to me, because they all support the team. It felt different, but on a par, with the climax to 2005 when I wanted my last, sign-off appearance with Bradford to be the most memorable. With so much invested at the Bulls spiritually and physically over the years as I was coming through, I wanted to leave on the right note and being able to do so meant everything to me.

Likewise with the Test whitewash against the Kiwis which ended the 2007 season. I feel so lucky to have played with the calibre of player I have at that level. To have put the Great Britain jersey to bed – for me and a lot of the other senior guys – in that fashion just does not get any better; especially after having personally waited seven years for a series win at international level. You only borrow that shirt off its previous incumbents and hold it for the next generation, and we were desperate to do it proud before we relinquished our tenure.

It is only really by sitting down and trying to write a book like this that you can properly reflect on such achievements – not that it means I am contemplating retirement; there are far too many new and exciting challenges on the horizon for that. If you try to evaluate too much while you are still in the midst of everything, it merely becomes self-indulgence. I've been fortunate in my career to have had lots of 'Sky Plus' moments, where you can programme in and record your favourite bits and keep going back to them. I've been involved in a lot of fantastic games and unbelievable nights that I'd like to play in again, if you could do such a thing. Cataloguing them has made me appreciate the huge enjoyment and meaning behind them even more, and how fortunate I am to have played in teams that have been successful. People know about those showpieces because they are well documented, but the events in your life that perhaps you don't want saving for posterity are the ones that make winning even more special and give the best times their true importance and significance. Writing about the ones I'd like to erase and, often, the despair that surrounds them has been equally important as the glory. Those experiences, as much as anything, have made me who I am today.

TWO

NO PRETENTIONS OR EXPECTATIONS

From the minute you see some kids playing sport, you can tell they are something special. I was never one of them. I loved being involved, it dominated my early years, but making a living from it or playing at its pinnacle couldn't have been further from my ambitions. Family life was centred on a typical working-class upbringing; hard work, honesty and loyalty were the watch words around the house. I've got two sisters – Amie who is eleven months younger than me and Sally four years my junior – so I spent a lot of time looking out for them from an early age. They are not massive fans of the game, they've got their own families and lives but, when they get the chance, they come and support me. Of course we used to argue a lot and as you get older you grow apart, especially if you're a different gender, but, even so, we remain tight-knit and mates.

Holidays were always spent in either Wales or Cornwall and they were fantastic trips, good times, and the house was always full of cats – I think we had about sixteen at one stage – but from the inside, to me, everything just seemed normal.

I did seem to spend a lot of my early years in hospital and maybe that is why, sometimes, you think that there are forces within you. When I was two, I nearly died. I was in intensive care for quite a while but they never really found out what was wrong with me. The medical people said it was mumps with complications; Mum still reckons that was not the case but I pulled through, even though I was pretty sick. Even before that I knew my way around accident and emergency because as an eleven-month-old I broke one of my legs, slipping down between two parts of the sofa, and I was forever cutting my head open. I'm clumsy anyway but because I always wanted to do things, I naturally just seemed to keep getting into scrapes. It was a regular trip down to St James's or Leeds General Infirmary for my parents.

Rather than put me off anything to do with physical contact, my stubborn streak just used to make me more determined to carry on. Such determination and dedication is genetic; my granddad on Mum's side was a professional boxing champion when he was in the navy and a decent footballer – he played for a while for Bournemouth. He was mad keen on the round-ball game but watches rugby league now and wishes he'd had the chance to give it a go. My dad is the hardest-working bloke I know; he has run his own business manufacturing false teeth for as long as I can remember and always made huge sacrifices, doing whatever it took to keep himself above the breadline and the family afloat. There was never much money around and in the days when interest rates soared and nearly sent him over the edge, he was regularly putting in sixteen- or even eighteen-hour days without complaint. He knew it just had to be done and that set a terrific example. Mum possesses the same virtues; she has been unstinting, never griping or moaning about her lot.

I began playing league around the age of four when I brought a letter home from school. Andrew Lightfoot gave it to me and it was from my local club Stanningley saying that they were looking to take on more juniors. Subs were ten pence a week; training began at 6 p.m. on Wednesdays with a match on the Sunday for anyone interested in coming down. That was the start. A lingering memory remains of playing in the park for them, down at the bottom end where there were some council-owned changing rooms. Winters tended to be a lot colder and snowy then and the ritual after games was plunging our iced-up hands under the hot water taps of the big sinks in those freezing huts to try and warm up. It stung your arms like hell but we had to do it to try and get some feeling back and it became something of a dare to see who could keep them under the running water or in the basin the longest. I always enjoyed those days.

School was okay, I went to Stanningley Primary which was a good one and then Intake High Middle School. My results were always quite good but it wasn't the most conducive environment for a kid like me. I knew how to do just enough to wing it; I could get through without having to hand in too much coursework or, especially, homework. I was pretty sound academically – especially in maths and sciences – but I could have done better if, maybe, I had been pushed, challenged or encouraged more by the teachers. Perhaps that was my problem; I was more interested in having a good time than going that extra mile with my studies. Intake was a strange place for the subjects that I favoured; its renown was in the performing arts. Learning was based around that, which didn't really suit me. I felt they were more interested in those potential entertainers who had come in from further afield and who wanted to be stars rather than the talent they had on their own doorstep. It was pretty easy to get into trouble and I often did. A lot of us took drama because it was easier to get a good mark in and there was more of a chance to mess about for an hour compared to dance and music, which were the other options. I was never the leading-man type but I didn't mind a mess about on the drums – although you only got a couple of months' shot at it before having to make up your mind what course you were doing – but dance was definitely out. It was a bit of a laugh but I never fancied a career as an actor and I could hardly imagine being in a musical.

Some of the friendships made at Intake have endured; Simon Priest and Chris Radford are still good mates, as is Paul McGinity – who, ironically, I had a fight with which saw him expelled. Generally I used to knock around with the older kids, playing football a lot in the park and around the back of the school. That got me selected for the school teams although normally in the age brackets above me; it was not due to the fact that I was any good but more because I always used to get stuck in. Perhaps unsurprisingly, I was a central defender, whose main asset was scything opponents down – finesse was somewhat lacking.

When it came to rugby, Dad coached me most of the way through until I left school. I don't think he was that interested in the sport until I started playing and he saw it as a chance to get out of the house socially on a regular basis. On many an occasion we used to be running around the old, rickety Stanningley club house after training while he sat at the bar. Unlike now, rugby at amateur level in Leeds seemed to be pretty disorganised. I used to turn up for the trials for the City Boys, and occasionally tagged along as a substitute, but it seemed as though I was never quite good enough to make the starting line-up.

As I progressed through the age groups, Mark Adams and Scott Denevan took over at Stanningley and they had a good set of players to work with and we were quite successful. In the early days, local rivals Milford were the team to beat with the likes of Gavin Brown, James Bunyan, Micky Horner and Guy Adams, who all went on to play professionally, in their ranks. We thought we were pretty sound until we came up against them. My interest waned when I hit my mid-teens and, like a lot of hormonal young men, I didn't know what I wanted out of life. Standing around with my mates seemed more appealing for a while than making sacrifices for sport. That phase coincided with an accident with a firework. It's tough sometimes in this country for youngsters when there's nothing much to do at night and you end up dicking about on street corners getting into petty mischief. A banger, which was being tossed around, landed on my foot and exploded, scorching through my trainers and causing second-degree burns. It hurt like hell and meant that for quite a while I couldn't wear rugby boots but that was also an excuse I was looking for. My dad was pissed off with me for giving up and it was the first of a number of times when something happened that could have stopped me making it. The group of mates I knocked about with were typical kids who preferred to be outside, trying to avoid getting into scrapes rather than causing them. We never instigated anything malicious – we were better termed as mischievous – but that used to find us in bother every now and then. I wasn't one to back down from any sort of challenge, which was great grounding for my later life in the game. I had a year out but by the age of sixteen I had regained my enthusiasm and started to enjoy rugby again.

Back at Stanningley I began playing successfully at both under-18 and open-age level, which meant two games a weekend. John Darby was the coach and the life and soul of the club. Sadly, he has now passed away but one of his legacies was to change my name. I arrived as James and almost immediately he started calling me Jamie. I mentioned to him that it was James and he said: 'Okay, Jamie, off you go.'

It's almost impossible to put an exact time on when it first dawned on me that I might be able to make a career out of the sport. I just enjoyed being a youth in the men's second team and the lads involved seemed to think I was making a contribution. At the same time I was doing well for the under-18s, we got to a cup final and I managed to claim the Man of the Match award even though we lost. I received a similar accolade when the senior side won a sevens tournament and things seemed to be progressing. I was happy to play anywhere; I guess I was as keen as I was versatile, so they threw me in at second-row, scrum-half, wherever. I was skinny, had a bit of speed and I loved it. The set-up really suited me; building up for games, having a great time with a good bunch of lads and then, invariably, going out on the piss after matches together – Stanningley was a great club for that. If there hadn't then been scouts sniffing around, I would have continued playing at amateur level.

I've never really suffered from nerves before a game; my only real worry when I was younger was to play well and not let my teammates down rather than be too concerned with the opposition or the stage. More than anything I had to overcome shyness and the prospect that, if there was a big crowd, people would laugh at me if I messed up. Nowadays, that is not a factor because I know that I have done everything possible to prepare thoroughly for a game with a routine that doesn't alter or vary too much. If I can do my job well, I know that it will help the team and I've never lost the anticipatory thrill of getting out there and mucking in. Such a philosophy is the basis of my captaincy, particularly for Great Britain. I'm not necessarily one for Churchillian speeches; it's more about stressing to the lads to do it for each other because we are all good blokes, and making sure the game plan is set and the emotions are intact. 'Play well for your mate, yourself and above all enjoy it' has always been my mantra. What you are good at, you revel in doing well, whether it is kick-chasing like Jamie Jones-Buchanan, smashing people in the manner that Gareth Ellis does so well or taking the big hits that I do every now and then. The sum of those parts, done to be the best of a player's ability usually means a team will win; there's no great mega-science or mystique about it.

I seem to have always had an instinctive timing and technique on defence. Whenever we did tackling practice, even as an under-nine, and were trying ten repetitions, nobody wanted to do it with me because they said I hurt them too much. That's always been in me, as has wanting to beat someone in whatever task I've faced. They were ethics which were reinforced by what Dad constantly drilled into me; he had me practicing all the time. Progress was helped by a growth spurt when I was around seventeen, which was important in the way I wanted to play. I've always had a wiry kind of strength but the added height enhanced my self-confidence. I wasn't one of those young kids I sometimes came up against who already sported a beard; I was a late developer on a number of fronts. Solving another medical condition about that time was another significant turning point, when I finally went to be fitted for contact lenses. I really couldn't see, I'm very short-sighted and even though I was thoroughly enjoying my rugby, that visit to the opticians improved it immensely. I started chasing the ball rather than carrier bags flying across the pitch, as Matt Elliott used to remind me. The first time he came down to see me play at Stanningley before the lenses were inserted, he saw this eager kid often running in the wrong direction. Suddenly, from barely being able to distinguish teammates or where the try line was, I could appreciate what was going on around me, my handling skills increased out of sight – excuse the pun – which was another great confidence boost and I never looked back.

I had wanted to stay on at school and take my 'A' levels but, in hindsight, to have done that I should really have gone to college; that would have suited me better. The school regime wasn't for me; I felt that that they treated the older pupils too childishly and I wanted to go out socialising. I left and got a job working full-time loading parcels for DHL and had some ambitions to go through the ranks there on the management and logistics side.

Soon after I started in the depot, I was asked to attend a trial at Wakefield Trinity. I played a couple of academy matches for them against Hull and then, ironically, Bradford. In that match they put me in at prop and I must have been the skinniest one ever to take the field. Peter Tunks, the former Aussie Test front-rower who had played for Leeds, was the chief executive at Belle Vue at the time and although he said he wanted to sign me for Trinity, the money was ridiculously low. Bradford said they were interested in the summer of 1996, just as Super League started but I had very little self belief in my ability to play at that level. My dad must have been sick of making excuses for me failing to show up for training but eventually I overcame my doubts and went up to Odsal. I didn't want to end up like one of those guys who sat around the pub telling no one in particular: 'I could have had trials or done that or achieved this'. I made up my mind to go and they threw me in against Castleford who were a top academy side at the time. Determined to make the most of the chance, I must have played pretty well because I got the Man of the Match award. That, though, left me with a problem. The Bulls said they were going to sign me to a professional contract so I left my job but it took them three months to come up with a firm offer.

In the interim, to keep body and soul together while I was in limbo, I was forced to get employment with a roofing company working twelve-hour shifts for twenty quid a day. Dave and Pete Rennie took me on to do the labouring and it was just really tough graft. The work didn't faze me but it was hard times, the kind which make you appreciate what you do eventually get that much more. We were on site at seven in the morning and I've never forgotten how exhausting and often inhospitable it was. Occasionally, even now, you need to draw on inspiration from elsewhere when it gets tough on the rugby field or in training and when that happens I remember and appreciate those days. It's often said that if you find a job that you enjoy, then you never do a day's work but that's bullshit. I love playing professional sport but there are times when it feels like the hardest work imaginable and that's when I think back that I could be on top of someone's house lugging pieces of wood instead. There were no inklings of being Great Britain captain when I was slung in the back of a van among various assorted materials and tools. Not every day is a great day, whatever job you do.

From the minute I saw it, I was impressed with the Bradford set-up, which had undergone something of a transformation with the advent of Super League and summer rugby. Even though I had supported Leeds from as far back as I could remember, and spent many an afternoon following the likes of Ellery Hanley – who had initially made his name at Odsal – from the Headingley terraces, playing for their great rivals was never an issue. Leeds never approached me throughout my junior days and if you've gone past the age of sixteen without being spotted then you rarely get swept up. I've always felt that although the scholarship systems and apprenticeships now provide an excellent grounding for a youngster, there should always be safety net for those who miss out in their formative years. Some young, talented players look superb before they get into open age and are then found out; Adam Hughes, who I played with in the Leeds City Boys squads, would be a prime example. Nevertheless, I was convinced that the Bradford deal was going to fall through so I carried on doing full shifts of manual work and then going training. The no-nonsense, deep-thinking, hard-nosed Aussie Brian Smith was the Bulls' revolutionary head coach and one evening, because his son Rohan was playing at Stanningley, he gave me a lift home. I was nineteen at the time and although I can't quite remember what he said, I know it was one of the most nerve-racking journeys I've ever taken – and that only one of us was doing any of the talking. I was seriously intimidated.

Eventually, going full-time at the Bulls was sorted out but it was an incredibly hard transition. The money I was earning was less than being employed and it was difficult to adjust, partly because being a young professional was such a new concept. In many ways, the first batch of signings were like guinea pigs, we were expected to be fully switched on to a life in the sport but we were entrenched in an amateur environment that included seeing your mates and going out for a good time, which invariably involved drinking. We had no mentors and it was never really made clear what was expected of us. Looking back, I don't know if I ever really got to grips with it. It was very long hours; we trained in the mornings, would go out to work with schools in the afternoons and then come back to train again in the evening. I can see why a lot of the lads who were around at that time fell by the wayside. My early career ran almost parallel with another of my Stanningley teammates, Craig Horne. He went up to Bradford and then on to Featherstone and ended up playing in France and we lost touch. He used to fight like mad with his brother Mark, they were always at each other, but Craig was a pretty determined winger and even though it didn't work out for him at Odsal, he made a go of it at Rovers, did a good job for them and was around when I later went over there on loan. That helped me and we used to travel together to Post Office Road. The only other one from our age group at Stanningley to spend a significant time in the professional ranks was Andy Bastow, who was one of the better players in the side. He got a run out with Wakefield, signed for Featherstone and then ended up at Hunslet. It would have been good to play against him but the only chance would have been in that ill-fated cup clash at Headingley which was the precursor to the drama with my hand, only he was out injured at the time. Another Bramley lad, Michael Banks and I came through the ranks together at Stanningley and we were almost inseparable. We signed on the Bradford scholarship scheme at the same time and the great bonus for me was that he had transport and used to give me lifts to training and just about everywhere else. He made one appearance for the Bulls first team in 1998 and eventually ended up playing back at our first club.

My roots have always been incredibly important to me, which is why I am only too pleased to try and help out with the coaching and I have an involvement back at Coal Hill Drive now. Brian McDermott said to me recently that when you have been through what we have as professional players, it changes you. I'm not the same as the blokes I used to knock about with at school, you can't help that. Top-level rugby league makes you grow as a person and a man, and although it might sound grandiose, those experiences – even though it is through sport – make you look at life differently. I've done some things that not many others have and that's not arrogance, it's just stating facts. But I come from the kind of background and a code that if you get above yourself you get shot down, and I like to stay close to those values. I don't just play the sport – I love it, and I'd go back and run around in amateur rugby league tomorrow if that was the only option. What I've achieved should show any aspiring junior what can happen. I'm fortunate that I was brought up within the middle of a good, supportive family, with a great set of friends and in Yorkshire. I have an undying love of the place and the people, who have few airs and graces. Rugby has taught me to be open-minded and I've been able to travel to other places and appreciate different cultures as a result of it but, no two ways about it, my favourite places are still among the Broad Acres.

THREE

VIA WOLLONGONG AND FEATHERSTONE

Gradually, I began to come to terms with the idea of being a professional rugby league player. For most of the 1997 campaign I learnt my trade in Bradford's Alliance side and found it to be really enjoyable, especially testing myself against more experienced performers. I thought I was doing okay and after the first team had romped to the Super League title with three rounds still to go, I hoped that I might be given a chance to make my senior debut. In those pre-Grand Final days there was nothing really left to play for and there were rumours going round that Matthew Elliott might pick a young side to face Paris, who were struggling by then, at Odsal in a fixture to celebrate winning the trophy. As it turned out, I wasn't included, apparently because he didn't think that I was physically big enough, although we easily won, 68-0. By then, the Paris pack was virtually made up of second-rate Aussies and they had already been told that their side was on the verge of disbanding. With them dispirited and away at the rampant champions, I could only see pitting myself against them as being the logical next step in my development. Unfortunately, the coaching staff didn't feel the same way and I had to wait. As it turned out, a year later I would cross the Channel anyway. Towards the end of the season I was playing with a sternum injury which meant that before matches I needed painkilling injections to get out on the field. Prior to one game I was in with the doctor and a couple of the lads waiting their turn for treatment outside the room heard this massive scream from me. When I emerged they looked shocked and asked if it was really that painful but I'd actually been stung by a bee just as the needle went in and ended up playing with a swollen head as well as a sore chest!

Whether it was part of my solid upbringing, I'm not sure, but even from the early days I understood and appreciated my place within the dressing-room hierarchy. I was young, impressionable, a little bit gullible and extremely conscious of the need to earn my right to be among guys who had hardened top-level experience. As part of the dressing-room culture, that sometimes meant being the butt of a joke or prank and, of course, being christened with a nickname. Jimmy Lowes was the self-appointed nominator and for a while, when I first came on the scene and I was so uncoordinated, he used to call me 'Brains' after the character in Thunderbirds. I really hoped that wouldn't stick and fortunately Kevin Crouthers came up with the less inventive 'JP' and that rapidly caught on. I'd already endured one partial change in identity and I wasn't referred to as James again until I became Great Britain captain and team manager Phil Clarke reverted to the more formal version.

Like in most work environments, I quickly came across some oddball characters that left their mark. Veteran Aussie Graeme Bradley was just a cantankerous, grumpy man but he was always good to me, although there were two sides to 'Penguin'. Stuart Fielden and I came through the Bradford ranks together and 'Peng' used to hammer Stuey all the time; he never let up on him, he was remorseless. It wasn't advice he was dispensing either, Graeme just constantly belittled him and did him down and Stuart didn't know which way to take it. It was relentless and probably got a bit out of hand at times – Stuart certainly doesn't like him much now – but Peng always toed the line with me. If we were out having a drink, I could quite happily sit in his company and found him to be engaging. He was someone who was always straight to the point and there were certain days, in particular when you were a young lad coming through, that you could see that you had to keep out of his way. He sometimes behaved like that because he could and that was the side of him that opposing fans hated but he also had a ruthless streak which made him feared on the pitch and that was a handy attribute in battle.

Stuart would be the first to admit that he is different to most, which is why some people who come across him see him as weird. He was someone who I could never beat when we did fitness work together when we first joined up with the first-team squad, and it used to drive me crazy. I never gave up on him – although enjoying the odd cigarette at the time probably didn't do me any favours – and I was never more than a yard away but his ultra determination to get to the top was the making of him; he's a genuine athlete. He broke through the year before me and everyone was raving about him in 1998 and rightly so. He's a complicated character, sometimes he doesn't understand whether those around him are taking the piss out of him or not and I think that's a legacy of 'Peng'. What I admire most is that he is himself, although that can sometimes be his worst aspect. He can be very self-opinionated but such stubbornness is one of his greatest features; he won't change for anyone. He'll do the things he wants to do the way he wants to do them. Occasionally, that made him an obvious target. He used to read in or around the dressing room and Jimmy Lowes, unfailingly, always moved his bookmark. Once, as the marker reached the end of a particular tome, he even ripped the final few pages out. Things like that probably hardened Stu's resolve and he was a great bloke to play alongside and the toughest to come up against, that's for sure.

At the beginning of the 1998 season and with a year of my original contract left, Matthew Elliott gave me a choice; either to go on loan at Dewsbury or to widen my rugby education by having a spell in the Australian country competition. He said that he could fix me up with Wollongong University who played in the Illawarra Carlton League, an industrial region with a great heritage in the code. As you move up the pyramid, you tend to get better guidance. By then, Brian McDermott had got to grips with me and told me that I needed to make something of myself at the end of a big argument we were having, and that sunk in. He thought that trying my hand on the other side of the world could only do me good. I still doubted my ability but recognised that such a trip could also prove to be a great life opportunity. The furthest I had travelled by then was to Spain for a holiday and the prospect was, simultaneously, exhilarating and terrifying. For a nervous, naïve twenty-year-old, the journey alone was an extreme test of resolve. It took three days and was a nightmare on virtually every leg. The flight from Leeds to London passed without note but on the next stage I was crammed into the back of an aeroplane to the Philippines. I sat beside what must be one of the few brown-haired Swedish women who decided that the only way she could cope with the long haul was to get progressively drunker. When we landed, there was a problem with my transfer hotel. Being relatively tall in a country where that is something of a rarity, I felt extremely self-conscious standing about, not speaking the language and surrounded by security guards with guns. Eventually it was sorted out but the following day the connecting flight to Australia was delayed which meant another night in very unfamiliar territory.

Finally, we set off for Oz but had to land in Melbourne as there are no night flights into Sydney and when I did finally arrive, there was no one around to pick me up. To say that by then I was in a genuinely tired and pretty emotional state was an understatement and some frantic phone calls to the club – who had set out a couple of times but had not found me there – led to another two-hour wait in a charmless airport terminal. Relieved to be collected, I was ferried to the steel city where club secretary Chris Bannerman was to become an invaluable friend in times of frequent need. On my first weekend the whole team went out together for a bonding session with the new boy which consisted principally of drinking games. I had already started to take the usual 'Pommy' stick and was determined to show them who could handle their beer the better. I achieved that, drinking my allotted buddy for the night under the table, Bramley style. We ended up in a bar that was sponsoring me and contained that day's opposition who began mouthing off against the so-called tough English guy whose name had been in the local papers. Inevitably, it ended in a scrap and with me being ejected by the bouncers who were then persuaded by my new teammates that they should let me back in as they were part-funding my stay. They relented and the episode had the bonding effect required but I was embarrassed by the incident and my lack of self-control born out of nervous inexperience.

The press coverage for Wollongong University was pretty good within the locality, where we were known as 'the Books', but it did not stop the players and staff trying to embellish it by fooling the media. Often when interviewed, the players would see who could get the most outrageous name to be published in the paper. For a while we apparently had a recruitment officer called Erskine Slidemuscle – that took some beating. Initially I was taken in by and stayed with the club's fitness trainer, David Boyle. I bumped into him again when I was over there for the Tri-Nations in 2006 and former Leeds teammate Mark O'Neill was giving me a tour round his old club Wests Tigers, where David is now working. We hadn't seen each other for eight years but he is a top guy, immensely fit and an excellent rower as well. He looked after me even though his life was in a bit of turmoil at the time; he was in the process of splitting up with his wife and moving in with someone else, but he was really good to me even with all that upheaval going on around him.

I was quickly singled out as the white-skinned Englishman but my initial attempts at getting a tan on the beach at Mount Ousley served only to give me a case of sunburn which led to much amusement among my new teammates. As part of the deal, I was supposed to get a job on a building site but that fell through and when I wasn't playing I stacked shelves at Woolies at night or worked on the doors or collecting glasses at bars in the town, including one owned by local celebrity and former Test and Wigan player Andrew Farrar. My first game was at the impressive Win Stadium in Illawarra in thirty-five-degree heat in a curtain-raiser before their NRL encounter against Newcastle Knights. As I was coming off, the likes of Englishman Lee Jackson, Paul Harragon and star man Andrew Johns were going through their pre-match routines and rituals, and it seems astonishing, looking back, that I eventually went on to face him at the top level.

For someone who had led a relatively sheltered life, the trip was a huge culture shock, not least in having to be independent and self-sufficient. I was indebted to the university coach, the feisty former Hull and Warrington scrum-half Greg Mackey. We didn't always see eye to eye, in fact, we once had a massive blow up at a club dinner and dance but his will to win was immense and left its mark on me. I still had an amateur mentality, which must have frustrated him, but unlike the guys he was used to dealing with, I didn't know what was required of me. In retrospect, especially, I can see that 'Bluey' was a wise bloke – albeit an abrasive one – and some of the firmest foundations of my subsequent career were laid by what he taught me. They were not so much game specific, but more the best way to mentally prepare for and conduct myself in matches. He impressed on me how to impose myself on the opposition and the methods needed if I was to win the psychological battle in my particular contest. Those lessons were invaluable and I'll be forever grateful to him for them. He wrote me a sheet when I left which I carried around with me for ages, and still have somewhere, which contained some crucial principles about what I needed to do to make it in my position. Also included on it was what I needed to change in order to achieve success and aspects to instil in my game that could make me different to others. Without natural gifts or an obvious skill, he stressed that I would have to develop other attributes that were possibly latent within me and he was a massive influence in helping me to see that and start developing them.

I had no money for the entire spell I was there and had to sleep on teammate Ryan Commerford's floor most of the time. We lived off noodles and bread for the majority of the week and when we got paid on a Friday, the first thing we did was treat ourselves to a steak. Characters abound wherever you play and our side had its share. As is traditional out there, we had a game on Anzac Day and before the start there is always a minute's silence.

We were lined up in position for the kick-off, rather than being grouped together, when the ref blew his whistle to mark its beginning and as the quiet descended all we could hear was this one bloke shouting, mainly obscenities. I glanced round and it was one of my teammates screaming, 'Let's get into these bastards, we'll show them, kill the...' and worse. It went on for about thirty seconds; he was just in a complete world of his own. He did eventually come out of his zone and realise but it was one of the dumbest things I'd ever seen – and we were supposed to be the university team.

While I was out in Wollongong I played alongside one of the hardest tacklers I've come across, an uncompromising forward called Jason Tassell. He was a genuine big hitter and that is a rare skill, on a par with those who can score tries out of nothing. Such intensely physical players are few and far between; Adrian Morley is another. Jason played a bit of NRL and was a biker who came down and only appeared in a few games with us. He was a good guy and gave me some useful advice. Also in our ranks was another fearless forward, Sean Skelton, who played for South Africa in the 2000 World Cup. I lost the bit of confidence I had initially gained because Greg was seemingly on at me all the time and I was grateful when my granddad came out to visit for a couple of weeks, which was a massive gesture and undertaking. Although he was seventy by then, it was great having a friendly and supportive face around the place. I certainly came back a different person but after six months I realised that I couldn't do it any more. Matthew Elliott had said that he would speak to me every week to check how I was going but I only heard from him once in a blue moon, though that was hardly surprising as the Bulls were struggling and in his predicament I must hardly have rated on the radar. Eventually I telephoned him and told him I was coming back. I was disappointed to leave and reflecting now it seems like the kind of soft option I detest but I needed to play more regularly if I was to progress. Learning the Aussie outlook on sport and witnessing their must-win mentality at first hand was a real help and an apprenticeship of some sort over there is something I would definitely recommend to any aspiring young professional.

Upon my return there was another culture shock in store: I was sent on-loan to Featherstone. By the time I got to Rovers the side was going well and on their way to reaching the inaugural Division One Grand Final which would see the victors promoted to Super League. Coach Steve Simms gave me a couple of run-outs over a three-month period, which I thought went okay, but he was generally happy with the players he had relied on before my arrival and stuck with them. I ended up principally being the 'rubber', doing the pre-game massages for those who were playing. I'd train at Bradford all day and then go up to Post Office Road hoping for a different type of hands-on role. It was an immensely frustrating experience because I knew that I was capable of being better than some of those who I was kneading; if only I could get a chance to prove it. Paddy Handley, who thought his place might be under threat and believed himself to be in some way superior, was one who went out of his way to make me feel unwelcome. Nevertheless, after the Wollongong episode, I was determined not to give in and to bide my time. Being involved on the periphery is nothing like actually feeling part of a team and able to make a genuine imact – it is the curse of the sportsperson. My senior debut was for Rovers as a substitute against Widnes at home in July 1998. I was anxious beforehand and we won narrowly, but I was still jeered by some of the more narrow-minded 'flatcappers'. I came off the bench and tried to get stuck in, as is my way, although I don't think I was particularly noticeable or remarkable; my performance was definitely nothing to write home about. That allowed a few of the Post Office Road faithful to have a go as I made my way back to the dressing room with jibes of 'Bradford rubbish' ringing in my ears, and even more laughably as I was living close to the breadline: 'What a waste of money.'

A better opportunity eventually came for me during the short-lived Trieze Tournoi, which gave some of the lower-ranked clubs the chance to play a few matches against sides of a similar standard in the south of France. By then Steve Simms had left and Kevin Hobbs taken over the reins, and he selected me to start at prop against St Esteve. On the journey over, I got involved in the card game 'chase the ace', partly to pass the time but also because I needed the money. The pot doubled after the first game was shared but I managed to stick in there and eventually take it, which cheered me up immensely. I was incredibly wound up before the match with this huge desire to prove so many people wrong and show them what I was made of and to earn the respect of those whose legs I had been rubbing. I ripped into the French pack and ran myself ragged from the off, forgetting that the temperature was red hot. By half-time I was physically exhausted and spent the entire ten minutes in what passed as a toilet. My initial shock at the primitive facilities quickly wore off as I simultaneously used both available holes in the ground, liquid streaming from each end. I won the medal for the Man of the Match but that was virtually the end of the season and my spell with Featherstone.

When I returned to Bradford there was devastating news; Matthew Elliott said that they didn't want to sign me again and that he thought that I wasn't going to make it. It took one of the scouts there who had spotted my late and latent potential at Stanningley to get me another shot – a one-year deal in the last-chance saloon. What the reprieve immediately made me re-evaluate was my social life. I was ready for a change but, more importantly, I needed to alter my priorities if I was going to make the kind of sacrifices needed to get to the top.

FOUR

THE BULL BEGINS
TO RAGE

A phrase I heard at about the time it seemed as though my dream might be over before it had begun has stuck with me since. It goes: 'The pain of discipline is nothing like the pain of disappointment.' Throughout the following pre-season I carried that thought with me constantly, along with a fair amount of anger. I can honestly say that I have rarely trained as hard as I did over the Christmas and New Year period going into 1999. I continually tested and pushed myself, even going out for a run on Christmas Day because I thought it would give me an advantage over those rivals who hadn't. I knew by then that there were players out there who were more naturally gifted than I was but that if I could take myself to places where maybe they would not go, then perhaps I could get one over on them. Something else I learnt very early on, predominantly from Brian McDermott, was the importance of mental toughness as being the vital extra ingredient for a forward. We have to be able to physically push ourselves that bit extra to compensate; it is our part of reading the game, and a much underestimated skill in itself.

I was fortunate at Bradford that in the season I made my breakthrough, there were so many natural leaders at the club. It bred a culture of encouragement and fostered a passionate desire to win trophies. The likes of Jimmy Lowes, Mike Forshaw, Brian McDermott, Bernard Dwyer, Scott Naylor and Stuart Spruce were all characters and consummate professionals. They knew how to work and play hard – and the right time to be doing it – and were the ideal role models for someone trying to make it in the big time. I just had to have enough intelligence to watch, digest and learn from them and their application and, gradually, their habits started to rub off. Three people who meant a lot to me when I was growing up and looking for heroes to emulate were Ellery Hanley, Dave Heron and Mike Forshaw. I always thought Ellery was a tremendous player with the way he carried himself around the field, the work he did to always be in the right place and the crucial tries he scored as a result; they're what you're most impressed by as a young lad. My Dad always liked to watch Dave Heron who used to sweep clear for some classic long-range scores, so I took a great interest in him, and Forsh was a real grafter who you had to admire. That was the craziest thing about becoming a professional, to find myself alongside him in the dressing room at Bradford. Jimmy Lowes was another who I'd watched from the ter- races playing for Hunslet against Leeds as a young scrum-half and I could never have imagined we'd end up packing down together.

Performing alongside Mike Forshaw I got to fully appreciate how much honest toil he put in and he looked such an intelligent player. Appearances, though, can be deceptive. He always had a funny tale to tell but had less common sense than most people. After training at Bradford we used to have dinner cooked for us by a lady called Penny and Mike, Jimmy and Brian McDermott used to hang around together. I made a point of going over to sit with them just to hear them either heckle every single person who walked into the room, or them trying to outdo each other with tall tales. It was hilarious and a great time. They started off with true stories to begin with but by the time they finished it was like the 'my fish is this big' boast and akin to being in the middle of Monty Python's 'Yorkshiremen' sketch; they used to make me howl. They have all been referred to as 'old school', as have I by Robbie Paul, and I take that to be a compliment. I think it's about respect and working for what you get, paying deference to experience and, where it's appropriate, socialising as hard as you play. There was a distinct order in the dressing room in which I grew up and that taught me the score about working your way through and truly earning your place. That's how I like to operate, even if it is an old-fashioned concept, of serving an appren- ticeship; adhering to and being prepared to take from those who know.

Condtioner Carl Jennings came into the sport in 1999 and revolutionised it for Bradford and possibly all of Super League. Everybody started to put loads of weight on and he played a major part in developing my physique, turning me from being willing but lanky into someone who could make a physical impact at the top level. He had an unjaundiced approach, coming from shot-putt and athletics and his techniques and methods opened eyes.

They shook rugby league out of any insular complacency. Too often we think that just because ours is the roughest, toughest game, with the fittest performers, that we can't learn from outside influences. I'd say his insight was on a par with how legendary coach Jack Gibson transformed the Australian game when he started importing and adapting defensive techniques from Gridiron. Mind you, 'Jenno' was mad as a wasp despite his fervour. He called me his 'Project X' and he used to absolutely destroy me; forcing me into extra training all the time. I'd be playing in the under-21s on a Thursday and then he'd have me doing extra weights on the Friday, Saturday and Sunday; there was no respite. It was all or nothing with him, but it not only helped me to add bulk but also to get a good training attitude. He'd put it in when he was an athlete and his dad is seventy-odd and looks twenty years younger and is massive, so their regime is obviously inherited. He made us ultra-fit and since he left and followed Matthew Elliott, he has done the same at Canberra – just look at how many of the extra-time games that they have been involved in they have won. He was frequently changing things and trying new routines to keep training interesting and when you are doing the slog, that is vital. I think he saw in me someone he could mould. I always had a willingness for work and occasionally that manifests itself in a bad temper. We once had a blow up when I was on a rowing machine in a public gym and he was shouting about how far I had to go and my response was short, loud and filled with every expletive I knew, in front of everyone. He put his head down and it all went very quiet, a few people in there sloped off for a while in case it started to kick off between us, but that was just our combined passion. There were also a few first-teamers in there at the time and they must have seen that in standing up to him I did have something in me. I was prepared to go the extra mile and I don't think that he would have put the time and effort in if he didn't feel that it was being reciprocated. More than that, I enjoyed it.

I achieved my initial goal of being awarded a first-team squad number but failed to make the starting seventeen, although it was not for the want of trying. I couldn't have done much more in the reserve side to get a shot; there was a spell when I won eight or nine Man of the Match awards on the trot. Just when it seemed as though there would be a chance of promotion for one of the younger guys from that team, Lee Radford was selected ahead of me. That was for a match away at St Helens and we got blitzed, which softened the blow a bit. Eventually, I was thrown in as a substitute at home to Wakefield. There were some nerves, not least about playing in front of so many people for the first time but mainly I was desperate not to mess up. It first really hit me that I was making my debut when I went out for the warm-up. In the week before, once I knew that I had been selected, I was relieved more than anything because it confirmed that at last the coaching staff must have studied the videos of my matches and seen something. My will to do well was centred on a fervent desire just to stay in the team and that spurred me on. I had to wait an hour on the sidelines to get into the action, in a game that wasn't particularly good to watch but by then I was desperate to give it a go. My first impression out there was how fast and physical it was but what I had on my side was that no one knew me and so they were wary. I've always been pretty strong and I made one particular run where I think I bumped off three defenders and you could sense a bit of a rise in the crowd, which was gratifying. I defended next to Robbie Paul and he was shouting at me to rip into the opposition; it was a lot more verbal and intense than what I had been used to in the Senior Academy.

I was relatively satisfied with how it went as I came off and with the buzz of feeling a real part of something. My first mark in the *Telegraph and Argus* was a six out of ten for my efforts and when you are young and impressionable, that kind of a measure in the public arena probably is important. It seemed fair for twenty minutes work, an above-average assessment. At the start of your career you are looking for affirmation no matter where it's from. If they were being honest, most players would admit that they do read things that are printed about them, although whether they take any notice of them is a different story. It is drilled into you not to put any store on what is said outside and to only pay attention to what the coaches are telling you but I have always been a firm believer that you know deep down whether you have turned up or not and you don't need anyone to tell you that. The hardest person to please is invariably yourself. At the start, I used to ask my Mum and Dad if had done alright but that was more often than not for reassurance when, perhaps, I knew that I hadn't.

My first big game was around a month later when I was on the bench to face Wigan at Odsal in front of over 13,000 fans. The night before, I was so nervous sitting at home that I must have read my game plan a hundred times over. You get tip sheets on all the players you are likely to be facing and there wasn't any part of their game or trait that I was unfamiliar with by the time I went to bed; if there had been an exam on it I would not have failed through lack of revision. In the end, I only got on for a few minutes but I was massively determined to do as much work as I could, especially as I was in awe of opponents like Denis Betts, whose career, in my position, I had avidly followed. It was a typically wet and cold Odsal night but I got fired into it for the brief time I was on and in the context of the season it was an important win for us. Wigan were the reigning champions and there was still an air about them even though they were starting to come to the end of their period of total dominance. Bradford, by contrast, were the new force emerging; we were wholeheartedly embracing the move to summer and full-time professionalism, which was seeing us catch up with and fiercely challenge the old guard.

I got my first experience of playing away at first-team level against Sheffield Eagles, in a match staged in the unusual setting of Saltergate, the home of Chesterfield FC. It was boiling hot, the dressing rooms were about as big as my toilet at home and we were all falling over each other while getting changed. The Eagles were starting to struggle a little in the wake of the euphoria of their sensational cup win the year before and Matt Elliott had told me that I would be getting more game time. I came on earlier, during the first half, and had the satisfaction of claiming my first senior try, powering over from close-in through a couple of defenders. Matt was a very observant and astute coach and afterwards he mentioned to the Press that he thought the game had changed with my introduction, which was the first time I had really seen my name in the papers. That meant a lot to me; I was chuffed to have made a discernible contribution to the team effort. I was starting to make gains along the way. More importantly, the performance kept me in the frame for selection the following week.

It was easier to come on after twenty minutes in those days and bust the game open as a wide-running, impact player and to cap it with a try was especially pleasing. Leon Pryce was one of the first to come over to me as I turned and walked back and his words of congratulation were 'it's about time'. I used to wear tape around my forehead in those days, which was of more use keeping my big ears held back rather than any hair out of my eyes. It was something I had started doing when I made the open-age side at Stanningley – the amateur game is full of such rituals and it becomes part of your psychology. After a while I realised it was more open to ridicule than portraying a hard-man image, so it was quickly dispensed with. From then on I seemed to be in or around the first-team squad most of the time. There isn't a point when you feel that you've made it or you completely get used to your new-found status – as I discovered at the end of that campaign when I was omitted from the Grand Final squad. If you start taking things for granted, that's when complacency sets in, but at least I had done enough to get a revised three-year deal. It was to be another full season before I could consider myself to be a regular first-teamer, when I was getting selected ahead of more experienced guys. I guess you know you've arrived when the senior players start to talk to you in the dressing room rather than just take the piss.

My first start came in the midweek game after the Sheffield clash against London at home. We thrashed them and the try-scoring run continued with a double, one of them thanks to a kick from James Lowes. We used to score quite a lot from that planned move in those days and I think Matt was pretty much the first coach to employ two front runners who were either props or second-rowers close to the line who Jimmy could either hit with a flat pass, use as a foil to find a half-back wider out or kick to. I was one of the lead chasers when he decided to grubber through and I managed to react quickly and land on the ball. There was no added pressure in running out from the off or any particular change to my routine, more a genuine enjoyment that I was getting longer spells of action. Although the 74-12 final score made it seem like an easy win, the Broncos were a really tough side, full of hard-bitten, mainly journeymen Aussies and it was a draining, physical effort for me throughout. The compensation for the bruising was the wage packet. We used to get paid weekly then and I was on a basic of £120, which was below average, but the win bonus was £500, which was also paid out every Thursday. I moan about the ludicrous demands of playing two games in a week now but I loved the midweek matches back then. All of a sudden I had an extra grand on me and going round Bramley I felt like a millionaire.

My first four appearances over a two-month period had all brought wins but that was nothing to do with me being a lucky talisman; the team was well coached and in good form. The game on the immediate horizon that I was desperate to play and do well in was the derby clash with Leeds at Headingley, a homecoming, albeit in the visiting dressing room. Around that time, the summer encounters between the two Yorkshire giants were just starting to acquire their massive interest, status and immense rivalry, and we were thrashed. We could not contain Andy Hay, he crossed for a hat-trick and the Rhinos were awesome. The result was a real letdown for the Bulls and their fans but personally it was a performance in which I felt I got added respect from our senior players. We were getting heavily beaten but I made myself available to do the dirty work. On a couple of occasions, as they put us under real pressure, we had tap restarts on our own quarter line. Taking the first hit when the opposition is on top and you have already spent massive amounts of energy constantly defending your own line is one of the hardest tasks in the game and I put my hand up a couple of times. Even in defeat, that day probably furthered my career. It marked a significant progression but I had been on tenterhooks throughout the week leading up to the game. My good mate Mark Adams kept saying to me that he couldn't believe I would be playing on the hallowed turf after we had watched so many of our heroes play there, and how he was chuffed for me. It all added to the tingling excitement. Of course I got there too early; there was no point going on the team coach when I lived so close by and what was more, I wanted to come round the corner to imbibe the majesty of the place and full realisation that it was now my stage. Fortunately, Jimmy Lowes was in the same boat and in situ well before it was necessary and it was also a big game for him. He had only recently and somewhat surprisingly left Leeds to join the Bulls, lived nearby, and was still the subject of the crowd's ire for his apparent desertion, so we stood together soaking up the building atmosphere. I settled straight into the game even though the team was underperforming. It was a record crowd and a hot day but fortunately, by then, because of the measured way I had been brought into the side, I was a bit more used to it and the sense of occasion helped inspire and bring the best out of me rather than be overwhelming.

As well as Chesterfield that season, we had another fixture at an unusual ground for the sport when London moved their home match against us to Welford Road, Leicester, as part of an awareness drive. I thought it was a great idea to reach out to a potential new audience. The game was played in midweek and there was a decent, loud crowd. Although it was the home of Leicester Tigers, a rugby union Mecca, we didn't have much contact with anyone from their ranks, although I can remember thinking that I wouldn't like to play on that size of pitch with fifteen-a-side; it was pretty narrow, although the stadium was great. The travelling was a pain – it was one of those trips that didn't justify an overnight stop but meant a fair bit of time sat on a coach and we got there about four hours too early – I think Matt must have thought that we were going by horse and cart and miscalculated how long it would take us. Then the kick-off got delayed because they didn't have enough turnstiles open to accommodate those who were queuing to get in. We ended up watching most of the curtain raiser between the amateurs of Coventry and Birmingham and teams like that get undoubted benefit from having Super League games scheduled on their doorstep, it's something the Rugby League should look to do more of. They should certainly keep targeting Wales, where the 'Millennium Magic' weekend is a terrific idea and maybe, now and then, shift a big game into places like the Midlands which are easily visited within a day – because rugby league fans aren't generally minted – for the overall good of the sport's profile. Although they weren't expected to, the Broncos gave us a real test that night, veteran Aussie star Peter Gill smashed me during the match.

Welford Road was a one-off and so, for me, in a Super League sense, was Wigan's famous old venue, Central Park, as it closed in 1999. I'd played there in academy rugby in front of about 500 people but I was conscious that it would be my only chance to run out at one of the sport's most historic and atmospheric arenas in a truly big game – even though it was a filthy night and it had rained all day. I felt that performing at places at like that, which held so much resonance, was an important part of my education and development. Playing in more and more high profile, meaningful matches was part of it, but performing well in the most hostile of environments and in the shadow of where the true greats had trodden was key. Wigan dominated us that night and it wasn't one of my best performances. I came off the bench and a couple of things I tried didn't come off. I attempted to bump off their prop Tony Mestrov to make a statement and the ball came free; that was naïvety, and not playing to the conditions. Nevertheless, it was a great place to play. The clash had been built up all week on *Boots 'N' All* and in the Press, and the Warriors did a job on us.

Atmospheres don't get much better or more electric than the return game with Leeds at Odsal in early September, which saw a competition-record crowd of over 24,000 packed into the bowl. Although it was early in my career, that match remains one of the finest Super League encounters I've been a part of, and one revered by the fans. The encounter was settled by a Michael Withers drop goal very late on to give us a nail-biting 19-18 win. It went by in a flash but I vividly remember that it was a tremendous feeling to come out of it with the points. Just before Mick's astonishing one-pointer, Nathan McAvoy had come up with a sensational play to pluck the ball out of the night sky from Steve McNamara's towering kick to the corner to get us level. That was the thing with Nat, he came up with some breathtaking moments of skill in big games for Bradford, but it was either rocks or diamonds with him. Even though it was Mick's first career drop goal, and such a crucial one at that, it came as little surprise to the rest of us; he could probably do anything and is undoubtedly one of the coolest characters I have ever come across in a dressing room. In training he was the most laid back and naturally skilful, and, at that time, injury free. He was one of the main reasons we won things at Bradford, especially in finals; his ability to score tries and come up with crucial plays in the big games was exceptional.

It meant a lot to me to beat Leeds but so did playing a part in a huge team effort. We weren't reading too much into that result because the Rhinos were on something of a downward spiral; they had won the Challenge Cup earlier in the season but it was the last few games of Graham Murray's reign and things were starting to ebb away – that defeat effectively broke their Grand Final challenge. Conversely, we were re-infused with belief that we could have a real shot at it, having been badly knocked off course by Wigan. We'd shown we had the necessary resolve to hit back and come up with the required performance and right result, under pressure and in front of a huge, baying crowd. What the Bulls achieved in 2003, when we did the treble and were virtually unbeatable, was founded on matches like that one with Leeds. The top sides have to learn how to come out on top in the big games. The team grew on the back of such encounters and gradually gained the knowledge of what was required to come up with the key moves and calls at the right time. We lacked a bit of that at the time but we gradually acquired the skills to shut out matches and eventually won trophies because of it. However, it is a process you have to go through together as a team. It's arguably the reason why the Aussies have dominated at international level for so long. It is not so much about comparative individual skill levels; their winning mentality comes from 'State of Origin' games. They may not always be the most attractive to watch but in such an intense environment, they learn when the big play is on and what is required to win when it really counts.

We thrashed St Helens in the play-offs to qualify for the Grand Final but by then I was already starting to feel that even if we did get through I might miss out on Old Trafford. It was a vibe I sensed about the way things were going on around me and I knew that I really had to play well that night to try and force Matthew's hand. Everyone else was back from injury, fresh and available and I realised that I would be the easy person to drop. I came on for the last twenty minutes and I was really, really pleased with my performance, I don't think I could have done any more. There was a lot of talk of how good St Helens were going to be under Ellery Hanley and we just blew them away. That was partly due to the competition for places, those guys who started knew that they had to justify their shirt and we were twenty points up in no time. I made a couple of breaks when I came on but as it turned out, they were not enough.

Because we had finished top of the table at the end of the regular season, we got a weekend off from the play-offs before the Saints game and used it as a bonding exercise. We all went up to Harrogate and had a good drink together as a team, although I'm not sure it was a great idea to schedule training on the Saturday morning and to try and instil in us some new set moves from tap penalties and scrums. Virtually everyone had a steaming hangover but because the plan to go away worked, we went back up there the following weekend to prepare for the Grand Final while Castleford and Saints slugged it out to see who would face us. It was just as enjoyable, although Saturday training was dropped.

After all the personal trauma surrounding the Grand Final, I didn't go to the civic reception which was thrown afterwards despite the side losing. I was in a pub in Bradford instead, even though Matthew rang and asked me to join the team. I was intimidated by and pissed off with him at the same time and I said no, which was, on reflection, a bit childish and selfish. I was the worse for consoling myself with a glass but equally, I really didn't feel an integral part of things. One person I did get on well with was assistant coach Mick Potter, now the head man at Catalans Dragons. He gives out an impression of being pretty dour but I always found him to be a really smart operator. When it was time for him to tell or teach you something, you switched on but he also knew how and when to enjoy himself. He was exactly what an assistant coach should be, he was able to have a laugh about the place with the players and act as their go-between with the head man. He was incredibly fit and showed us a few tricks and different exercises on the running machine and you could tell that he had been a very profes-sional player who had played in Grand Finals. Back home, he was awarded the 'Dally M' medal as the competition's best player – and no mug wins that – and you could clearly see why he was regarded as one of the best never to play for Australia. He was a good bloke to be around and chat to. Steve McNamara was one of the senior set who did not have too much to do with me as an up-and-coming junior, but you could tell he was a smart guy and a teacher and that he was destined to make his mark in coaching. When he rejoined the Bulls in that capacity I learned a terrific amount from him and he gained my respect that way.

The issue of mergers, a word that blighted the introduction of Super League, reared its head again at the end of that season with Sheffield and Huddersfield and, more bizarrely, Gateshead and Hull forming unpopular alliances. They were never destined to work, not least because of the distances involved, and were more or less takeovers anyway but it did begin to refocus a debate that had started with the arrival of summer rugby. It's tough to say what's right but as a player I can imagine how strong a side that contained the best of Castleford, Wakefield and Featherstone would be. If you look at Australia, two of their most famous names, Balmain Tigers and Western Suburbs – who were never going to take out a title individually – got together, became a force, and won a Grand Final. There is a lot more culture and tradition over here, though, and that has to be respected. I got my three-year contract extension on 20 December, which was a nice early festive present and a relief. It wasn't the best of deals, partly because of Nick Fowler, the agent who brokered it, who was recommended to me by Neil Harmon. He's not on Adrian Morley's Christmas card list either and I ended up having massive arguments with him which necessitated getting the then renowned Bradford chairman Chris Caisley, a noted solicitor, involved. Fowler once made the mistake of ringing my house and asking me for money, which got the tersest of replies. Years later, I couldn't believe it when we were in camp with Great Britain and I got a shout from Moz saying Fowler was a contestant on *The Weakest Link*, which somehow seemed appropriate.

FIVE

ON FIRMER FOOTING

After the despair of just missing out on the biggest game in my career so far, there was no way I was going to suffer from second-season syndrome. I wasn't going to be the bloke you read about one minute and who has then disappeared off the radar the next, like Paul Deacon when it's time to buy a round. Resting on my laurels because I had tasted first-team rugby was not in my nature and now I had the added incentive to take the next step up; to prove the doubters wrong. I relished the pre-season regime; I knew my limitations and that I would have to apply myself more than anyone else around me if I was to succeed. The three months of sacrifice and hard slog paid off and within ten games of the start of the 2000 campaign I had gone from failing to make the Grand Final squad to starting in the Challenge Cup decider.

The two big signings Bradford made, Hudson Smith and, especially, Brad Mackay played in my position so that gave me an extra push. Brad was a massive influence but their arrival brought out my competitive instinct. I was determined not to whinge about it but to prove that I deserved a place in the starting thirteen; I was definitely not going to miss out for lack of effort. Brad was an ideal role model, something of a wild man off the pitch when he was younger before becoming a committed Christian with a terrific work ethic and ultra-professional habits. We soon found out why he was known as 'Test Match' back home in Australia and that it was not because he had scored a hat-trick in one of them for the Kangaroos. As a youngster, he used to train with the enthusiasm of someone who was making their international debut at the end of every week; that was how dedicated he was and we were unfortunate only to have him for a season at the Bulls because his family never properly settled. He made a real impression on the senior players; Mike Forshaw behaved like he was in love with him, he was his shadow, and the other guys used to give Forsh some real hammer over it. To be fair to him, Mike just wanted to be the most consummate professional he could and saw someone competing for his shirt who could give him some vital pointers.

Although the massively popular Boxing Day game has become little more than a lucrative exhibition since the move to summer rugby, I was eagerly looking forward to breaking the punishing training regime for some proper contact. We faced a strong Leeds at Headingley, who included the likes of Barrie McDermott, Aussie hard man David Barnhill on debut, Willie Poching and Adrian Morley. I was desperate to prove myself in what turned out to be a fierce friendly. The real foundation for a good season was laid for me on the pre-season training camp in Lanzarote; it was great to be among the senior players who now accepted me a bit more. Four of us shared a little billet together, including Brian McDermott and Lee Radford, and we used to get hammered on protein milkshakes, we just couldn't get enough of them. It was a funny time; Brian would open the floor to us, we could ask any question we liked and he would always have an answer. It was rarely the right one but by sheer volume of words and accompanying wisecracks he would often convince us otherwise – or so he thought. He was the nearest thing we had to Jeremy Clarkson. Fans might think that going abroad to train is living the life of luxury but you become like an athletic zombie; wandering, dazed from fatigue, from one rigorous session to the next with what feels like five minutes rest between them.

Before the season started, Dad came round waving the trade newspaper *League Express* at me. They had profiled each club and looked at their prospects and he was thrilled to see that I had been picked out as Bradford's 'Young Gun', especially with the crop of talented mates coming through together at the club, not least Paul Deacon, Stu Fielden, 'Radders' and Leon Pryce. I was pleased; it was nice to have been noticed but the only people I really wanted respect from were the coaching staff and my teammates. At the end of the calendar year, Dad was round again with their *Rugby League Yearbook*, which had me down as one of the five personalities of the season. I'm not sure what impressed him more, my form throughout the season that warranted the inclusion, or the fact that my name was in a book which was easier to display than the yellowing cuttings he was compiling in a scrapbook.

I felt my all-round game was beginning to develop, I had always had an offload in me and was punching the line with more confidence, therefore setting up chances for teammates who were starting to see that I might be worth supporting. I was getting noticed for my assists, but the other side of the coin was that I also became more of a target and started appearing on opposition tip sheets. It's a compliment in kind but it just means that you have to keep trying to come up with new skills to defy them. That was certainly the case early in the season at Huddersfield where I was singled out for a lot of heavy treatment. Every time I got near the ball, three or four defenders piled into me. The tactic worked; I didn't mind rising to that sort of challenge but I ended up trying too hard, had a poor game and made some costly errors. I was dragged into touch and spilt the ball a couple of times attempting reckless offloads. I gave Matt the excuse to bring out the hook and substitute me. Unforced errors are a cardinal sin for a young player trying to make an impression. An experienced operator is allowed more of a licence because they are tried and tested, and the coach has ultimate faith in them. I was nowhere near that level and I was fuming with myself.

There was no point sulking, I've no time for players who do that after a poor performance, instead I set myself two new goals. First, I decided that if things were not going my way, I would resist the temptation to try some flashy, gimmicky piece of skill to get out of it. Instead I would front up and try and unsettle the opposition with my attitude. If they wanted to continually bash me, fine, but that would not stop me running at them as hard and as often as possible until they were sick of the sight of me. If they missed me, great, then I was away. It was a realisation that I needed to be sharper, more focused and better prepared. Physical training was not enough if I wanted to stay in the side, I had to have a mental edge and I've invested heavily in that area since. Also, I vowed that I would never play that badly at that stadium again and now the Galpharm is one of my favourite venues; I have been fortunate to have won some terrific games there for club and country. Although not a key match against the Giants, it was an important experience and a stepping stone in my career. I was determined to remember the lessons learned that day.

Tactically, my first start of the season, against Warrington at Odsal, could not have worked out better. Often the Bulls' game plan under Matt revolved around exploiting a particular side of the opposition and to attack as often as possible down that channel. Fortunately, it was my time in the spotlight because everything was targeted down the right and Jimmy Lowes and

Henry Paul made sure I got a lot of quality ball. I managed a few noticeable runs, which won me the Man of the Match award and that meant a lot to me. Even more fortunately, it was the week before we played the same side in the Challenge Cup semi-final and I was conscious that a good display might give me a chance of playing in that game and, possibly, my first final.

We rarely got celebrities up at Odsal but around that time William Hague arrived to promote a joint-learning initiative, something that the Bulls were renowned for, and we were required to take part in a photo shoot with him. A few of the guys were taking the mickey out of him, asking daft questions, but rather than relying on his oratory skills to retort with a witty or sharp comment like most politicians would, he just started to stammer and seemed lost for words. It was the first time that I had been in such exalted company and he did not come across well; he was clearly not that interested in speaking to us at all, although Seb Coe was there as his minder and it was great to meet him.

Much has been made since the sport moved to the summer that the Challenge Cup has lost something of its edge or mystique. Before the final was moved to late August, there was a feeling in certain circles that it was in danger of just becoming a pre-season tournament and losing its lustre to the Grand Final. I've never subscribed to that theory. For the players it is still extra-special and something that we were brought up with and revered. It's what we all watched on television as youngsters and went down to Wembley to be a part of. Being a product of Super League, I have never known it any different. For me, the cup had never started three-quarters of the way through the season. Beginning it early seemed to give the lower division sides a better chance of shocking the top teams because they would not be in full swing. Rugby league is a brutal sport; it's not like football. If you are not up to the physical requirements and skill levels, you will get blown away. It is very unforgiving. Nowadays, the Challenge Cup is half of what the season is about when it comes to silverware; the other trophies have gone and every player values it.

In the early rounds against Sheffield and Wakefield, the key factor was that we did not concede a try, which illustrated the hunger in the side and set down a marker. Matt showed what a smart coach he was; he knew that if we improved our defence on the standard set in 1999, then we would be in with a chance of winning silverware. Defence is the most team-orientated part of the game because if your weakest link goes, the opposition score. The full squad wanted penance for the Grand Final and we were prepared to go that extra mile for it. The semi-final, against Warrington at Headingley in late March, was a seminal match in my fledgling career and the most important one that I had featured in thus far. Matt told me early in the week that I'd be starting and I was jumping; my Dad was really chuffed and all my mates wanted tickets. It was a noon kick-off for the BBC, which was great because there was no chance to be nervous. You get up, have breakfast and then it's into the car to the game. It helped me that it was on the turf I was so familiar with; that was awesome. I parked in my favoured spot just round the corner, no doubt annoying the local residents.

It was a tough, end-to-end game for a while; I managed to get over for a late try and our forward dominance and the Paul brothers' guile saw us through to the final. That was a tremendous feeling and I went out in Headingley to some of my old haunts with my mates to celebrate but there was a bit of trouble. The 'Skyrack' pub got shut down because a lot of Manchester City fans had come over on the back of it being Warrington, looking for Leeds United supporters, who they found easily enough, and it all kicked off. The pub ended up looking like something from the Wild West, with everything smashed up, but it would have taken more than that to wipe the smile off my face. All that initial hard work had quickly paid off and I stood on the verge of getting my first medal in the game. It was all a new experience to me and I tried to learn as fast as I could. No matter what players may say and coaches would have you believe, there is part of your mind that is set on the big day from then on. I was aware of it as a positive spur going into the league matches leading up to the final. You do worry about injury – Leon dislocated his shoulder and missed out – but once the action starts your instincts take over anyway.

The constant reminders of the size of the event came in everything that surrounded it; people asking you for tickets and getting arrangements for our nearest and dearest sorted out. There was a real buzz around the city, although the Bulls were a much more intimate set-up in those days, with the club based around a couple of portakabins because of the Odsal re-development, which lent itself well to the family atmosphere they'd generated. We were always there hanging around them, making plans and finalising details. It was over fifty years since Bradford had won the trophy and we were overwhelming favourites, which brings its own pressures. The senior guys were constantly reminding us to ignore all the predictions and that no matter what their poor form going into the game indicated, Leeds, our opponents, were the holders. They also had some hardened, big-game players like Adrian Morley and Iestyn Harris and they saw the cup final as the ideal chance for them to turn their season around. At the time, Bradford had the reputation for being chokers in finals and there was a fierce determination among those who had been there before and lost – like Brian Mac, Jimmy Lowes and Bernard Dwyer – to put that right because it was galling hearing it. I wasn't particularly bothered that the game was at Murrayfield and not Wembley as the cup final went on the road, although there was a tinge of 'what might have been'. I have not yet managed to play in the national stadium and it remains a huge ambition. I even missed out on performing there in the under-11s curtain raiser because I was a year below when it was the Leeds schools' turn. I was just grateful to be in the final, Edinburgh is a beautiful city and it was good to get away with the boys.

The team flew up there, which was another indication of how seriously the club were taking things. Again, you are guided by the senior guys and when they start getting excited by that prospect, it rubs off. We got there in the middle of the operation to clear the ground of intense flooding, which seriously threatened the event. At one stage the stadium was submerged under three feet of water. We were slightly divorced from all that, I couldn't see them postponing the cup final, even though there was talk about it in the idle chit-chat between those hanging around the team hotel. We had to remain focused on the game and Matt had already told me early in the week that I would be playing, so that was my sole train of thought. The three guys who were left out of the squad, Paul Deacon, Neil Harmon and Lee Radford, seemed to be having a whale of a time. Neil being Neil had convinced Brannigans that, as part of some sort of deal, they had agreed to give the squad free beer and every time we got on the bus to training, the trio of them were at the back stinking of it, they'd be quiet but were clearly the worse the wear. Neil or 'Le Chateau' was another, somewhat unsung hero in my continuing progression through the ranks, giving me lifts to training throughout most of 1999 and 2000, and invariably saying the right things. I was glad I wasn't one of them for once; I was just on a natural high with the prospect of playing in such a high-profile fixture that had worldwide interest and attention.

Once again I was rooming with Brian Mac and he had been asked to do a video diary for one of the local television channels, which was a mistake. We all had to be interviewed and went along to Jimmy Lowes' room when it was his turn. Jimmy went to the toilet and Brian started stripping off and filming himself naked in the mirror when we heard Jimmy shout:

'Come and have a look at this.' I don't know how, but he had somehow produced something that looked like a pair of small honeydew melons. It didn't look physically possible but he wanted them recorded on film. Brian had to delete that scene and most of the others. It would have made interesting viewing for the Youtube generation. Brian had also written the Bradford player profiles in the match programme with his usual off-beat humour. It was the first time something like that had been given over to the players and it is an idea which should be fostered, giving a chance for the public to understand the wider personality and character of those that they watch. In them, he called me Inspector Gadget, which was something Matt Elliott had come up with because of my long arms and ability to keep my limbs going, but it was a pretty crap nickname to have out there in the public arena. Mind you, Aussies are not exactly renowned for their sense of humour; they're not a nation overflowing with well-known comedians. Brian was complimentary, as well as taking the piss out of all of us – it was an entertaining piece that we all appreciated. The night before the game I was struggling to sleep and Brian started reading me passages from the standard-issue hotel-room *Gideon Bible*. Neither of us was religious but it was his way of lightening and calming the mood, until I asked him about the first Gulf War. He is another to have come to the sport relatively late and by an unusual route, having spent time as a professional boxer and a Royal Marine. We used to joke that he was just a potato peeler in the catering corps, even though we knew he had seen service in Iraq. Trying to fill the time, I asked him, half jokingly, if he had ever killed anyone. The atmosphere changed instantly and it became incredibly tense as he went silent before he commented, almost monosyllabically, that he didn't want to talk about it. I was never sure if he was serious or not.

Our assistant coach, Brian Noble, commented after the final that by standing in the dressing room as we were preparing, he just knew that it was going to be our day. Sometimes you get that feeling before the most important clashes; it's not arrogance, more a sense of an innate belief in each other. You look at people and you can instantly tell the mood. You are together in a confined space and it defines the phrase 'you could cut the atmosphere with a knife'; there is a real charge between you and from everybody. It's like a radiated energy to feed off; there is a collective will to achieve a common goal that no outside force is going to stop. You can almost see it and feel it. Because we weren't allowed to do much warming up out on the pitch, there was a lot of beating the crap out of each other on the tackle shields in the dressing room that set up another positive force field; it was like the 'Ready Brek' advert, we would certainly have shown up on any thermal imaging camera.

I really enjoyed walking out into the stadium to be greeted by the huge crowd; a few people had told me to have a look for my family and get that out the way. I did, but of course I couldn't see them; you never can and I've stopped bothering now. I didn't even mind greeting the dignitaries, that's part of what gave the occasion its special feeling. All that pomp and waiting around can affect some players, making them freeze, but my thoughts were more with those coming round to meet us. I couldn't help thinking how many of the blokes in the line had gone for a quick piss either prior to the warm-up or simply from nerves before going out and had not had time to either wash their hands or dry them properly. The same thought crossed my mind when we were introduced to Prime Minister Tony Blair, again before the cup final, the following year.

The start of the game could not have gone better for us or worse for Leeds winger Leroy Rivett, who was peppered with high balls which led to two early tries. That was Henry Paul sizing up the situation and being smart. I felt sorry for Leroy. It was the plan to put him under pressure, he wasn't the tallest and we were hoping to jump over the top of him with our big outside backs but for him to drop the first couple was jackpot. A year before he had been a hero as the Rhinos won the cup for the first time in a generation. That sunny afternoon in London, he had become the first player to score four tries in a cup final to take the Lance Todd Trophy. A season later and he was a late draftee into the Leeds side, becoming one of the quickest riches to rags stories in sport. He looked like one of those cartoon characters who was trying to catch a piano thrown out of a block of flats and after he had dropped the first bomb, he carried a haunted look of sheer fright. The big clash in the forwards was between our pack leader Brian McDermott and Adrian Morley for the Rhinos. They had an almighty collision in the first minute – Macca head-highed him – and that sort of set the tone for the rest of the game and they were constantly at each other. Henry won the Man of the Match award but for me it could easily have gone to either of them. Having completed my stint, I witnessed at the closest of quarters one of the most outrageous pieces of individual skill for a try ever seen in a cup final. Nathan McAvoy broke clear, chipped over Leeds skipper and full-back Iestyn Harris and sensationally regathered to score. It was one of the flukiest touchdowns I'd seen; David Boyle – who had replaced me – was screaming for the ball on the inside and should have gone in unchallenged, all he needed was an orthodox pass. Instead, Nat unbelievably chose to kick and somehow came up with the goods; if he hadn't, he would have been torn to pieces. We built a big lead and although we were under siege at the end, we always felt that we could hang in there. The second half seemed to drag on because of a couple of long video referee deliberations and I was itching to get back out there after strutting and prowling the side lines for nearly an hour and what seemed like a thousand times. That had sapped my energy and when the final hooter eventually went, the best I could do was punch the air. I'd made up my mind as I was going up to collect my medal that I was going to kiss the trophy when it came to my turn to lift it and I was hanging on the tails of the senior guys for the subsequent lap of honour.

The celebrations in the evening were amazing; although we were in a hotel in the centre of Edinburgh, we stuck together there and didn't split up and go out into the city. They are the best times, especially in the Challenge Cup because you are all together as one in an unfamiliar place. It's not like the Grand Final, which is played at night in Manchester and as soon as it's over you are on the bus back to your club. With the cup final being played in the afternoon, it is champagne in the dressing room and then you regroup back at the team hotel. It is not just the players, it's everyone who has a role in the club; the people who sell the tickets, those in marketing and on the front desk, the kit man – everyone was there celebrating with their partners at the party. I'm sure it was as good a feeling for them as us and the club really looked after us all. I didn't have a particularly early morning; I found my bed alright, although there were a few sore heads on the coach trip back after breakfast. There were even more beers on there and that is my favourite part. Everyone is together, there's nothing to distract anyone, no one can go anywhere, they can't sit by a slot machine or need to be worried about being harangued by anyone. It's just you, fifty-square metres of bus and a lot of beer and that's sometimes where teams are made. Some of the greatest times I've had have been on long bus journeys back from places like London, Edinburgh or Cardiff. Everyone gets to be honest with each other and it's a very intense kind of meeting. Once back in Bradford, it was onto another bus, an open-topped one to Centenary Square which was another thrill and a bit different to the ones in October after the Grand Final when you are freezing. I wasn't at the front with the extroverts like Henry, Robbie, Leon and Tevita; I was quietly waving at the back alongside Scott Naylor, just chilling, soaking the atmosphere up and taking it all in.

To keep us fresh and focused after our good start to the season, we spent a couple of days up in Durham doing some arduous training during the day and having some excellent nights out as well. At the end of one of them the police were called because Paul Anderson insisted on walking around the corridors of the hotel we were staying in with no clothes on. It was an act of bravado from the big man, but as soon as he heard those sirens he absolutely shit himself and scurried back into his room like a mouse. Paul was another cornerstone of the Bradford pack but what you see with him is not quite what you would expect, for one thing he is deceptively intelligent. Despite his imposing size, 'Baloo' would be the first to admit that he doesn't wear the trousers in his relationship, they belong to his missus. He was a good one to have around the place; he used to travel over in the car with Lee Radford and Steve McNamara and they used to ruin him at training but he took it in the good-hearted, humorous spirit that was harboured in that unique, dressing-room environment. It's what is so frequently referred to by sportsmen as the craic and what they miss most when they retire or move on. 'Baloo' was the smelliest, dirtiest man but he played on it; he'd be getting the piss ripped out of him for his physique and hygiene but it would roll straight off his big, hairy back and he had a very dry sense of humour in response. For a young second-rower, playing behind the likes of him, Brian McDermott and, later, Joe Vagana was fantastic and they were such a good mix.

They say that what goes around comes around and the contrast to the previous season against Leeds at Headingley could not have been more marked. In an almost exact form reversal, we absolutely hammered them 44-2 and weren't far short of our peak. Although it was only May, that was our defining match of the season. Having felt cheated out of the previous season's Grand Final by a couple of astonishing video-refereeing decisions, we had a burning desire to win something to make up for that intense disappointment. Lifting the Challenge Cup a month earlier dampened that feeling a little but there was still some talk from Leeds about how we had not deserved to win and we wanted to show them by how far we were the better team. What stood out in the early weeks of the season was the meanness of our defence. There was enormous satisfaction looking at the Super League table on Teletext and seeing that we were the only side who had two digits in the 'against' column rather than three. I don't think that's a record which has ever been bettered for the opening half of a campaign and against the Rhinos everything fell right for us.

As part of our rehab after matches, we used to go swimming on a Saturday morning in the baths at Bradford University. Following one such session, we were in for a rude awakening when we climbed out of the pool to find that the coaching staff had swapped our clothes for dresses, wigs and handbags. Their plan was to take us out to Otley for the day and having got over the initial surprise, we found ourselves walking down the High Street in drag and beginning a pub crawl at eleven in the morning. It was some sight in the quaint old market town, twenty-six big rugby lads dressed as women frequenting the hostelries. I'd never seen Brad Mackay have a drink but he seemed to be enjoying himself although there was a slight scare around four, when we stumbled into the preserve of about fifty bikers, which led to an interesting initial stand-off. As a bonding exercise, it definitely worked and stories – although fortunately not too many pictures – still abound about that one.

Just when we thought we had a winning formula, our fifteen-match unbeaten run came to an end in a bad-tempered encounter at Warrington. They had the brilliant Australian scrum-half Alfie Langer pulling the strings for them and Tawera Nikau at stand-off who was a fierce competitor even though he was nearing the end of his career. The Wolves were a side that always raised their game when they faced the Bulls and 'T' took that to another level; he had that kind of forceful presence. You knew you'd done well if he came up to shake your hand and was sweet with you after a game. Slowly and surely our rollercoaster was starting on its downward run but not before we had beaten our nemesis, St Helens, at Odsal in the follow-ing round. I was back in the starting line-up for the first time since the cup final and we pipped them, 17-16, in a Grand Final rematch and I took the Sky Man of the Match award. I've still got the Tissot watch they gave me, somewhere in the attic. Ian Millward had just taken over at Saints and it was my best overall first-team performance to date. It poured down but my stats were good in all facets and my name started being mentioned as a possible candidate for the England World Cup squad from then on. Brian McDermott had already impressed on me that subbing was like trying to read a book from halfway through and if I had serious international ambi-tions, I needed to measure myself against the likes of established stars Paul Sculthorpe and Chris Joynt who were in the opposition ranks that night.

The clash also had added poignancy in that Bernard Dwyer – who was such a Trojan for both clubs – officially called it a day after suffering torn biceps in both arms. He was incredibly tough and it was a terrible shame how his career ended. He suffered the first injury early in the season and recovered in time to make the cup final seventeen. However, the following Wednesday we had to play our delayed league fixture at Hull after having been out celebrating for two days solid. It's hard backing up at the best of times and as we slugged out an eight-all draw, his other arm went. He was distraught but his body was telling him something and, being the pragmatic guy he is, he just decided to get on with the rest of his life. Bernard meant a lot to a whole load of us, a real players' player and someone who you wanted to have around you, especially if you were learning your trade. He took me under his wing when I was breaking through and a lot of what I subsequently achieved I owe to the likes of him for showing me what was possible and how it could be attained. There was a fitting tribute to him on the big screen after the game to him which we all watched intently.

We immediately followed the Saints win with another tremendous, mid-week encounter which saw us draw at Wigan and go back to the top of the table. I was beginning to feel I was making a bigger impact and having a greater role and that if I played well, the team had more chance of winning. I spent a fair bit of time that night trying to tackle Jason Robinson – a near impossible task – who was in his final season before going to rugby union. Attempting to hound him on a kick chase was a nightmare and as I tracked him for the umpteenth time I can remember thinking to myself: 'How good is this guy?' Around that time, one of my mates said to me that I was getting there. We were having a beer outside in the sunshine at a pub and I asked him what he meant. He got out the *Daily Mirror* and there was a report of the previous day's match with my name in the headline. I felt some self-satisfaction and thought that I must be going alright until he reminded me that he only bought the paper because of the racing pages. I was fortunate to play in a Bradford side where there were no real show ponies, I viewed most of the guys as soldiers; skilful players but hard-headed and that suited me. I've no frills and their no-nonsense honesty helped me adapt and integrate. A lot of hard work went into trying to establish myself but the transition into a first-team regular almost seemed to happen almost overnight. A lot of the time – especially when the outside world started to take notice – I was often pinching myself and thinking: 'what are you doing here?' I was so made up with playing and the little bit of extra money I then started getting, that I was just really enjoying life. The only thing that unsettled me was being in the spotlight; I found being asked for my autograph and stopped before and after games difficult. I wasn't being rude, it's just my natural shyness and I still find that sort of acclaim awkward but as you grow up in the sport you get more confident within yourself and find out who you are as a person.

I was lapping up everything and fulfilling my dreams, and felt that I was making progress, especially by performing well against the best. That tag could not be applied to Salford, who we thrashed at Odsal by a competition-record score of 96-16, a game which brought me my first professional hat-trick. There aren't many forwards who get them and I wouldn't say it was devalued by the standard of the opposition; you can only play what is put in front of you. It meant more to me than getting the Man of the Match award would have done, although any delusions of grandeur were quickly shot down by my mates who were happy to point out how limited the resistance had been. That try treble came in the middle of a rich vein of scoring form which was probably due to more than just good fortune. After the epic, beer-fuelled Challenge Cup celebrations I decided, over a six-week period, to be really disciplined in my life, including regulating my drinking, and the results showed on the field. I saw how good things could be.

Where the Salford game did not help us was in preparation for the huge return clash with Wigan. The ease of the victory against the City Reds possibly had relaxed us a little but, equally, someone had left part of our player assessments of the Wigan players written on a whiteboard in the visitors' dressing room. The Warriors probably didn't need extra motivation anyway but to spend their waiting time before going into battle reading where we thought they were weak and could be exploited handed them, and their astute coach Frank Endacott, a vital psychological edge. Our 30-18 defeat ended a run of thirty-one consecutive home games unbeaten but considering I came up against the toughest pack I had faced – Terry O'Connor, Terry Newton, Neil Cowie, Mick Cassidy, Denis Betts and Andy Farrell – I felt that I had done pretty well. That awesome six brought the best out of me and I was rewarded with some wider recognition when I was named in the initial forty-man squad for England's World Cup bid that autumn.

It was a natural buzz to be in John Kear's sights but I played the selection down and tried to remain realistic and grounded. In the space of just over half a season I had gone from the fringe of a club first team to the edge of international selection. That was all well and good, but with Great Britain splitting down into the home nations for the three-week tournament, there were probably only fifty guys in form and eligible for England anyway, so I wasn't going to get carried away. I did celebrate with a try in a narrow win against London at The Valley though. We still seemed to be cursed in travelling to matches against the Broncos, however. This time we flew down but went to the wrong airport and still ended up with something like a three-hour coach journey to the ground, which saw us arrive just in time. We felt like Steve Martin in *Planes, Trains and Automobiles*, it was a nightmare.

Speaking of nightmares, so was Brad Mackay's weekly column in the *Telegraph and Argus* the next Thursday when he alluded to an incident in a nightclub involving some fish. When I had a drink back then, I could go a bit crazy. It was exuberance – an enthusiastic release – and at Penningtons in Bradford they used to have koi carp swimming around in a tank in the toilets; it was all very classy. I decided to liberate one of them and asked a member of staff behind the bar for a champagne bucket to capture it. I spent about half an hour leaning over the tank, fishing with the bucket and eventually got one. I took my prize back into the club and positioned it on the bar for the remainder of the night and anyone who wanted a drink had to kiss the fish first. It was all good-natured and the fish was returned to its more natural habitat without being traumatised. Looking back, events like that embarrass me now but it was all part of my rollercoaster life at the time and part of growing up. In some ways I was something of a fraud, occasionally short-changing myself and the team. There was little moderation, I was training as a true professional and then sometimes pissing it up like an amateur.

One of the most physically demanding clashes of the season, as it always was, came at Halifax. It would be good to have them back in Super League; they are missed, especially when it came to the much-anticipated derby with Bradford – to some of the Bulls fans it meant everything to beat them and vice versa. That match was at the old Shay, where the teams got changed in portakabins right next to each other. They had a tough pack and during one confrontation, Robbie Paul was on the ground and got kneed in the ribs. We looked round and he stayed down but we just expected him to bounce back up like he usually did. Afterwards we realised why he hadn't; as we were battling to a twenty-all draw, he was suffering from a punctured lung – not that it stopped him from rabbiting on all the time. As the regular season began to come to a climax, we had the chance to catch Wigan at the top when we went to the JJB Stadium. We were 19-2 up at one stage but lost in the last minute after Scott Naylor and Stuart Spruce had been sin-binned by referee Russell Smith late on. We had a tremendous first half but were poor after the break and they deservedly got themselves back into contention. Understandably, our frustrations mounted, including with Russell and instead of keeping a calm head, he started to struggle a bit. As I think he would admit, when matters on the pitch began to get emotional, he had a tendency to get involved in them rather than remain detached, which is the acknowledged sign of a good ref. In those frantic closing stages, with eleven men, we were desperately trying to chase back and cover but they got the ball wide to Kris Radlinski and we were beaten. With that defeat, realistically, the best we could finish was third and the disappointment boiled over in the dressing room afterwards. Matt Elliott was obviously gutted at seeing the season's work potentially slip away and came in and said: 'I hope you're all as disappointed as I am.' Jimmy Lowes just lost his rag, pointing out in typical Belle Isle style that it was us that had sweated the blood and tears. It was another turning point; Wigan were getting better and better and we just couldn't beat them that year. Jimmy had taken over the captaincy and, by then, a campaign had started on Sky to relieve him of it because certain pundits thought that the added responsibility was affecting his play. That was just nonsense and annoyed us, although I suffered the same thing in 2005 and realised by then that it was just part of the media's role to look for excuses when things aren't going well for a side but without knowing the facts.

I was compensated by being named in the final England twenty-two and selected by a group of worthies for the mythical Super League 'Dream Team'. I went for the specially commissioned shirt and photo shoot with Stu Fielden and we commented that we were in really stellar company. Once there, I quietly went about my business and merely said a few 'alrights' because I was in awe of the others who had been included. I was rolling with the flow, things were going well personally but we bombed out in the play-offs. In the first match, at St Helens, Chris Joynt came up with arguably the most famous try of the summer era, ending a length of the field move as the hooter went with the winning score, which famously saw Matt captured by the cameras seemingly falling off his chair in shock. I was even more gutted because I was on the sidelines at the time having been substituted by Hudson Smith. I like him but in the lead-up to that score he gave up chasing back and if I had been out there, I definitely would not have done – whether or not it would have made a difference. The game had gone well for me, I'd scored a try and we were in a winning position but by the end I was helpless and desolate. We weren't unlucky, we should have just shut the ball down.

In the aftermath, Matt announced publicly that he would be leaving at the end of the season to go to Canberra. We'd had an inkling, rumours had been flying about for a while and the players were formally told just before the Press got to know. I don't think we were affected by it; there was a resignation among us that the whispers had been confirmed and from the way he had been acting we could kind of tell. It was not as though we had turned up for training one morning to find that he had been sacked or just gone. The Board did not wait long to promote Brian Noble who, amazingly, was the only British coach in Super League at the time. There were a number of second-rate Aussies holding down positions, which was similar to many of the playing rosters, although the youth system was not fully in place at that point to provide sufficient up-and-coming talent on the field. It was the right decision by the management at Bradford; Nobby had bided his time, served an apprenticeship and I liked the element of continuity. I knew where I was at with him and he probably knew a little bit more about me than Matt did, having watched me a lot with the academy team; it probably did me a slight favour.

We recovered quickly from the St Helens heartache to dispose of Leeds pretty comfortably at home – another supposed last-ever game at Odsal – but at the final hurdle, Wigan again showed they had the measure of us with a victory of equal ease and magnitude. We weren't helped by the fact that Brad Mackay cried off at the last minute when he was sick on the bus. Unusually, we went to a hotel first which was not the norm and wouldn't have been the preference of the players. However, it is a bit of a ballache getting in and out of the JJB Stadium. So we thought we would go early and rest up there for a couple of hours, which was different but not necessarily the right thing to do. For someone like Brad to pull up sick, he must have been ill and he looked green sat at the back of the bus. I'm not sure that was as much a reason for our eventual defeat as Wigan's desire to make the Grand Final. We'd fulfilled our ambitions by winning the Challenge Cup, our first trophy since 1997, and some of our guys couldn't match them for passion. I remember as they began to get on top of us, feeling increasingly pissed off throughout the second half and not wanting to believe that the season was ending in such a tame fashion. It was a real comedown having led the competition for part of the year that we hadn't made it to the defining night. It was a shock but we all know now that although the regular season rounds have a bearing, it is solely to do with how you perform in the gargantuan games in the play-offs that decide success or failure. Some teams who have been shoddy all year can come into them in the right sort of form and really shake them up; we were the reverse.

By then I'd begun coaching the open-age side at Stanningley. They used to have a plot of land that has since become the fire station, which I'm sure Councillor Arthur Miller secured for them in the first place because he knew that it would become valuable one day. The club were between homes, having had that one knocked down and the new venue at Coal Road not yet having been built. As a result no one was really taking an interest in the open-age side but the club were under scrutiny from Sport England who were providing a £1 million lottery grant to top out the new facility. Contingent on receiving that was running teams throughout the age levels and they asked me to take over the coaching of the senior side to help them out in the interim. I wasn't the greatest coach – I was only twenty-two – and it was mainly about having a laugh with my mates, but I wanted to do it. They only had about eight or nine who'd turn up at training – such as it was – but we'd scrape together enough for a match at the weekend. That got us through a couple of years and served its purpose, the money came in and a terrific community facility was constructed. I had the honour of being pictured starting the building work, along with other products of the club Mark Calderwood and the current coach there, Rhinos teammate Jamie Jones-Buchanan. The club has since gone from strength to strength under him.

One Saturday we played down in Nottingham and the lads followed me in a convoy of cars, although it was the first time I had driven on the motorway. That lasted twenty minutes, I was doing sixty-five miles an hour on the inside lane and they got fed up and all shot off and I had to catch up with them. I just got to the dressing room as they were starting to get warmed up. We only had fourteen men and the opposition were a big set of mining lads. Almost from the kick-off, I was getting more and more agitated on the sidelines as they began to bully and intimidate us. Lads from Stanningley are all game, they might not be the biggest but they'll always give it a go and after half-time I could take it no more. I had an old pair of pumps on and some shorts without underpants and put myself on as a substitute. I knew I shouldn't have done it, Bradford would have been furious, but I couldn't help myself. I managed to get a couple of tries, smashed a few people and although they were only amateurs it felt good, like I was doing something right. We got close and then they began pulling away again and I took myself off before the end so as not to risk injury. I'd calmed down by then and as the sides were leaving the field together I laughed when I heard one of our opponents say: 'Who did that No.15 think he was, coming on for a bit and thinking he could turn the game?' Because they wouldn't have seen that much Super League down there, they didn't have a clue about me, which also served as a note that I shouldn't get too carried away with any delusions of grandeur. It wasn't appropriate to have scientific coaching methods or theories or to base my style on anyone; when you've only got a handful at training the best you can hope for is having a game of touch and pass, a bit of craic with the lads and then head off home. More time was spent ringing round trying to get people to turn up in the first place and Darren Robson was a massive help to me in that.

It was even difficult for me to go for a drink with the guys after training because virtually every pub around us was full of Leeds fans and I was about as welcome as Paul Anderson in a beauty parlour. It's a problem I've always had. When I was at Bradford, Leeds fans wanted me to do well as long as I didn't beat their side. Now, the Bradford fans I meet, because I'm at Leeds, want me to lose and not play well because they think that I am a Judas. Verbal abuse is one thing but what started to surface around the time we were physically battering and terrorising sides in the first half of the season was the constant insinuation that the Bulls were complicit in substance abuse. Those rumours have been around for years but I have always maintained that the people who moan about it the most don't know what hard work is. That was where being part of the international set was great. Top players mix from all different clubs and the others could see the how hard we trained in the gym and what the Bradford ethos – set by the likes of Carl Jennings, Brian McDermott, Jimmy Lowes and Mike Forshaw – was. Among them the understanding was that you always go in there and tear yourself to bits. We had the best weights regimes, supplements; protein, creatine and nutritional advice through Carl, he was a pioneer – a market leader in the sport – in many ways. There were times, coming out of his sessions, that we could hardly move, never mind throw a rugby ball. We'd be thinking: 'How the hell could we do skills drills after that?' even if it had only been an intense forty-minute session. The motto was always: 'Go heavy or go home.' It was almost a competition to see who could train the hardest or lift the most. When you get that kind of attitude and desire, it does tell against those who look for shortcuts. What we did when we were away with our national sides opened a few people's eyes and, hopefully, they started to understand a little bit more of what we were about. I'm pretty convinced that people who do take drugs in our sport – and there are very few – are not doing it to cheat but more out of worry as to whether they can make it or if they are going to be good enough.

SIX

DIRT TRACKER TO ROLLS-ROYCE

England coach John Kear's comment about me transforming from 'a dirt tracker to a Rolls-Royce' during the World Cup seemed to sum up the way things had gone for me during 2000. He had a young squad, not so much by choice but because the older guard had gone, as internationals had become so infrequent. The first graduates of the academy and scholarship schemes were starting to come through and that investment in the new, up-and-coming breed was beginning to pay off. Eight of us were selected from Bradford, so I immediately felt at home and that made it easier to gel into a squad. I feel for those guys who are the sole representatives from their club, it must be extremely hard for them to come into that potentially intimidating environment on your own, when you don't really know anybody at a time when you need mates around you. When I eventually became one of the more experienced players, I made a conscious effort to welcome those guys on board, to make them feel a valued part of the team. Hooker Paul Rowley from Leigh was in that boat in 2000 and although he was older than me, I went out of my way to try and include him in what we were doing, especially when we were in America for our pre-tournament training camp.

Looking back now, that was the best rugby-related trip I have ever been on and not just because a bunch of young lads were let loose in Disneyworld. We were so well looked after and catered for – it was a great hook up. The night before we flew out of Manchester, they took us to the Grand Final at Old Trafford to see Wigan and Saints play. Me, Scott Naylor and 'Sprogger' Spruce weren't going to watch that, having come so close to being a part of it and we just mooched around in a bar in the corporate area having a few cold ones instead. To us it was like rubbing salt into our wounds. We could understand the England management's good intentions but the last thing we wanted was to see our main rivals battling it out in the best domestic game of the year; it wasn't rudeness or disrespect, it was just more painful than Brian McDermott's dress sense. Virgin flew us out and I know that they like to gloat about how everything is bigger in the States but when we arrived at our 'Magic Kingdom' hotel, well, the rooms were just ridiculous. Normally when you're 'on tour' there's a rickety bed that's two-foot-by-six-foot if you're lucky, in a damp, smelly, crowded, cheap room because that helps the club cut costs. These had a massive double bed each, four televisions, a jacuzzi, everything you could want. 'Sprogger' and I, who were sharing quarters, couldn't believe it. We kept thinking: 'this is the life, this is what international football is about.'

I was somewhat star-struck to be among so many great players but that didn't stop them taking the odd liberty. I loved John Kear's enthusiasm but even that was tested during one training session that was open to the Press. We were supposed to be showing them some of the intricate, highly skilled drills that we had practised but every time the ball got to Mike Forshaw, he messed up. Whether it was deliberate or not, John's patience and good humour gradually began to wane and after a while we were ordered just to go back to basics. We did some hard training when we were out there and the real character was Harvey Howard. We used to do six big hits on the tackle bags to end the sessions and John would be wandering around us shouting: 'That's excellent, excellent.' Harvey would be yelling 'one more, one more' and by then John was backing him up and those in his group ended up doing almost double the amount of hits. It was warm out there so we trained early, which left us time to do some other great stuff around the complex. As VIPs we got straight to the front of the queues for all the rides and we were in a private, sectioned-off part of Epcot for an astonishing firework display which was outstanding; I couldn't speak highly enough of how they looked after us.

To finish our preparations we played the United States national side but that was never going to be anything other than an opposed training session. The best thing about them was their kit, which looked fantastic, and we ended up winning 110-0. Going into it I knew I had to perform well because I was down the pecking order behind the likes of Forsh, Adrian Morley and Andy Farrell and I was new to the set-up. I got a try and thought I put in a really good performance for the team, notwithstanding the quality of the opposition. I did as well as I could have, being voted the Players' Player of the Match. After the non-contest, we went back to the 'Floridian' hotel for an official reception which was out of this world, not least for the quantity and quality of the food. Again, though, my inexperience and gullibility was to cost me. I went out for a drink or two with Sean Long; we were both young and impressionable and somehow got into an argument with some blokes over women. We quickly scarpered as it threatened to get out of hand but we were easily identifiable and it wasn't long before the local police came to the hotel to search for the culprits. I was looking incredibly sheepish, and chastising myself for having let the side down, when they tried to arrest skipper Andy Farrell because they thought he was me. Not surprisingly he didn't see the funny side and I'm sure that as a result of the incident I missed out on facing Australia for the first time in the opening World Cup group match. That devastated me when I realised how close I had been. We all thought then, and I still do now, that there is massive potential for rugby league in America. The public genuinely love their sport and the great athletes they naturally produce would, I'm sure, take to the physicality of it. If it ever did take off in America they would be a huge force. Someone would need to spend a lot of money and show great enterprise to raise the profile and that is something we lack.

Before the tournament, nobody gave England a chance; it was felt that the Aussies just had to fly over to pick up the trophy because Great Britain had been distilled into the home nations and we were raw. John Kear used that as a motivational tool. Everyone has a skill and his is undoubtedly the ability to galvanise disparate people and fill them with pride and passion for the task ahead. He was very smart that way and came up with some novel ideas. His record speaks for itself; he is the only coach to have won the Challenge Cup twice with teams outside the so-called 'big four' clubs in the Super League era. I like watching the guy and his genuine love for the sport; it knows no limits and rubs off on those around him. He was great for me at the time, very different to Matt. Some have questioned his technical ability but he has learnt and adapted and the way he inspires for one-off games is second to none in this country. He has the ability to instil belief and often through unusual methods; he had us watching *Zulu* as part of the build-up during the World Cup. It was full on out in America and we flew back to set up camp in Staines for our opening match against the Aussies at Twickenham. John told me before we went into a big press conference for that game that I wouldn't be playing and, being an emotional person and absolutely gutted, I was struggling to hold back the tears. It would have meant everything to play for my country and Scott Naylor, who could see what I was going through, had to pull me to one side. He said: 'Don't do it here in front of all of those people; if you want to get upset about it, go elsewhere.' That forced me to get a grip and, ultimately, to work harder to break into the side.

The immense disappointment of missing out hit me in a big way; I ended up going on a couple of nights out in Staines with the other lads who hadn't been selected, which the coaching staff encouraged as a way of relaxing and letting off steam, as long as we didn't disturb the others. One of the mornings after, we went to train at Eton and Stuart Fielden and I were still the worse for wear but we were inexperienced at all this. John had to call an early end to the session which didn't please him in the build-up to a huge match. He walked up to skipper Andy Farrell and said in a loud but clearly agitated stage whisper, 'Jamie Peacock is as white as this wall and Stuart Fielden is looking straight through me; we have to do something about this.' We were shocking and held our hands up. We had two really good team meetings in the lead-up to battle, which was another of John's strengths. In the first get-together, everyone had to get up in front of the rest of the squad and the staff and say what their best and worst life experiences were. The room was only small, it held twenty people sat down at best and the atmosphere was highly charged with emotion. People like Steve Carter, the masseur and conditioner, who we knew as 'Scrapper', is a top bloke and had been in the SAS. He told us some really harrowing tales of being on duty and things going wrong, particularly a time when he had been stuck in a tank somewhere awful.

The other member of the back-room crew who made us all sit up and reflect was kit man Stan Wall. He is a legendary figure in the game, having been a top-class referee before looking after the dressing room at St Helens. He told us about a mine collapsing and that he was forced to pull the bodies of thirteen of his mates out of the rubble. He said it was simultaneously his worst and best time; on the one hand he'd lost some of his closest friends but when the final body was retrieved there was a sense of elation because he knew that they could be properly laid to rest. It opened my eyes and put missing out on a Grand Final – which was my contribution – into perspective. It also reaffirmed something about the honesty and integrity that runs through the core of the people involved in the sport. Perhaps being through such hard times is what attracted them to this toughest-of-all codes in the first place. Although I've had to get used to it, I don't like speaking in front of people so I found the whole exercise very difficult and not my kind of thing. I knew the audience but I didn't know them as people so I think my contribution lasted all of about thirteen words, 'I won the Challenge Cup and got left out of a Grand Final'. It was a hugely worthwhile exercise, though, at breaking down barriers by sharing secrets. People who spend the year working out how to smash each other will always be a little guarded when they come together and it was a good idea from John to get us to open up a bit and see a different side of each other.

The second time we joined ranks was to hear a motivational talk from Francois Pienaar, the captain of South Africa's rugby union World Cup-winning outfit in 1995. He was a physically massive bloke and spoke influentially about how they drove themselves to overcome the odds and had some good things to say. It was Pienaar who came up with the phrase 'dirt tracker' when referring to the 'midweek' side and how anyone could come through to make an impact if the set-up was right. Our meticulous preparations were thrown into turmoil the night before our first game when Francis Stephenson was arrested after wrongly being accused of rape, a charge which was later dropped. I was already seeing my future wife Faye by then and had sneaked out of the hotel to meet up with her but when I got back everyone was in the foyer and we all had to go down to the police station in turn to give statements. Andy Hay took Franny some clothes as his were all in for forensic tests and Paul Deacon was caught up in all the furore and thrown into a cell because he had swapped rooms and was in the one where the incident supposedly occurred, which was duly taped off. The story made the papers the next morning and Franny was so devastated by it that he didn't even go to the match – I'm not sure that his career ever recovered either.

For a while I suffered some self-pity, wondering why those sorts of thing always seemed to happen around, or to, me but I resolved to knuckle down and force my way into the England side for the remaining group games against the lesser-ranked sides. The disruption gave the senior guys something to talk about as they killed time before going to the stadium and they performed creditably against a star-studded Australian line-up, in the seemingly endless rain. I got my shot in the next clash against Russia at St Helens and in many ways it was the perfect introduction to the international arena. We were never likely to lose and things came off for me, I managed to grab a couple of tries and I remember feeling immensely proud when I rang Faye to tell her straight afterwards because she was in Spain. She had hoped to be there but it was the first time her mum and dad had seen me play, and I hoped that the performance had left a favourable impression. The only thing that annoyed me was being booed by the Saints fans when I neglected to put home favourite Paul Wellens in for a try. The ball had slipped in my hands and I decided to hold on to it after making another break, Paul had been supporting and would have been clear for the line on the inside. They thought that I was being greedy and had denied their man his moment in the spotlight by going for a hat-trick and not passing but that is not in my nature. Nevertheless, I did what I set out to, the tries topped off some hard graft and the overall performance was a combination of dirt tracker and Rolls-Royce. When you first come into a new team, you have to prove yourself and show that you are prepared to get involved in the muck and bullets, and be there in the trenches. It's a way of saying to your new team-mates: 'I might be the young lad but give me the ball, I have no fear. I'll work for you and, when we are all blowing a bit and fatigue is trying to make a coward out of us, I'll be there, you can trust me.'

I felt that I proved myself to the England camp in the same way I had eventually done at Bradford and showed them what I was all about. I'd been like a spare part and I wanted to make sure that I wasn't going to be the one left on the sidelines any more, I was desperate to be involved and wear the jersey of my country. I was awarded the Players' Man of the Match which left an afterglow. The guys in the thick of battle tend to value those who show wholehearted endeavour as much as the candidates who make the obvious headlines, usually through their scoring exploits. The gladiators' opinions are invariably different to those who watch the game, either as sponsors, spectators or members of the media. The most difficult thing was that again, when I went up to collect the little trophy, I had to make a speech in front of the lads. I can't remember what I said but I guess I mumbled some thanks, went red for about ten seconds and sat straight back down again. The performance meant that I kept my place for the game with Fiji at Headingley, which was on the BBC. Three of my best mates – Gaz Fearnley, Neil Gibbins and Simon Priest – came up to watch and to go out and celebrate my call-up afterwards and we had even more to commemorate as I ran in three tries in a 66-10 victory. It was a cold, crisp, real rugby league day and the Fijians were very tough – I chipped all my back teeth running into their loose-forward Atunaisa Vunivalu who absolutely monstered me. You might score tries against them but you earn your bruises as well. They could certainly hit and they had Lote Tuqiri captaining them who was class and stood out a mile. Being on the national stage, I was thrust into the public eye with numerous national papers wanting to interview me after the match, which was a bit daunting. It's never so bad straight after a game because the endorphins are still racing round your system which makes you chatty and on a bit of a natural high. Now, with the benefit of experience, I am a bit more guarded.

I also had to do the post-match press conference alongside Andy Farrell and I was more nervous about that than I ever was going into a game. As it was the World Cup we had to wait for a cue from *Sky Sports News* who were showing it live and that made me even worse, especially as we had not been given any formal training on how to handle those sorts of situations. It's another area where players could do with more help; I learnt by being self-aware and I tried to improve by watching and copying those who I thought were naturally good at it like Robbie Paul and, later, Brian Carney. Because my performances had been eye-catching in those two games, I was selected in the 'World Cup XIII' after the group stages. That was some honour bearing in mind the talent on display but I was realistic enough to know that I hadn't achieved that yet – I was yet to face the best. In fact, it did not even get me a place in the starting line-up for the quarter-final against Ireland a week later, also at Headingley. In the build-up John Kear had gone out of his way to keep mentioning my contribution to the media but it didn't bother me that I was chosen on the bench. You want to be out there when the battle is at its most intense, snappiest and most aggressive but I had had two good games against a pair of poorer sides and John was justified to revert back to what he thought was his strongest line-up. When I did get on, I got the chance to turn the game with a try just before half-time that edged us into a 12-10 lead. It came running off Sean Long and we struck up a good combination. We got along as people, we were from a similar kind of background and it was just like playing alongside Henry Paul. They were both consummate passers of the ball who were also great organisers and playmakers. Back then I was the kind of player who could break the game out wide and that was the role John had in mind, once the initial sting had gone out of the encounter. For the first time I was in a match where mate was playing mate as club loyalties were put aside. Admittedly, for me, the only familiar face in the emerald ranks was my good pal Mick Withers and he was the exact opposite of an up-front, aggressive player. The real clashes were between the likes of Adrian Morley and Barrie McDermott and there was a genuine passion in the match which the crowd picked up on. Barrie also took on Stuart Fielden with a high shot and that is where their cameo rivalry started.

Chris Joynt came up to me after the Ireland game and said: 'You've had a very good season mate, keep it going.' His comments meant the world to me. He was unquestionably one of the best in my position in the competition and for him to mention that after his side had just been defeated was the mark of the man. He didn't just score tries; he worked himself to a standstill on defence. Once I'd got to know him better, when we were in camp with Great Britain, he'd always have a quiet, unassuming word. The quarter-final was a tight, competitive, fiercely passionate game that felt like a proper international at the time and I relished the confrontation; they are the ones you want to play in – where the guys really commit to each other. They mean the most when you win and sting the hardest if you lose, which we did, pitifully, in the semi-final.

A fellow Bull did haunt us that afternoon at Bolton's Reebok Stadium; Henry Paul had a sensational match as the white-hot Kiwis absolutely blew us away. Some said that we had gone into the game complacent or were overawed but the truth was that we simply weren't good enough. The New Zealanders had a hell of a lot of experience in their ranks and it was the first of an unwanted trifecta for me. England's 49-6 wasting was their biggest-ever home defeat and I was subsequently to follow that up by being a part of Great Britain sides that suffered their worst humblings at home and on foreign soil. We went into the semi honestly thinking that we had a genuine chance of winning it and getting to the World Cup final but all their players were up to the necessary standard. The only slight saving grace was that it had been announced during that week that Bradford had signed Joe Vagana and he was awesome that day, unstoppable; he dominated everyone, especially Darren Fleary.

Daz was great to get to know during the World Cup, he was very quiet off the field, the exact reverse to how he played on it, which seems to be a common trait among most of the sport's true tough guys. He could hit hard which gave his side an enormous lift and he was the perfect example of what pure application can do combined with the right standard of coaching: it has to be a complementary, two-way street and when it's the right mix it can take you to a different level. I could have worked as hard as I wanted at Bradford on my limited skill base but listening to the smart people in the game, the role models around me, also shaped my future as much as my determination and focus on what I wanted to achieve. I needed the tips and specialist tuition to harness that to best effect.

Although the defeat against New Zealand was humiliating, I got nominated for the tackle of the tournament when I tracked back over about seventy metres to halt Nigel Vagana just as he was about to score. It looked spectacular but the truth was that I was coming off the bench and was as fresh as anything. I'd just done three tuck jumps on the sidelines as part of a warm-up and someone shouted 'you're on' just as Nigel made the break. I sprinted after him and because he had been playing for half an hour or so I managed to get to him. I had a real willingness to not give in but I reckon it's always easier to chase than be chased. In the end it didn't matter because they scored straight after it anyway. I was directly confronting Stephen Kearney, another who I had watched in awe on television when I was coming through so that I could pick up tips on the business of being a second-rower. He was always looking to advance his game and was another with a reputation as a tireless trainer. Studying him, I used to think 'I like the way he does that' or 'I'd like to add that to my game', although after the semi-final he left me stunned when I asked him for his shirt. He refused the swap because he said it was for someone else and I was a bit dirty on him for a while after that. I was just starting to make my way in the game and he was up there so it would have meant a lot, especially after the pain of humiliating defeat. Obviously now I realise why; I get a lot of people requesting things like that from me and I can't exchange jerseys after the battle all the time. Having got to know him a bit better since, and understanding the pulls on a modern sportsman, I know he was not just being rude.

Losing the semi-final was a bittersweet feeling personally, things had gone so well for me during the year that I was still a bit wowed by everything but failing in the last four was a huge disappointment, especially as, once again, I didn't get the chance to face the very best, the Aussies. We'd heard that Great Britain would be reforming to play in an Ashes series the following year and that was a constant spur during pre-season. I realised with the likes of Chris Joynt and Mick Cassidy playing for Ireland and Adrian Morley, Andy Hay and Mick Forshaw vying for places that I needed an even better season if I was to be in with a chance of making the GB squad and fulfilling that dream. I resolved to kick on again to try and reach that next level and decided to immediately give up smoking. I had always been one for a secret or furtive cig but it was time to make further sacrifices.

The semi-final also made me realise that you couldn't spend too much time congratulating yourself if you really wanted to succeed. For the next few years, the thing that would infuriate me most about representative rugby was that, with all of the series losses, I had never ended a season on a high. Sometimes, though, that's what gives you the burning desire to try and continually better yourself. Throughout the World Cup adventure, Harvey Howard had been brilliant for morale. He is a genuinely funny, slightly off-beat guy who was also a bit of a prankster. I was honoured to be awarded the accolade of outstanding contributor by the England management while he was designated the best trainer but he secretly swapped our trophies and to this day I have never got my true one back. At the time, he had just won a Grand Final ring in Australia with Brisbane but for a while he struck up a hilarious double act with Neil Harmon when they were together at Leeds. My other compensation for defeat was that after the tournament, the annual 'Golden Boot' rankings were announced after taking soundings from journalists around the globe and I was adjudged fifth-best second-rower in world rugby. Individual accolades are nice, and measure progression, but this isn't tennis or golf.

SEVEN

AT LAST THE AUSSIES

The big signings at Bradford for 2001 were Lee Gilmour and Daniel Gartner and they went on to play significant roles in the success that followed. Gilly was a great attacking addition, with a mouth as big as his talent. We captured him from Wigan and it was good to see that the club still had a focus on signing the best British youngsters, following on from the likes of Radders and Deacs. That was mirrored in Brian Noble's coaching staff when he made Bernard Dwyer an assistant and took on Karl Harrison. 'Rhino' or the 'Big Turk' was the kind of strong character Brian needed around him in what was, by his own admission, a difficult time stepping up, taking over from Matt and establishing himself and his style. Karl's a funny guy and one of a dying breed since the advent of full-time professionalism – they don't make them like that any more.

For pre-season we went to Jacksonville in Florida – I think we were among the first to go on a training camp over there – and it was pretty crazy. The ten days we were there was probably too long, we trained very hard for the first four of them and then were given a couple of rest days and we made the most of it. It opened my eyes as to how much the Americans rely on fast food; we just couldn't get a decent meal anywhere. On one of the nights off, we went out for a drink to relieve the steam built up by the almost constant physical conditioning we were doing. At the time Tony Yeboah was still a cult hero at Leeds United and, being fans, me and my mates used to follow the Elland Road habit of taking our tops off and swinging them around our heads chanting his name when we were out on the town. I somehow got all the Bradford lads doing it at around three in the morning in a café.

Within about twenty seconds armed lawmen were there in force. I couldn't believe how quickly it all happened. As they came over I asked: 'Are you real police?' To this they replied, extremely politely: 'Sure, we certainly are sir, would you mind putting your clothes back on.' We did, of course, and went straight off back to the hotel. There was no malice, we were just being loud and brash and throughout the trip the Americans could not have looked after us better, especially Robbie and Henry – they loved those Paul boys.

I always marvelled at Henry Paul because when I was coming through, he was the main man, an outstanding playmaker and the mainstay of the Bradford side. I got to play outside him for a couple of years so I could appreciate his talents close up and I owe a lot to him. He was such a skilful player and he engineered so many breaks for me; I'm in no way dumb to that fact and I remain very grateful. I was fortunate that the team, at the time I got into the squad, was pretty settled. Henry, myself and the right-sided centre and wing pairing of Scott Naylor and Tevita 'The Chief' Vaikona quickly gelled as a unit. It felt as though we had played together forever and we were good for each other; it was a strong weapon in the Bulls' armoury and that combination was one of the main reasons why I enjoyed myself so much. We were all different but got on so well, socially as well as in battle. We were in awe of Henry a bit because he was such a great player; he was incredibly dextrous and immensely dedicated; he wanted to work hard and he was fit. Often, those who have the most natural ability don't want to put the effort in, but he did. He also didn't court a higher profile, that's not really for him – that kind of thing is more for Robbie – although the pair of them did seem to get carried away by the idea of being rap stars for a while. Most of the Bradford boys cringed for them, they can play rugby but, let's face it, they are no singers; it's not as though they're Eminem. Robbie likes to think he's some sort of fashion icon but no Kiwi has got much dress sense either. When they were together, the sum of the whole was more than the parts in those kinds of things, they'd egg each other on and they were great for the Bulls as a marketing tool. They put themselves forward and undoubtedly appealed to a different and wider audience and you have got to admire that.

We had four more days of intense training in America after the café incident before flying home. Brian Noble hates aeroplanes almost as much as I do and for the ten-hour return journey Jimmy Lowes gave him four sleeping pills to get him through it. Six hours into it and Nobby was grabbing the seat in front of him, sweating profusely and generally looking very uncomfortable. It turned out that Jimmy had deliberately switched them for caffeine tablets – while we were all soundly asleep, he was awake throughout twitching away and pacing up and down the corridor. Being the kind of coach that he is, Nobby's great skill was that he copped it on the chin and took it in the spirit it was meant; some coaches' egos would have been too big to cope with a prank like that.

None of us had heard of Danny Gartner but he turned out to be one of the greatest guys I've ever played with. He ended up living close to me at Calverley and in his first game – a friendly at Wakefield – the pitch froze at half-time. He was always calm, collected, good for an expression and such a smart player when either supporting the break or clearing up others' mistakes on defence. I've never seen a bloke wear so much ice after a game – it was all around him in the dressing room – I'm surprised he didn't suffer from hypothermia after matches. He was a real bolter, he'd struggled with injuries back home in Australia but always had the talent and played alongside Test men Steve Menzies and Nic Kosef at Manly. One of Nobby's scouts had told him that Danny was the best of that trio and they were probably right. I still keep in touch with him now.

Odsal as a ground is full of character, so when we had to move out to Valley Parade while essential maintenance was done to the stadium, I felt we lost something. I loved to play in the old bowl, to train there and use that unique field. You get familiar with its little quirks, not least the turned up corners in the in-goal areas, and that's what home advantage is all about. Bradford City's stadium was a much smaller pitch and the dressing rooms were built for eleven-or-so lithe footballers, not a squad of twenty rugby players and the necessary accompanying entourage. There was no soul to the place, we'd just arrive to play and then head off; they were tough times for the club. Odsal is unique, other teams generally found it to be a bit of a throwback and that was a maxim we lived by; to make sure that they didn't like going there. It's different to any other major rugby stadium so the opposition never quite got used to it and, initially, I found it tough going back there once I'd moved to Leeds. The best aspect of Valley Parade was that in having Henry Paul and Paul Deacon in the side, we could kick goals from the halfway line – I remember Ian Millward when he was in charge of St Helens moaning about that. Headingley, on the other hand, is the kind of ground opposing teams just love to perform at. Irrespective of it being a local derby, whenever I was running out there for Bradford, I used to relish the lush pitch and tremendous atmosphere and just be ready to perform, it was always inspiring. At Odsal, you had to have the place virtually full to generate the same kind of backdrop. At Headingley, you could always guarantee that it would be loud and the play would be fast which tends to bring the best out of you.

In defence of the Challenge Cup, we racked up big wins against Widnes and, somewhat surprisingly, in a televised clash at Halifax which made a few people sit up and take notice. Brian had said on taking over that he wanted us to play with more flair; he had noticed that what had let us down at the end of 2000 was our rigidity on attack. The focus under Matt had been so much on defence that we had become predictable with the ball which was why we had signed Lee Gilmour. The start of the season, though, was tough for me and I struggled. Teams had seen what I could do and there was an extra emphasis to stop me after my World Cup exploits. Coming off such a good year, there were occasions when, subconsciously, my desire was a shade lower.

We started the Super League season well, beating newly crowned World Club Champions St Helens at our stand-in home in a terrific match, before a near-capacity crowd. That backdrop certainly generated a hot, hostile atmosphere. Another of our newcomers, Shane Rigon, starred with a hat-trick. His introduction to the British game had also been somewhat traumatic; we played a friendly against Hull at their inhospitable Boulevard ground with snow in the air and on a bone-hard pitch. He received a proper broken nose and suffered near-frostbite and was hardly a picture of happiness in the dressing room afterwards. I hadn't played but made a point of saying: 'Welcome to England, mate.' He was a good bloke, quiet and reserved and he struggled a lot with injuries, which meant that he was in and out of the side. His wife didn't particularly enjoy it over here and when it got towards the end of the campaign he was gutted at the likelihood of being released to go back home, especially to play with South Sydney who were propping up their competition, rather than staying with a winning outfit here. He was small in stature but Bradford added three inches to his height in the official player profiles they sent out in the club handbook.

The cup quarter-final was away at Wakefield and we blew them away 38-0 with Henry at his absolute best. It was around the time that all the rumours were starting to surround him about where his future lay and that the English rugby union had approached him – along with a lot of our other youngsters. We gave him a bit of stick about the mega-money they were reportedly offering when we were bidding against him at cards but he had a thick skin. I was never on Twickenham's shopping list; I'd have struggled with the idea of a ruck and when it comes to kicking I've got two left feet.

I started to get my form back a month into the season with a couple of long-range tries in a big win in front of the cameras at Salford. I've always found the opening weeks of a campaign difficult because of the residue of playing internationals. It's not so much tiredness, more that the guys you are competing against and playing alongside have had two months extra preparation, training and fitness, and I was finding that out the hard way for the first time. After the representative season, you finally finish at the end of the calendar year and you've four weeks off over Christmas. Your coach is telling you to rest up but my instinct is to get out there and at least do some running. No matter how much you do on your own, though, you are always a couple of percentage points behind the lads when you rejoin them and it takes a while to catch up and get your body attuned to the sport's demands. I was quickly conscious of the need to try and nullify the head start of others by training harder and longer. Even though I'd by now played against some of the world's best, I was still finding my feet and total confidence after such a meteoric rise.

Lee Briers – who is such a smart footballer on the big occasion – was on fire for Warrington as we met them again in the Challenge Cup semi-final, this time at Huddersfield. It was cut and thrust for an hour but I managed to barge my way over from five metres out to break their resistance, thanks to the standard top-quality service from Jimmy Lowes. After I'd touched down we looked at each other as we celebrated and knew, although it was unspoken, that we were on our way back to the final. That kind of play, at such an important time in a crucial match, meant a lot; especially as I was starting to be regarded as more of an established player. That was why making the cup decider was a different feeling to the year before. Then it had been, 'I hope I've done enough to play, wow, someone pinch me'; now it was more about making a decisive contribution in seeing a winning game plan implemented. I learned a valuable lesson in the build-up to the big day, however, which has stuck with me since. We went down to London four days before the game and I trained every session in the lead-up as though it was the final because I was young, enthusiastic, eager to maintain an impression and such a potentially daunting stage was still so unfamiliar. Scott Naylor again had to take me aside and said: 'You need to pull back a bit, you're not going to win it by working so hard in midweek, it's what you do on Saturday that matters.' It was good advice; you've got to have intensity in your training but not at the expense of wearing yourself out. I wasn't even bothered that we would be facing our so-called hoodoo side, St Helens. Rather than worry about it being them again standing in our way of a trophy, which I know a lot of the Bradford fans did, I saw it as a golden opportunity to finally put one over on them.

Before then, our tag of so-called invincibility came to an end with a surprise defeat away to Wakefield at the start of the Easter period, when we blew a ten-point lead. Nevertheless, you can't read anything much form-wise into those two, more often than not, derby clashes over an extended weekend. Invariably sides win one and lose the other, as we showed when hitting back to defeat Wigan in a lunchtime kick-off at Valley Parade. Like so many of those second matches, it was understandably a bit sloppy but we dug in to put down an important psychological marker for later on in the season.

The week before the Challenge Cup final we went to Hull and drew. We were pegged back in the final minute, despite my best efforts to chase and haul down Tony 'Casper' Smith but, more importantly, we lost Stuart Spruce with a shoulder injury that eventually caused him to call time on his Bradford career. It was not the kind of news we needed in the lead-up to such a showpiece event. He was one of our leaders in the trenches and the dressing room and we missed his vocal presence at the back as much as anything. There was a huge irony about the 100th Challenge Cup final with it being played at Twickenham, the headquarters of rugby union. I had thought that it would be a great venue but I had been spoilt by Edinburgh and the tales of Wembley. A key part of the build-up is the fans lining the streets, waving their colours and cheering the coach through. Twickenham, however, was underwhelming. We passed a couple of shops emblazoned with the England flag and before you knew it, we were in the dressing room, that was it and it didn't seem right. There was no special feeling on the way there, which is usually such an integral element of that particular day. The journey in is when you really appreciate what it means to the fans – of the game as a whole, not just the competing clubs – and how universal the occasion is. We'd won the toss and got the home dressing room, which was probably a further drawback because it was so huge. The team becomes a little bit disjointed as everyone is getting changed in separate areas and little corners, you are spread out all over the place and it is hard to create an atmosphere. St Helens had the one that was plain, concrete and small but that forces sides to get together more.

When we got out on the supposedly hallowed turf, everything was against producing a spectacle; the crowd was muted, enclosed within a part-built stadium in driving rain and the grass was too long. If that wasn't bad enough, we lost in what was at best a dour clash and didn't score a try. Saints had the smart players who could adapt to the conditions, especially half-backs Tommy Martyn and Sean Long. Their short-kicking games for the only two tries were the difference, which shows what a grim contest it was. For me, that final was a real non-event and even if we had won, somehow it just wouldn't have had the magic it should. I got substituted, officially because I'd damaged my arm but I suspect because I just wasn't playing well enough. Somehow, Neil Gibbins, one of a group of my mates who had come down on a coach and spent most of the time getting blind drunk, had managed to make his way close to the dugout where I was sitting and he was shout-ing to me: 'Come on, you need to get this sorted out.' I glared at him, told him to shut up, wind his neck in and gestured to him to go back to his seat sharpish. He couldn't apologise enough afterwards but he was just upset at the way things were going. He felt like we all did, and couldn't help himself. All round it wasn't a brilliant day for the city of Bradford as our landlords got relegated but my allegiance to Leeds United meant that that was the least of my concerns.

After such a disappointment we had a run of really high-scoring wins back in Super League, especially at home. Our desperation returned and we were determined not to let the campaign peter out like it had the year before. We regrouped, realised we were a great attacking side and started blowing teams away to the extent that many of them were beaten at Valley Parade before they had even arrived. That sparked confidence in a squad that had, for the most part, been together for a while and where the com-binations were settled. Things were becoming consistently instinctive. We were physically the biggest team, playing on a small ground which helped us. We quickly gained field position and we were very good at finishing moves in the opposition twenty. Added to that, opponents knew that with Henry in the side, they couldn't afford to give away penalties virtually any-where on the field; he was regularly kicking goals from the halfway line. It was a double whammy – we were either going to take the two points on offer or put the ball right where we could hurt them the most.

The only defeat in that great run came, almost inevitably, at St Helens where Paul Sculthorpe was at his destructive best, scoring a couple of tries before half-time which broke us. He was untouchable, a true 'Man of Steel', and around that time one of the best players in the world. He set new standards with his ability to attack with the ball close to the line and when he got his angles right, which was more often than not, he was virtually unstoppable. Their coach, Ian Millward, banged on about how they had the formula to beat us which was good for the papers but that was about it. He was never quite as magnanimous in defeat – when he used to bitch and whine – as he was boisterous in victory and verbal battles between the clubs became something of the norm while he was in the Saints hotseat. Knowsley Road has always been one of the hardest grounds to win at but, more often than not, I found that stimulated my performance; it was the need in me to prove people wrong coming to the fore again, I suspect.

Inter-county football was back on the agenda in the middle of the season, the revived Yorkshire *v.* Lancashire clash billed as a genuine Test trial with the Kangaroos on the horizon. The match attracted 10,000 fans to Headingley, so they believed in it, and the entire White Rose pack was from Bradford with Jimmy Lowes the skipper. I could understand why David Waite, the GB coach, was behind such a move. Although Super League was undoubtedly raising standards, there was still a lack of week-to-week intensity for the top players. Sadly, over here, such a fixture does not seem to inspire the same passions as the 'State of Origin' encounters between Queensland and New South Wales, which borders on war without the weapons. For some in those matches there is genuine hatred in the colour of the opposition jersey. There is immense pride in, and something clearly definable about, representing Yorkshire. Even though they won this game, Lancashire probably ceased to really exist after 1974, being replaced by big-city conurbations. They had all the superstars in this match and, typically, we were the grinders; straight, hardworking Yorkshire folk, typical of the image.

Lee Crooks and Peter Roe were in charge of us; Lee was making his way in coaching after a distinguished playing career and Peter was very much from the old school. Everyone used to call me JP but Peter, who is a real character, got it into his head to label me 'Peaks', which stuck for a while. We were practising doing sets of six in training and I'd been taught that when you were called to take a drive in and then play the ball, you used to drop to the floor to simulate a real tackle. When it came to me I did my usual and Peter asked what was going on and told me to get up. I explained to him that I was waiting and timing the play-the-ball so that the others could align their runs and readjust. We did the drill again and I did the same thing and again he shouted: 'What's he doing? It's like he's got a spider on his back.' It wasn't that well organised to be honest. Crooksy had been an idol of mine and a great leader on the field but in a team meeting he showed us a sheet on which he tried to explain his strategy. He'd written 'defence' with a big capital 'D', little 'e', little 'f', big capital 'E', big capital 'N', little 'c' and a little 'e'. We couldn't see what he was on about and the system he was wanting us to play. He tried to explain himself on a flip chart using a pencil on a white sheet but because we were in a conference-sized room, all we could see when the sun shone in were some indentation marks he had made on the paper. He meant well and was probably nervous; it was his first major appointment in that capacity by the Rugby League.

As part of the build-up he got Peter Fox to come in and rally us, who had been great in the seventies and eighties when his underdog county sides ruled the roost. I'm sure he was a terrific motivator in his day but now we'd reached a time when playing the sport was advancing at probably its quickest-ever rate with video analysis, scientific attacking strategies, focus on nutrition and highly detailed preparation. Peter stood in front of us and all he said was: 'We'll just tackle, tackle, tackle,' and 'Never mind kicking to the corners, put the ball up near the posts, the floodlights will dazzle them.' He went on for nearly an hour dispensing advice like that and basically telling his life story and many of the lads were struggling not to burst out laughing. We stayed at a hotel in Bramhope and just before we went to the ground, they wanted us to watch the inspiring Al Pacino speech from *Any Given Sunday* but Lee couldn't get the video to work. The harder he tried the more we were slumping into our seats with embarrassment. Peter Roe came on instead and started talking about the pride in the shirt and was nearly in tears when another great ex-pro David Topliss had to come up and lead him off, it was well meaning but madness trying to recreate the old days.

It was a strange game as well; there were nine tries in the first half but only one in the second. The players in both dressing rooms were annoyed that the opening forty minutes had been little more than an exhibition and in the second the concentration was much more on defence and we tended to snuff each other out. The best thing about the contest was that the man of the match was given the 'Roy Powell Medal' and I used to love watching him play, especially for Leeds when I was a fan there. He tragically died in his early thirties at a training session and it was a great touch to remember him that way. Hopefully, his total honesty and constant hard-work ethic has rubbed off a bit on the way I play the game; he was a tremendous role model. He showed how far you could get with desire and endeavour and he was an inspiration for those of us who aren't blessed with innate talent.

After we'd beaten Leeds at home and I'd scored the game-breaking try, a story broke that the Rhinos had put in a bid for me. Bradford told me that a faxed sheet had come through from Gary Hetherington with, 'we'll give you £65,000 for Jamie Peacock' scribbled on it. There were two schools of thought at the time; that it was a genuine bid because they had just announced Iestyn Harris was going to rugby union in Wales which freed up some salary cap money, or that it was some kind of a smokescreen, a publicity stunt in the light of that news. Perhaps in a bid to deflect criticism from their fans, they wanted to be linked with a locally born lad who just happened to play for their biggest rivals. Certainly Gary is a shrewd operator and it got the Rhinos some good positive coverage but there was no actual contact with me directly. It was pretty weird because I kept getting texts off all my mates – a lot of whom were Leeds fans – asking me if it was true. The Bulls played it down and gave the impression that they weren't taking it seriously but I don't know whether that was just to keep me sweet. I laughed it off, there are always rumours flying around, and I had no reason to leave anyway because we were on the verge of achieving something special at Valley Parade.

The spark for that was a defeat in a game I didn't play in at Warrington; that jolted us out of our groove. I got rested that afternoon and I was pretty upset despite having played in a midweek international for England against Wales at Wrexham. That was an ad hoc fixture, the way things were then when it came to international planning and preparation; a bit like the Origin clash. It was a decent enough crowd and the camp beforehand was fun; Brian McDermott just mercilessly hounded Paul Anderson through-out the two days we were together. We were down in the match early on; they were pumped up on typical Welsh passion, as we'd expected, and we just couldn't get hold of the ball. However, their side was made up of a number of lower-league players and they ran out of steam in the second half. I managed to add to my representative try tally and we went on to win pretty comfortably in the end, although it didn't feel like a proper Test, in spite of their commendable efforts.

I was in the dressing room toilet at Wilderspool before the Warrington clash when Nobby came over and said: 'You know I'm resting you for the right reasons; you've played a lot of rugby.' Even so, I pleaded with him to let me get out there. It was the perfect eye-opener; not a confidence-busting loss against the Wolves, more of a reality check, which strengthened our mental resolve to finish the regular season on a high. Not that there weren't the odd distractions along the way. Playing Leeds again, at Headingley, we were confronted by a naked duo of each gender midway through the first half who were supposedly protesting about defections to rugby union and had slogans written on certain parts of their anatomy. The odd thing about that was that Faye had told me someone was going to do it over a week beforehand but I had dismissed it. She knew of the guy concerned; he was a professional streaker who lived near us, in Pudsey, and what he was planning was all around the town. I was probably the least surprised of the lads when I turned round to see what the commotion was, I just remember surreally thinking: 'Ah, she was right, what a crank.'

Our best display of the regular season came against our major summer rivals St Helens, Henry's faultless kicking seeing us turn them over at home. Ian Millward, who was never short of an opinion when we played them, seemed to think that there was something wrong with us kicking penalties from the halfway line but it would appear that the rules don't bear that out. His crowing might have created an atmosphere of 'them against us' for the Saints players but he just seemed to infuriate everybody else – and that made me want to beat his sides even more. The victory was important for our confidence in view of our recent past results against them and dented their hopes of making the Grand Final. We were denied top spot for a while when Wigan turned us over at the JJB stadium, even though we dominated for the first hour. David Furner was in their ranks and he was another tough Aussie in the Gartner mould who I loved to watch and admired when he was playing in the NRL or for the Aussies. He was a tough competitor and we had some terrific battles against each other in the back row where no quarter was given but he was never underhand.

I got to meet him a couple of times off the pitch, once when we did a promotion for Asics together and we just sat and chatted for a couple of hours swapping notes and anecdotes and then again when I was in Oz during 2003. I'd bumped into his Wigan colleague, prop Craig Smith, when I was revisiting Wollongong, where he had starred. I was desperately trying to get hold of some Robbie Williams tickets for Faye – he was playing at the Sydney Cricket Ground – even though the 'sold out' signs were up. Over there the rugby league players are superstars, like the soccer lads here, and when I mentioned it to Craig he said that he had some pull and I should leave him my hotel phone number. True to his word, a couple of hours later he rang and gave me a contact who sorted us out and we went with Michelle Gartner, Danny's wife; that was the measure of the man.

When we got there, despite there being 30,000 people in the ground, I bumped into Craig and Dave Furner wandering around somewhat the worse for wear and waiting for the crooning to begin. Again they were great company and once the music started, we agreed that Duran Duran, who were the support act, played the better set. Alcohol is banned in stadiums over there, so most people arrive pretty much tanked up and the atmosphere was great. By the time Robbie came on, the euphoria had died down and hangovers set in.

An example of the bloody-mindedness in the Bradford team, a quality that made us stand out, was that we took things like defeat to heart; so when we came up against Warrington – by then struggling in Super League – we blitzed them at their place, inflicting a record 84-12 home defeat on them on a sunny afternoon. In the last round of the regular season we put Leeds to the sword at Valley Parade to finish top of the table and in pole position for the play-offs, but in those days there was nothing to commemorate the feat which left a bit of a hollow feeling. There should always be recognition of that scale of success and it was soon afterwards that the lobbying began, which saw a League Leaders' Shield presented in future years. It is a huge achievement in itself to finish top of an increasingly competitive division after so many weeks of slog. My form was recognised by inclusion in both the Super League 'Dream Team' and the Opta side of the year, collated from the comprehensive weekly statistics they compiled, so all bases were covered. The best thing about the Dream side was that it only ever met up to be presented with a bespoke shirt and to have a photo taken. Those jerseys really meant something because of their uniqueness and the company you were in to get one.

We were confident going into the qualifying semi-final against Wigan because we were at home where we had been near impregnable. Henry's goals were again crucial as we took the shortest route to the Grand Final. Wigan had emerged as our most likely challengers; they had got stronger as the season went on while Saints had self-destructed. The Harrogate formula had worked again on our week off before we faced them and when the hooter sounded, the realisation that I would be playing in the seminal match I had missed out on two years earlier was especially sweet. I'd gone into the clash with the Warriors knowing that, barring injury, this time I would be part of the occasion and that was a major motivating factor. I just had to get there and ensure that the wheel had turned full circle.

Getting to the major domestic night of the year first up means that you only play one competitive game in three weeks. There are two ways of looking at that, on the down side you may not be match-hardened – but we were mentally ready, we'd been preparing ourselves for big-match football for the previous twelve weeks. So, conversely, it was good to have some additional time off to freshen up. After the Wigan match we went down to JB's to celebrate, had a few days off to get away from everything and then came in to train hard. We watched the qualifying semi together as a team on the Friday night and the following Monday we started to focus precisely on who we were to play and how we would set about beating them; we couldn't wait. I didn't care that it turned out to be Wigan rather than St Helens, who seemed to have the wood over us in finals at the time, we weren't looking for omens. Despite the inevitable hype, the whole squad was chilled out, there was supreme confidence in each other's ability, we'd got better as the campaign had progressed and the experienced campaigners had the necessary calm heads.

As always, early in the week before Old Trafford, the 'Man of Steel' awards are presented at a prestigious black-tie do. Bradford won nothing. If ever we needed an extra edge, that was it. There were no accolades for the performances we had consistently put in. Paul Sculthorpe deserved the top gong, he was a constant standout performer, even when his side were struggling but there was a feeling that Henry Paul's case had been overlooked a little because he was on his way to rugby union. In his first year as coach, Brian Noble should have been up there and we all got extra motivation from him being brushed aside in the final nomination.

Old Trafford was everything I'd heard about and the contrast to Twickenham earlier in the year couldn't have been greater. We met at the Cedar Court Hotel in Bradford and a couple of luxury coaches were laid on for the journey over, one for the players and the other for our families and kids and the drive across the border was incredibly relaxed. We got to the stadium really early and went for a wander on the famous turf. There was no one much about and a few of us ended up playing cards – a game of euchre – on the stage in the middle of the pitch that had been set up for the pre-match entertainment; that's how chilled we were. Even though he wasn't due to join us until the following season, Lesley Vainikolo was there as part of the squad and he was wandering round like a kid. He'd been at the Cedar for about a week after flying in from New Zealand and had run up a food and bar bill of around £1,000, which the club had to pay. He was swanning around with his rucksack on his back like he'd been at the club three years, never mind three minutes.

We took that mood into the dressing room and it was translated into our start, boosted by a long-range penalty in the first set of six. Those two points were never going to win the match but psychologically they were absolutely massive. For us, they confirmed our feeling that things were right while the Warriors visibly slumped a little when they saw the ball sailing over from fifty metres out and were behind before their heads had even cleared. Much as we knew it was our time, they must have sensed that their name would not be on the roll of honour. Every opportunity we carved out in the early exchanges, we took. It was one of those rare magical moments in your career when anything you try comes off and Mick Withers was the chief beneficiary with a breathtaking hat-trick. The other early incident that set the tone was when Scott Naylor pulled off a terrific tackle to halt Wigan's danger man, Aussie Test star Steve Renouf. Scott was an expert at that and he has unsettled some of the game's greats; he was horrible to them, getting in their ear as well as giving them a physical working over and, more often than not, it put them off their natural game. They were suddenly too busy being wary of him. Scott was incredibly under-rated but he was a great mentor for me. He is a genuine salt-of-the-earth, unassuming type, he knew what his abilities were and always played to the best of them. Mind you, he loved to moan but that was his way of getting through training. By the time he got to Bradford, his body was knackered but he did the best he could. He was a nightmare for the opposition but he looked after me, even socially, and we had some good times together. You need players like that in any successful team; guys who are prepared to be great defenders. You won't necessarily see them scoring spectacular sixty-metre tries but you find that those wearing the other team's colours who should have been influential are being completely bottled up. He was a great club man, a good, honest bloke who was true to people and loyal – and he could drink, but he knew the right time to have a beer. He wasn't the hardest trainer but he always did his job once he'd crossed the whitewash; he played through the pain barrier on a vast number of occasions.

At half-time we went in 26-0 up amid a feeling of some incredulity. Beforehand, Nobby had quoted Sir Alex Ferguson, as we were in his back garden, saying systems don't win big games, players do and that's what had happened. For the first few minutes back in the dressing room at the break, there was almost a giddy feeling, a sense of amazement with some questioning if it was really happening. The margin meant that Wigan had to score five tries in forty minutes to beat us and deep down we already knew that victory was ours. Brian and the senior players had to try and bring us back to reality and although the stock phrases and clichés like 'we've won noth-ing yet' started to come out, inside I was thinking: 'Yes, we have!' I'm sure Lowesy and Brian Mac – for whom the painful memories of agonising Grand Final defeat still burnt bright – felt the same and were visualising the champagne corks popping and fireworks exploding but they did their best to keep a lid on things. We knew we had to nail the first ten or fifteen minutes of the second half to snuff out any remote threat and once we had, the remaining time was immensely enjoyable. Nowadays I prefer the feeling of winning in the last five minutes, the sense of satisfaction doing that is enormous but that was the club's first Grand Final win and to do it in such style without any pressure at the death was immense. I played the full eighty minutes and got cuts to both eyes which required stitches but there was no way I was coming off; I was proud of my battle wounds.

On the final hooter, Brian did an impersonation of a man throwing a monkey off his back after all the pre-game analysis had centred on us being chokers on the big occasion and it certainly felt like that. Ultimately, though, we didn't just win, we put in a defining Grand Final performance; we totally dominated Wigan physically and mentally but we needed to. That group of players had to show that we were not the nearly men but worthy champi-ons and the manner of the victory was a vital part of my development; it was spiritually enriching, it made a statement. It also had implications on a wider stage. Bradford had suffered riots during the previous summer and our win was heralded as starting to restore some civic pride and worth. It was important for the community, and especially the people behind the scenes who lived and breathed the club and what it stood for. It put out a positive message at a time when perception of the city was poor. It meant a massive amount to the fans that Bradford could produce a sporting team of note on the national stage. A lot of them had suffered with the riots and the way things were handled in the aftermath but this was an indication of the wider, positive value of sport.

After the euphoria has died down, there can be a feeling that because you've attained your longstanding goal, what else is there to achieve? – but I just wanted more. A couple of days after, because all the emotion had been sucked out of me, there was a dazed sense of numbness but that soon passed, not least because the team had arranged to go straight to Amsterdam for a week, which delayed our civic reception. Jimmy Lowes chose the destination and the trip was so good that it ruined me for a fortnight after-wards. The Dutch hotspot is probably somewhere you should only go for a couple of days at the most if you are a touring party of young, lairy lads. We'd not exactly been reluctant to celebrate in the immediate aftermath of Old Trafford and the trip was chaos. It was great to be away with the boys but it was pure excess with very little sleep. When we got back a few of the guys had to stop their cars driving out of the airport to be sick and when I finally found the sofa at home I was convinced I was going to die; mind you, I was nearly hallucinating by then.

One of the most enjoyable legacies of winning the trophy was that I got to take it out, as all the players did. That gave me the opportunity to exhibit it at my old club at Stanningley, which meant a lot to me and them. The big silver vase also made a trip around a few of the pubs in Bramley with my mates and ended up back at home with me, dented and stained – I'm sure the powers that be have to straighten it out every year when it's returned. At the club's 'Player of the Year' celebrations I got the 'Best Forward' award which meant a lot when you looked at who else was in the frame and because it was chosen by the coaching staff. They are the ones you aim to please and they see every game in the minutest detail; it was humbling, especially with the hard start I'd had to the year. The only downside to the event was that when Henry was chosen as the 'Player of the Year' – which he unquestionably was – a few of the so-called supporters in the room booed him because by then he'd confirmed that he was going to 'the dark side'. People like that have crossed the line of being fanatics if that is the level of respect they show to someone who had exhibited exceptional skill and commitment on and off the field in the quest to bring glory to them and the club. That behaviour, just because he had chosen to make a career move, appalled me. Those who resort to such levels tend not to have the guts to come up and confront players directly about it and they obviously don't understand what character and sacrifice it takes just to run on to the field as a rugby league professional. Thankfully, true fans are nothing like that.

Having missed out on facing the top nation in the World Cup, my fervent dream of playing against the Kangaroos nearly didn't happen. So many moral issues and dilemmas were raised after the events of 9/11 that discussions about whether a sporting tour should go ahead or not seemed incidental, no matter how much it meant personally. The Aussie players' initial decision to call the tour off seemed a bit of a knee-jerk reaction to me at the time; you have to soldier on with some things. The carnage on an iconic pair of buildings in New York, as well as at the Pentagon and in a Pennsylvania field, had brought the perpetrators the international notoriety they were looking for and it was hard to think that a further attack on guys playing what, to the rest of the world, was a minority sport, would feature high on their agenda. I'm sure it was different for the blokes who were deciding whether or not to fly over. The initial hype seemed to miss the point that they were more concerned about some other terrorist plot happening when they were halfway round the world and apart from their loved ones, rather than them being worried for their own personal safety. There was a campaign mounted in some quarters that called the Aussie players wimps, especially because their union counterparts had already pledged to tour here but I never bought into that. That is the last thing rugby players are and every time I read or heard it, I found myself saying to no one in particular: 'Get a grip.' I certainly wasn't going to be regarding them as spineless if I did line up against them, that green-and-gold shirt still meant everything to the guys wearing it. To put your family first is honourable and loyalty of the highest order, not the act of a coward but I thought that not coming over was giving in to terrorism and, if it stops people undertaking their normal activities, that's when it succeeds.

One of most outspoken voices in Australia was television pundit Phil Gould, who – not for the first time – used the dispute to rubbish the state of the English game and to try and get the players there a rest instead of touring after an arduous domestic season. 'Gus' has been incredibly successful in the sport as a player, top-level coach and leading analyst, but his rampant xenophobia, at times, borders on a kind of racism. He is one of those Aussies who bang on about the beaches and the weather over there and, as far as I know, that's not something you can construct, invent or own. It is a beautiful country that is fortunate to have some amazing natural resources and fantastic people. His derogatory stance towards our game at the time was part of his brief as a high-profile commentator in the Australian media. He was being paid to be controversial but it was vital for the credibility and finances of the sport, especially over here, that some form of tour went ahead. In the end it was salvaged by only having three Test matches on consecutive weeks and dispensing with the other games. I was relieved that at least we knew what was happening and could start to prepare, but the revised format did play a little into their hands as they were used to such intensity with the huge success of their annual trio of State of Origin matches.

It was a massive boost to be named in the GB squad and unquestionably the highlight of my career at that time even coming off the back of a winning Grand Final. I've grown up with it being the greatest possible honour to represent your country and, in rugby league terms, the pinnacle of that was playing in the Ashes. It had meant such a lot just to watch those matches as a young, impressionable fan and to now have the prospect of playing in them seemed sensational. At that time, if we were going to beat them, then we needed all our top-line players on board and it was a blow that we went into the series without the Saints pair of Keiron Cunningham and Sean Long. Nowadays we have a squad of about thirty who can handle the international stage quite easily but then, our talent base was not as strong and there were few who the Aussies really rated or respected; but they did respect that duo. I was one who was untried and certainly not tested at that level.

We had two camps, one in Worsley near Manchester, the other at Brighouse and coach David Waite, who was conscientious and technical, was just what we needed. He'd been brought in from the top echelons of the Australian game to revamp the methods, systems and the performance department at the RFL and, according to the more established guys in the squad, he'd immediately made the whole set-up more professional and akin to what was going on at the more progressive Super League clubs. Things had improved during the 2000 World Cup and he had taken it up several notches again. He had inside knowledge of the Australian players to pass on – the NRL wasn't on television over here then – and it was like coming out of the dark ages; we were the Eastern Bloc seeing what was available in the West. He was also very detailed and absolutely specific about the way he wanted us to play. That enabled guys coming together from different clubs, and therefore used to a variety of game plans, to gel much more quickly. Although he had some mixed press, his public image was something of a mask and he was probably too surly with the media, which gave them plenty of ammunition to criticise him. I'm not sure that was the right approach but he certainly had a great way with the players. He possessed an aura of confidence that rubbed off, although he was perhaps too thorough in that first year.

You could tell right from the off that he was excited about coaching the elite players. I first met him during the 2000 World Cup; he acted as an observer around the England squad and Sean Long kept calling him Terry all the time, after the well-known hostage, but who was to know he would take over the reins a year later? David is a very smart man and a deep thinker, not just about matters affecting the game, and he liked to talk. Jimmy Lowes instantly respected him, which said a lot, but initially he was overbearing.

We did a long video analysis session in the lead-up to the Ashes series looking at all of their players in intricate and minute detail. Normally there are a few clips of each of them highlighting things like which hand they tend to carry the ball in, which shoulder they lead into the tackle with, which foot they step off, which is their weaker side and so on but this was something else. We were in there a couple of hours and the footage of someone like Shane Webke had gone back more or less to his days in the under-nines. By the time the film had finished, we felt that we knew where he lived, what hand he used to steer his car, what he bought for tea – the whole session was too long, intense and ridiculous, especially when you've got Leon Pryce sat behind you farting all the way through it.

To his credit, David learned from that and the following year cut back and tailored his preparations to suit, which showed a great degree of understanding and trust in his players. That ability to adapt is the mark of a very good coach. It is a very fine line between pandering to the players and allowing them to run the team and having an authority to get the necessary points across. He, like Nobby, trod it very well. Some criticised his team selections and the fact that he played people out of position but he could only work with what he had. I would prefer to play alongside someone who might be in an unfamiliar role but up to the standard mentally, physically and skilfully rather than another who gets picked for playing in a position just because they usually wear that shirt number. Not that I felt I had got off to the best start with David, thanks to the trip away for a post-season, warm-weather training camp prior to the Test series. I don't like flying and the doctor had given me something to calm me down before taking off. David came to sit next to me and as soon as we were airborne he started getting his charts and statistics out and showing me all the details of the Kangaroos I was likely to be facing. The next thing I knew I could feel my eyelids getting heavy and when I woke up we were in Spain; I was really embarrassed and convinced I'd slept my way out of the team.

As part of the preparation we played a practice match of 'grab' rather than full contact against the GB under-21s behind closed doors at Odsal. I really set my stall out to do well in that to prove to a whole new set of teammates and management what I was about. The Bradford guys knew where they stood with me, what they were getting and what I was capable of in matches. I might have made an impression with some of the rest of the squad when I had come up against them but the quickest way to gain their respect was to show what I could do when alongside them, so that session was an important stepping stone. Guinness came on board as our sponsors, which was welcome, but I never saw signs saying, 'there's a crate, help yourself'. I was rested for our warm-up Test match in France but I wasn't worried that absence from it would harm my Ashes chances. David was very good about it; he told me that I needed a rest because I'd played a huge amount of rugby having had a lot of game time in virtually all of Bradford's matches. He also told me that I needed to be mentally ready to face the Aussies because I would be starting in the First Test. It was not only a fantastic feeling but brilliant coaching on his part; it gave me all the time I needed to take it in and get my head round it because I was in unfamiliar territory. I'd heard for years about how great they all were but I, along with a lot of the other British lads, had never faced them and didn't quite know what to expect. It wasn't fear, far from it, just the uncertainty of not know-ing how deep the water was when you took the plunge into it.

It helped having a core of Bulls around me, including Mike Forshaw who had come out of international retirement and, bizarrely, Aussie Michael Withers who was suddenly eligible as British because he had played for Ireland in the previous year's World Cup. He was drafted into the squad but never used. We were close friends and he spoke to me a lot about whether he should make himself available. He'd been the form full-back in Super League and capped it off with his Old Trafford try treble, but he was in turmoil about whether to don the red, white and blue or not. In the end, he committed himself but the selectors didn't and it hurt him being in camp but not in the frame while all the time he was ridiculed and slagged off back home for being a turncoat. I still think that was a mistake; if he had played, his clinical support play could have been crucial. There was an immense feeling of pride putting the shirt on for the first time for a photo shoot in the days leading up to the opening match but an equal buzz getting all the training gear. I'd got the cherished jersey but now I needed a performance that would grace it.

After the French clash, we spent five days warm-weather training in La Manga, which was very useful despite the in-flight embarrassment en route. As a new squad repetitively practising drills, there can be a lot of standing around and Manchester in October is not exactly the ideal place to do that. It always tends to rain there at the best of times – and more often than not come Grand Final night – so to get away to a temperate climate increased the quality and amount of work we could do. We familiarised ourselves with the designated style of play and David got his methods and points across better without the players' minds wandering because of the damp and cold. It aided concentration and gave a greater focus and helped with the bonding process. We got to have a few beers together which is the best way of breaking the ice; the next day you've got something in common other than the rugby and almost always tales to tell about the previous evening's escapades or hilarities. Apparently David Beckham was in the complex at the same time but our paths did not cross.

We knew, going into the opening rubber at Huddersfield, that we were unlikely to have a better chance of victory because the Kangaroos had only flown in a few days before. I felt confident and privileged in the lead-up to the game which, fittingly, was played on Remembrance Sunday, a date that always means a lot to me. Rugby league is an honourable sport, it's tough and you've got to do some brave things at times but nothing in comparison to the blokes that went over the trenches and made the ultimate sacrifice in war. To have the chance of representing your country on a day when such deeds are recalled added another dimension and meaning to my Ashes bow. I felt an added sense of duty to the fallen because we were taking the flag into a different sort of battle and I drew inspiration from their heroism. I was nervous because I wanted to show my best but without fear as virtually all the squad had not even been born the last time Great Britain had won an Ashes series in 1970. That was our call on the field when things got tough; someone would yell 'seventy' at key points to spur us on and remind everyone that we were doing it for each other, to bring the pride back to the country and in recognition of past glories. I always love singing the national anthem; I'm very patriotic and felt myself to be an ambassador for everyone who played the sport in the country as I shouted it out.

The Australians kicked off and I already had it set in my mind that I would be the second person to get my hands on the ball. A prop normally takes the first carry but I wrapped round to make sure I got the next one and a feel for things straight away. I was lining up ready to charge into the likes of Robbie Kearns and Jason Stevens and thinking: 'right, it's on here, let's see what it's like to face these so-called supermen' and when I made ground and realised that it was just like any other game, my belief lifted further. I was expecting to get absolutely smashed by them in that initial tackle but it didn't happen. The Aussies were something of an unfamiliar bunch to the watching public at the time, especially with a relatively young pack, but they did have three 'generation' players: Darren Lockyer, Andrew Johns and Brad Fittler. To my eyes, you have world-class players and then ones that only come along once in a generation. Usually there is only one but they had that trio.

What happened after that first skirmish I could scarcely have scripted and even now it still raises a tingle to replay it in my mind. We'd done a lot of work on kick pressure and at the end of their first set of six I rushed up to try and shut Lockyer down, as instructed. The ball clipped me, Gary Connolly picked it up and was away and as I sprinted up with him, he gave me the perfect pass and all I had to do was flop over the try line, barely ninety seconds into my Ashes debut. It was mad, startling. I didn't want to over-celebrate, no matter how much I felt like hollering from the top of the stand, because it was so early in the match. I was dying to kiss the badge and give it the big ones but, because of their renown, the sensible side of me said: 'What if we end up losing by forty points to four?' I just couldn't do it. I didn't have a clue either that I'd just won £1,000, put up by the sponsors if anyone scored in a quicker time than it took to pour one of their famous black pints. It was certainly 'worth the wait' as far as Stanningley were concerned because the money had to be donated to a junior club. I was told about it immediately afterwards and that gave me another massive buzz which meant as much as anything. They'd just had their new clubhouse finished but lacked the money for a big screen, so that cheque paid for it. Mind you, by the time I came out of the dressing room and rang my mate Mark Adams – who was the coach there – to tell him the good news, he had already been celebrating the award and made no sense at all.

Early on in the game, Aussie prop Jason Stevens was censured for stamping on Terry O'Connor which got a lot of publicity. I wasn't close enough to the incident to see if it was deliberate or not but, given the size of Terry's head, it would have been difficult for him to miss it and I don't think it would have done too much damage anyway. There may have been some malice intended but given what was going on throughout the match, the incident was blown up out of all proportion. We'd gone thirteen points up just after half-time but midway through the second period the game was in danger of slipping away from us. They scored a try from distance and it seemed so easy for them as they cut us to ribbons to come back to within a point. Suddenly I was now witnessing first hand what I'd seen so often as a spectator from the Aussies, but I was determined that, on my debut against them, history was not going to repeat itself. With a similar collective will, we dug in for Paul Sculthorpe to claim a great winning try near the end. I was so wrapped up with and fascinated by the events that I didn't even notice we had won with sixteen men and that Paul Wellens had not been used by David Waite. That probably said something about the lack of depth in the British game; he had to manage his limited resources for a compacted three-match series in the knowledge that there wasn't too much back-up if any of his starting squad got injured.

When the hooter went it was awesome; we'd confounded the critics, I'd scored a try and had a win in my first crack at the world's best, and I felt ecstatic, euphoric and privileged. I felt I'd played well, the team had performed; it was everything I could have dreamt. I met Dad in the stand afterwards and he was spewing. Every match I played in he put a bet on me to be the first try scorer and on this occasion he would have had the most generous of odds, at something like 30-1, if he could have placed it. For some reason there was nowhere open to take his hard-earned pound within the McAlpine Stadium.

I spoiled things in the aftermath when I allowed myself to get carried away by the euphoria of the triumph and all the hype surrounding it. I had every right to celebrate my achievements but went out and got wrecked until about five o'clock in the morning and committed the cardinal sin of failing to wake up for the following day's team meeting to analyse the video. It was the first and only time I have been late for something like that and I only realised when assistant coach Graham Steadman was sent to find me and was hammering on my hotel bedroom door to wake me up. My misfortune wasn't helped by the fact that the door to the conference suite where the gathering was being held was at the front, so there was no chance of sneaking in sheepishly at the back of the room, hoping no one would notice and that things wouldn't be disrupted. I had to walk past all my teammates who had been in there for ten minutes or so and I was incredibly embarrassed, it was a desperate feeling that has stuck with me and acts as an occasional reminder of, and antidote to, excess.

As expected, the Aussies grew into the series but we struggled a bit because we had no real comparable experience to draw on. The play-off series and Grand Final was still pretty new to us and I certainly wasn't used to backing up one really big performance with another immediately afterwards and that was one of the reasons we suffered in the Second Test. Had I appreciated what was involved I would not have got too carried away first up but you learn from such experiences and disappointments. We just did not have that sort of knowledge and insight then. Much was made of the fact that the Second Test was to be refereed by Australia's top whistler Bill Harrigan and he was likely to keep 'a big ten metres' between the teams to allow his countrymen to fully display their skills. I hate it when I hear things like that, ten metres should be just that, although I have known some unfit whistlers shorten it to make it easier for them to keep up with the play. What concerned us more was that the Kangaroos would be better acclimatised, stinging from losing and would have a referee who would naturally interpret a game in a way that they were more familiar with, so there would be several factors against us. Subconsciously we might have been a bit too relaxed going into the game and there was also a feeling of disappointment within the squad that it was taking place at the Reebok Stadium, Bolton. The only relationship we had with the ground was losing there twice to the Kiwis, the previous time humiliatingly in the World Cup semi. It didn't feel like a home fixture straight away and perhaps we should have picked places that were more familiar to us rather than level the field.

We were conscious of the weight of Ashes history but to keep hearing that we were eighty minutes from making it became a cliché. What did annoy us was the usual conspiracy theory nonsense that was trotted out, that it was fixed for us to win the opening rubber so as to keep interest going for the entire series. Aside from the insulting insinuation that rugby league players could be bought in such a way, I have never come across an Aussie who would deliberately lose at anything, let alone a whole team. It was a preposterous suggestion that beggared belief and was the product of people with too much time on their hands. Perhaps it was passionate British fans grasping for a reason as to why we seemed to be able to get up for one match but seldom went on to take the ultimate spoils. David Waite came in for some criticism for not changing his team and supposedly his tactics for the second game. The simplistic line was that he seemed to be trying to cram his side with as many loose-forwards as possible but he was limited by who his best players were, not the position they played in. We made a decent start to the second encounter but on the back of Andrew Johns' renowned kicking game we were quickly submerged. Their ability to score three or four tries in quick succession to put a game out of reach was more evident then and they punished every mistake we made and any weakness shown. The only positive for me was that I didn't miss any tackles but I was dropped to the bench for the deciding Test. David let me down gently when he told me that he wanted to do things a little bit differently at Wigan and although a lot of the lads came up and kindly said that I shouldn't have been the one to have relinquished my place, he was probably right, no matter how desperately deflated I was.

The Second Test wasn't my greatest performance in a struggling team but I didn't do myself any favours turning up late and in a state to that meeting. He could tell that I was probably jaded, the drink does that and when you are in camp all the time, it's not like being at home where you can refuel yourself properly and do your own thing to get back into top shape. It was a hard lesson but one that I needed to learn. With the Aussies' convincing win in the Second Test, everyone believed that momentum had changed. After Bolton, we did a review again on the Sunday morning with footage from a camera position behind the posts. Normally, the get-together would last around forty minutes and be based on about fifteen minutes of footage taken from the whole eighty. This, however, was the full game. It took about three hours to analyse and everybody copped it. It was the longest session I have ever been involved in but in the Third Test we certainly got our pride back, if not the result.

We made a great start, Paul Johnson went in at the corner, we really took it to them and they knew they were in a game. I came off the bench absolutely determined to show what I could do after losing my starting spot and made a fifty-metre break before half-time that just lacked support but seemed to get the crowd going. Even though we were narrowly behind, we got a standing ovation when we came off at the interval. We never backed down physically; it was a drop in intensity which eventually beat us, although it was a massive effort from everybody. Barrie McDermott summed up our resolve. I first came up against him in 1999 and he tried to dominate me, using me a few verbals, pulling my shorts up my arse and giving me a few elbows but I made it clear that I wasn't going anywhere and if you do that with experienced campaigners you tend to gain their respect and they start to leave you alone. In that Test, the Aussies were certainly running scared of him. Early in the second half he said to me, 'It's on here'; I replied, 'What is?' to which he countered, 'Just watch'. The next minute a scrum erupted and he started steaming into each of their front rowers in turn which fired everything up. From then on you could see the fear in their eyes every time they packed down wondering what this mad guy was going to do next and for the next ten minutes the game was in the balance. Sadly, we didn't have the players available to capitalise but it took some bottle for him to do that. I always enjoy playing internationals at the JJB; it's probably my favourite stadium for them and I know that goes for a lot of the boys. In the week leading up to that deciding game there was a lot made of the fact that there were a number of guys from Wigan in the side; the fans really got behind us because of that and they are probably the most vocal when it comes to Test matches. The noise is energising and it is no surprise that we have had some good results at the home of the Cherry and Whites in recent times.

The Kangaroos' score just after the interval made the gap, at three tries, too wide for us to close although for seventy minutes it was a classic encounter. That series taught me a tremendous amount. I quickly realised that in Test matches, unlike in Super League games, where you can build up to a peak, there is no time to ease yourself in. You've got probably around twenty-five appearances at that level in your life tops and you have to maximise your potential in them straight away. You can't be a novice coming into the national side, trying to find your feet; you've got to be up to the mark immediately and contributing. The understanding of that was the biggest eye-opener for me and has been a real help since; I took on board that those sorts of matches are few and far between. What, perhaps, proved to me that I could play at that level was that even though I didn't start in the final encounter, I emerged as Britain's top tackler and the official stats said that I didn't miss one throughout the entire series. I'd only been playing Super League a couple of seasons and that helped dispel any natural doubts I might have had about keeping such illustrious company. I'd first come across Andrew Johns watching him in the main game at Wollongong when I'd been out there – and I recalled thinking at the time, 'how special is this bloke?' – and here I was lining up against him three years later. My self-esteem and belief increased as a result, in spite of the overall defeat. As it turned out, after the Third Test, Brad Fittler retired from international foot-ball and it was good to have been able to pit myself against him before he put the boots away for good. Players like that don't come around too often, although I wouldn't have minded too much if he'd been injured during the final encounter – that might have helped us.

Another of the great talking points was the suspected heart attack suffered by Aussie coach Chris Anderson at half-time at Wigan. We had no idea until afterwards but it just showed the pressure that surrounded the match on both sides and thankfully he made a full recovery. They knew they had to take us seriously; fitness levels had increased markedly since Super League had turned the sport full-time, but the Kangaroos were still so much better at taking chances. David Waite showed us a statistic in the final appraisal that in every game we had made as many opportunities as them but we didn't finish them. Their greater talent pool to choose from means that there are more players with the natural ability to do that within their ranks. They could also sense when there was a lull in the game better and their world-class names could take full advantage of it. Fortunately for me, I had an unofficial fourth Test on the horizon because as Super League winners, Bradford were set to take on the NRL's finest to open the 2002 season in the quest to become World Champions. I didn't need any greater incentive to keep pounding the streets again in pre-season.

EIGHT

WORLD CHAMP AND IN THE DEPTHS

Most people carry an image of what they expect rugby league players to be like; especially of the big, tough lads who play in the pack. More often than not, we like to try and live up to it but sport is an intensely emotional business, not least with the amount of effort that we invest daily without any guarantee of a return. Andrew Johns' well-publicised plight, when he confessed to being a drug user, highlighted what even the greatest have to endure psychologically. He took them to cope with the pressures of bi-polar disorder and constantly being in the spotlight, after being caught with an ecstasy tablet returning home from the 2007 Challenge Cup final, where he was a guest. For that reason, I'm not one who wants to question or re-evaluate his contribution and right to legendary status. What he took recreationally enabled him to thrill and enter-tain, it didn't enhance his ability. I am not in the same league as him when it comes to the intense media focus that the top players have to cope with in Australia, where league is the dominant sport. The way Johns' every move off the field is scrutinised, coupled with the huge expectation to perform when on it as the widely acknowledged best in the world, makes him the equivalent of David Beckham in the thirteen-a-side ranks. When he candidly spoke of suffering depression, though, I could relate precisely to what he was saying. In our line of work, the downs are much further in the depths than the highs are up. He talked of finding it difficult sometimes to face going out of the house and his revelations struck an instant chord with me. It was something I experi-enced midway through 2002, which was a strange season of peaks and troughs anyway, after I had faced Johns and his green-and-gold gladiators in one of the most ill-conceived matches ever undertaken in the sport.

International rugby league was one of the initial casualties of the move to Super League and the summer, and while short tours over here were just back on the horizon, we were suddenly pitched into travelling over to Sydney for a one-off Test, the first time our national side had played in Australia for ten years. I don't know whether the senior Great Britain players were consulted about the idea but coach David Waite didn't want it, not least because the NRL top performers were coming off the back of their exceptional 'Origin' series; their combinations were set, in top form and ready to play at the highest standards. By contrast, we were expected to compete in a league programme that had been brought forward on the Thursday night, with the GB lads then being minibused straight to Manchester airport after their respective games to fly off early the next morning for the match-up exactly a week later. It was a flawed idea from the start and the ultimate – hardly unexpected – result set respect for the British game back a long way Down Under. We should have waited until either a complete tour was scheduled or done it properly so that we had at least a ten-day lead-in rather than get there sore, properly jet-lagged and be expected to virtually run off the aeroplane steps straight into the Sydney Football Stadium. Back then, the Aussies definitely had a better weekly competition and a larger pool of higher-quality players to choose from and yet we were expected to roll up part fit and beat them on their own turf. To compete with the very best you have to be at your absolute peak and during training some of our guys were falling all over the place still suffering from the effects of the journey and sleeping tablets; it was shocking.

Paul King and Lee Gilmour got the best out of it because, after they were told they wouldn't be playing early in the week, they became ping-pong champions. The flight was arranged as professionally as the Rugby League could, we travelled business class and for a big guy like me that was a luxury – all a bit different from when I was on my way to Wollongong, trapped in economy next to a pissed-up Swede. When we arrived I knew the media greeting us would be big time; the *Illawarra Mercury* had devoted its back six sports pages to rugby league while I had been out there. We also knew we were going to get slaughtered in print. The day before the game we went to a dinner and they had footage running of Barrie McDermott saying he wanted to 'bring back the biffo' which became the headline; I thought he was talking about some kind of bear. They also gave us all a rating and description of our talents beforehand which were universally awful. Publicly everyone in our camp commented that we genuinely thought we had a

chance but you've got to say those things. Our belief was growing, especially after the experiences of running them close the previous autumn, but
we knew that we were really up against it with so many of the odds stacked
against us. As sportsmen, you've got to have confidence in your ability to
battle against adversity or how can you expect anyone else to support you?
It's at times like that you have to back yourself the most, no matter how
seemingly forlorn the cause.

We were based in Manly and it was good to go on the famous beaches
there because I had always been too skint to visit the place when I was with
the university boys. The hotel was beautiful and it is a terrific spot but the
management made a bit of a mistake arranging for us to walk on top of
the Harbour Bridge as a sight-seeing tour because we were so knackered.
Paul King bottled out of it; he got the jelly legs halfway up the first ladder
and came straight back down. They tried to arrange things for us to do
each of the days we were there but I didn't intend to play the tourist; I just
wanted to get myself right for the Test. Some coaches like doing things on
the morning of a match to keep the players fresh and relaxed and there was
a game of beach cricket organised but I've never been one for holding a
bat. I'd rather just be by myself in the build-up, especially when the contest
is something as massive as an Ashes Test. I was a little nervous on the coach
to the ground, thinking about the guys I would be playing against. It was
the one and only time I faced Gorden Tallis and he was an idol of mine. He
was coming to the end of his playing career, carrying a serious neck injury
and wasn't in the best of form but I remembered watching him play in a
Test match in 1998 when I was in a social club in Illawarra and thinking,
'this guy is unreal, how much intensity does he play with?' He had a kind of
freakish strength and watching him you could see he was a great example
of how to use emotions in such a positive way. He was another who, out of
the battle, was the complete opposite of his rampaging image – just a quiet,
nice guy.

I was knocked out by the Stadium when we got there, it's one of my
favourite venues and although that night it turned into a graveyard for
British rugby, I was determined – like at Huddersfield early in my Bulls
education – to go back there and put in a performance one day. I knew it
would be a great place to win a game, which we eventually did so dramatically in 2006. Being back in the GB starting line-up was a confidence boost
and we were in the contest for the first quarter-hour or so but by the break
it was 34-0 as the Aussies unveiled their full range of talents. Russell Smith

refereed and, as was the fashion then, he kept a wide berth between the sides which played even more into their hands, giving them space to work and us more sapping ground to make up. We also ran out of players as injuries took their toll and by the time the Green and Golds brought the likes of Jason Stevens, Steve Menzies and big Willie Mason off the bench to wreak havoc, our confidence was shot. The way Mason smashed through us that night made his name and reputation; he had a massive game. We were so short of fit troops that the word came out from David Waite that I was to play on the wing when we had the ball and to defend at left-centre. I was marking Lote Tuquiri; he looked at me quizzically as if to say, 'What the hell are you doing out here?' Then he just shrugged his shoulders as if to add, 'Don't worry about it, mate'. Our only shining light that night was Paul Sculthorpe; he was at his peak and outstanding in a team beaten 64-10.

I felt humiliated by the whole experience, not least because I struggled with the notion that it could be the last time I pulled on the national jersey. The hurt was immense and lasted for a long while afterwards, which is why I could relate to Andrew Johns and his reasons for taking various substances. The Great Britain management, which was put under immediate, unfair scrutiny, called a team meeting to discuss the fall-out the following morning before we left Oz, but none of the players knew about it. We'd gone out as a group to drown our sorrows and then found out when we got back in the early hours that we had this surprise get-together which had been scheduled for around noon. Some of the boys had only just rocked up from King's Cross, they'd been out all night and went straight to the conference room; the whole thing was a bit crazy. For the one and only time I can remember, Stuey Fielden was late for a gathering. He always used to cut it fine and tended to get to things literally a minute before the appointed time. It's one of his traits but he prided himself on his punctuality, although it used to frustrate some of the boys and the staff who frequently pleaded with him not to take it to the wire. On this occasion he didn't make it but still blamed everyone else. There were inevitable calls for David Waite to stand down in the Press which was ridiculous and all the players rallied round him. Headline writers and reporters were looking for an easy quote and the way some ex-players jumped in to condemn him and us was disgraceful. David remained confident, he knew that things would turn round and Wayne Bennett, the Australian coaching guru, also had a lot to do with that. He could see that there were signs of progress but that we needed more competition between the best in the world, not less, to improve the

standard. He also wanted to bring back respect for the flag and the prominence of Test-match rugby as the game's peak, which was being overtaken
by the spectacle and standard of the State of Origin series. Around that time
he re-formulated the Tri-Nations concept, which took off in 2004, and I
will always be grateful to him for liberating international rugby league and
putting it back on a firm footing.

There was also some talk in the aftermath about central contracts, like in
cricket, to lighten the workload on the top British players and to help them
prepare properly for the challenge of elite rugby. It's a nice idea in theory
but how it would work in practice, with players prevented from turning out
for their clubs, who are the game's strength, is difficult to see. I'm not sure
the central governing body has the finance or will that would be needed
anyway. All the talk in the media at the time was that the international game
was finished; we'd tried desperately to perform but we'd been shafted by
administrators and I was absolutely gutted that I might not have another
chance to conquer my personal Everest. It was a soul-destroying thought
that would not go away and the upset was felt by everyone involved. My
inner struggle to come to terms with what had happened and its possible
implications was made worse by being involved in a car accident upon our
return. I couldn't sleep on the plane on the way home and was suffering
from severe jet-lag when we landed. I was feeling sick, awful and completely
disorientated. We'd been invited to a barbeque, of all things, the day we got
back and I wanted to go but I was in no fit state to drive, so Faye did. On
the way there, she was just going through a set of traffic lights when an old
dear with a passenger just turned into her, writing off their car and having
to be cut out of the wreckage. Fortunately, they were alright, although we
were all severely shaken and shocked, but the incident served to deepen my
darkest days. It's hard to quantify depression but, like Andrew Johns, I just
didn't want to go out and face the world for quite a while afterwards.

All that was a far cry from the start of the season which had begun
superbly for Bradford, with Johns again figuring prominently. The match
with Newcastle for the mantle of World Club Champions immediately concentrated the mood and a lot of the Bulls' pre-season focus was on winning
that game. Some of the boys who had been omitted by Great Britain in the
Ashes were eagerly looking to mix it with the Knights. Others who were
coming to the end of their careers and hadn't tasted representative football
were equally desperate to take a shot at the best side from the other side
of the world. All the hype in the build-up centred on the debut of Lesley

Vainikolo and how the 'Volcano' was set to explode. Les has a heart of gold and you can tell that straight away when you come into his company. I reckon you can see the moral compass within people as soon as you meet them and his was well set. Even though he had played for New Zealand and come over from Canberra Raiders, he was very naïve. His birth certificate might have said he was in his early twenties but in his head he was about seven years younger. England made him grow up and he just got better and better but that first season was hard for him, especially because he arrived with such a big reputation. I found it tough to come to terms with that when I moved to Leeds; people expect things of you that you might not be capable of and you have to grow into your role. He was suffering from a lack of confidence, especially as he came over after being out for six months with a knee injury, but by the time he arrived the marketing people at Bradford had done their job superbly and everything was centred on him; he was the main reason why bums should be on seats. It was hardly surprising that the crowd expected a try with every touch of the ball and I felt a bit sorry for him being put under such immediate pressure but he came through in the end to attain legendary status and was one of the best I have ever played with. He struggled in that first season but it was the making of him. A lot of imports have headed straight home after coming here, maybe thinking it would be easy but finding that it isn't, whereas his stature grew with his hair.

Brandon Costin, our other major signing, came from Huddersfield and went back to them the following year. Sometimes you get guys who are top names at the less successful clubs who struggle when they become a smaller fish in a bigger pool. It was always going to be more difficult for him to shine in a team like ours because there were brighter sparks around him. He could rub people up the wrong way even though he was a very talented player. It was always going to be a tough act taking over from Henry Paul but coming in and immediately bossing blokes around didn't go down too well. On-field signings capture the public imagination but there was an equally important addition to the staff off the field when our new conditioner, Martin Clawson, arrived. 'Clogger' was another filling big boots, despite being a short-arse, after Carl Jennings decided to rejoin Matt Elliott in Oz. He immediately stamped his personality on the role, did a great job for us and I've got all the time in the world for him. Steeped in the game, his dad was a great player and uncompromising prop; he won people over by his knowledge of conditioning and his demeanour. He quickly became a very important cog and a perfect link between the coaching staff and the players. I really enjoyed what he brought that was different to Jenno, namely, grittiness and reality. We had a new crop of youngsters coming through at Bradford with the likes of Jamie Langley and Rob Parker but, even though I'd now won things, I wasn't a fully fledged senior professional when you looked at the roster. I was in that mid-ground but I did get squad number twelve which was an important landmark for me and further vindication of what I was striving for. It's a number I've always liked, I was grateful to receive it and it felt like another rung up the ladder of recognition.

As build-up for the World Club Challenge, the Bulls followed Great Britain's example and booked in to La Manga to prepare. It was good to be back, not least because they've got the greatest beds in the world. The constant training is always going to tire you but the beds are like being sucked into the sandpit in *Star Wars* and you're asleep the minute you get into them; they are amazing and I wasn't complaining. There had been talk in the lead-up, like there is most years, that the game might be played over in Australia and we would have jumped at that chance. I'd certainly favour alternate hemispheres, or better still a neutral venue like South Africa or America. Being the beginning of February in Huddersfield, it was naturally cold, wet and blowing a howling gale to greet the Knights but that advantage for us was tempered by the knowledge that we would be facing Andrew Johns again after his mastery in the Ashes Tests. Conversely, we knew very little about the rest of the Knights squad. All we'd really had to go on in training were big, colour headshot photos which turned out to look nothing like the players concerned when we came face to face with them. We'd also heard rumours that they had come over to have a few beers, which made us even more determined to show them how seriously we were taking it.

We played well from the off and continued that throughout the first half but what stuck out for me was the way Jimmy Lowes ran the show in the second period. We were trying to tire Johns out, making him do a lot more tackling than he was used to by directing the play at him and Jimmy was relentless. You're going to get whacked when you run into Johns, he's as tough a battler as he is a genius with the ball in hand, but Lowesy kept taking it for the team and it paid off as we won quite comfortably. It was billed by the Bulls' marketing machine as the most important match in the club's history and even though Newcastle didn't have their strongest team out, we felt like genuine world champions. I'm not sure how much one match says about the respective competitions; both sides had changed personnel since winning their domestic crowns anyway and the momentum in achieving the right to be there had ebbed away. To be fair to the Knights, though, they copped defeat on the chin without making too many excuses, whereas some other Aussie club sides have come over with their long list of reasons why they were disadvantaged already written out. Some of the Bradford fans had been worried that we would be a much less potent force without Henry Paul to guide us, so to score within two minutes of the first competitive match without him – brother Robbie doing the honours – and then go on and win by a margin was good for us. It showed that as good a player HP was, clubs move on. One man can make a difference to a team, but not make a team. Some tried to make capital out of us having six overseas players in the side but they all enhanced the competition, they certainly were not journeymen. I've no complaints with guys who improve the standard and all of ours were an asset to Super League rather than taking the place of a youngster.

The match was also the first club game over here to be played under the then international rules which meant increasing the number of interchanges from six to twelve, which has now become the norm. That helped us maintain our relentless forward pressure and Brian Noble played the card superbly but I would favour dropping it back to eight now. Defences are getting tighter each season and to restrict the number of players who can come back refreshed after a short stint off the park would encourage more flair. Before the trophy was presented, most of the players swapped shirts because it is a unique clash and souvenirs from it are at a premium. That made the following morning's pictures in the papers look odd but invariably, you never get the exchange you want. I was after Billy Peden's jersey – he was someone who I had watched and admired for a long time – or that of Steve Simpson, who was on his way to becoming a Kangaroo but I had to settle for Daniel Abraham's instead.

One of the truisms of sport is that it's always harder to retain something than win it in the first place and that proved to be the case with the Bulls come the start of Super League. It's not something you can anticipate or easily counteract; it is more to do with desire and the hunger to keep achieving. The added impetus of having lost something makes you strive that little bit more, although deep down you are not even aware of it. When you're a defending champion you still think you are doing things as purposefully, but when the shit really hits the fan the pain of previous defeat is an extra, unquantifiable percentage within you that fights the prospect of repeated failure and which creates its own impetus. Bradford had dominated physically the year before but that then became the template for all the other Super League clubs and in 2002 there wasn't a small side in the competition. That, combined with the continued effects of full-time training, meant that we had lost a little of our advantage. Others might not have had the same calibre of player but they matched our physicality which is when you need to take your mental strength to a higher level. In the week after the Newcastle match, assistant coach Karl Harrison was reported to have said that he thought the Bulls could go through the season unbeaten. I wouldn't have been surprised if something like that had come from Robbie, he loved all the attention and was the master of the flash remark and I would occasionally pick up something he'd said on Ceefax and think, 'What the hell is he on about now?' I wouldn't have expected it of the normally phlegmatic Turk. He was probably misquoted or said it tongue in cheek – there is a big difference between could and should – and, of course, the next game it came back to haunt him.

Leeds played very well to beat us in the Challenge Cup at Valley Parade, our first home defeat for a year and a half. Right from the start you could tell that the Rhinos were up for it and we never really felt that we were in a position to win. It was a rare occasion when the bookies got the pre-match predictions ridiculously wrong, having Leeds at 20-1 and they seemed ultra determined to make those odds look like the insult they were, especially in a cup tie. The Rhinos were one of the sides who had bulked up and signed some experienced professionals like Adrian Vowles who collectively gave them a much tougher edge. I liked Vowlsey; he might not have had the biggest physique or been a natural playmaker but you could never ask any more of him when he was out there; his commitment was second to none. He was a proper 'Man of Steel' winner in 1999. That's what the prize should be about, not necessarily who scores the most tries. I'm in favour of their being two awards, a genuine 'Man of Steel' as depicted by the title and an 'Entertainer of the Year'. There are some tough half-backs who have won it, who get their heads knocked off as well as setting up and scoring the points – like Sean Long and Iestyn Harris – but, for me, there should be a distinction; one award for the glue that holds a side together and another for the tinsel.

I always hated losing to Leeds irrespective, but that defeat meant that we gave up the chance of holding every available trophy in the same calendar year which was an early aim dented. We'd been brought immediately back down to earth from our world high by our deepest rivals, and it was a bitter pill. Robbie succumbed to an injury he was carrying into the game and that gave our critics the chance to say that the forward-dominated Bulls lacked creativity, but that line seemed to be trotted out whenever we were beaten. We had loads of game plans, not just the one we were credited with, although our strength was our forwards, so we played to it. It's not like American football where you can bring on a special team to suit. We had variety but we liked nothing better than simple rugby – to get forward quickly, smash the opposition and then play sparkling stuff off the back of it. That defeat gave us a soul-searching jolt but we used the enforced three-week break to refocus on retaining our Super League crown and we began with a first-ever win at the JJB Stadium, in the Grand Final rematch with Wigan. Going into the game I had an infected leg and felt horrible and afterwards the dressing room was described as being like a M.A.S.H. unit with all the various treatments that were being administered, but it was an important early pointer and another indication of our ability to hit back after adversity. The first game of the year is often one of the most brutal and that one was no exception. As is often the case with the fixtures, having waited to get stuck in, we went from famine to feast, especially as Easter was early that year, with four games in a fortnight. With the first of those invariably being the toughest, the intensity and quality lessens with each clash. Any fans who prefer to just watch tries being scored should head for the final match of that punishing schedule as by then defences are invariably too knackered to chase back. It's just a case of patching yourself up and doing the best you can while feeling shattered. The quartet began with an ugly win at Widnes and a confrontation with their Aussie prop Robert Relf. Some players you just like getting into arguments with while you're out there and I seemed to spend the whole eighty minutes remonstrating with him, although the final whistle was where the animosity ended. Involving myself in something like that can make me play better and sometimes, if I'm a bit down, I'll go out and pick a verbal disagreement with an opponent because it will get me emotionally involved in the game. It's incredibly hard to get up for every match and, if I'm struggling, that can be a trigger. Leeds assistant coach Franny Cummins pointed that technique out to me years later after he noted it in my play.

Someone had the idea of taking the Bradford squad to see a screening of the film *Ali* as a way of group relaxation during that tough run. Although we all admired him as the greatest boxer ever, most of us had already seen it on pirate video and after about half an hour we'd all sneaked out. Our sub-sequent winning run came to a tame end in London and we again got back on track with a big win over St Helens. However, like so many of the games between the sides in the Millward era, it was shrouded in controversy. It was the week before they were due to play in the cup final and, as well as resting some of their top liners; he chose to play the final twenty-five minutes with twelve men. It was disappointing for those who had paid their entrance money and the wider-watching television audience who'd expected a great contest, but some people think that they are bigger than the game. Millward was at it again in the return fixture at Knowsley Road when he called the Bradford fans unsportsmanlike for boycotting the game in protest. I never really got to know the bloke but I remember how much he used to piss me off with the stuff he'd supposedly said. No doubt he was sitting at home laughing that he was continually winding everyone up and that might have been great if you were playing for him. We eventually learned to take that kind of thing with a pinch of salt and in the end he became a bit of a pan-tomime figure. Now, at least, the early squad-naming system in the run-up to games means that the fans know what to expect. I could just imagine how the Saints supporters who travelled over must have felt when a virtual academy line-up was revealed on their arrival at Odsal, although there was worse to come for them further down the line.

I got my only try of the season in that unsatisfactory home game, which was another indicator of how much of a struggle the year was for me. Soon after, though, I signed what was to be my final, three-year contract at the Bulls, although I didn't know that at the time. If I am being honest, I was in a comfort zone; my edge and absolute desire had lessened. Subconsciously, there was not as much fight as there had been when I was desperately trying to establish myself. My own second-season syndrome had come a year late. I put pen to paper soon after Brian Noble had done likewise and that was an important factor. He was the guy who had the most faith in me, he'd spot-ted and watched me when I was at Stanningley and said he might be able to do something with me – although he wasn't sure what – and had then guided me through the under-21s and the transition into the first team. I didn't want to be anywhere else, even though the negotiations had gone on for some time beforehand, which is always a pain.

We completed an important double over Wigan with one of the greatest penalty goals in the history of the competition, Paul Deacon dividing the sides with a shot from inside his own half in the last minute. Games against the Warriors were always among the most competitive and enjoyable but we were just starting to pass each other on the slopes around that time. Richard Moore made his debut for us in that clash having been recalled from a loan spell with London after Paul Anderson broke his arm. Another who has been labelled old-fashioned in the way he plays the game, he has been something of a loose cannon during a tempestuous career. He's a very talented guy and I'm glad he's got his career back on track now at Wakefield and is on the fringes of the international scene but he is a moon unit. He possesses one of the best singing voices I have ever heard, he's got Lionel Richie off to a tee, but he can only manage one song. He's so short-sighted that I don't think he can see any of the words on a karaoke machine.

Even though we were top of the league, crowds were decreasing at home and in our next game at Valley Parade, which we eventually won late on against London, we were booed off at half-time, which was a rare occurrence. Spectators have always been difficult to get at Bradford as of right and the marketing side of the club has traditionally worked incredibly hard to attract the numbers. There are a lot of people in the massively diverse city who are never going to be rugby fans and it needed the delivery of silverware to convert others. It took a little while for them to understand the Grand Final concept and realise that you didn't have to win all your matches throughout the season, it was how you finished on the last night that mattered. Also, off the field, the club signed a deal with a new nutrients company Bio-Synergy whose products didn't go down as well. Carl Jennings had not only been great at the fitness and conditioning side but with his athletics background had brought new business to the club, not least in the shape of EAS who undoubtedly offered the best range around at the time. When Jenno went we lost that deal and the replacement stuff, which was supposed to be protein powders, seemed more like Nesquik so I gave it a wide berth.

The County of Origin was made into a two-match series over an extended weekend as a trial for the one-off Test in Sydney and Brian Noble was installed as the Yorkshire coach. The event was taken a lot more seriously and, with the number of Bulls involved, was also a good laugh. Lancashire were again the red-hot favourites, they had all the most-capped players on their side while we relied on a number of youngsters who were just breaking through. The Red Rose narrowly won both clashes, although the second one at Headingley was the most bizarre. In the first half everything they did came off and stuck and no matter what we tried, it didn't work; that happens around three or four times a year. As a result, they led 30-0 at the break. Nobby was calm during his half-time pep talk and told us to stick with it and weight of possession would even up. It did, and we nearly pulled off the most dramatic turnaround. I was fortunate enough to receive a lot of the accolades for leading the revival but I couldn't stand the thought of an embarrassing home defeat in the Yorkshire shirt and that spurred me on.

After the Sydney debacle, and no matter how inconsolable I felt, it was straight back to Super League action and the culmination of the fractured campaign. Comfortable victory over Leeds included Barrie McDermott being sent off after what was becoming a predictable spat with Stuart Fielden. Their confrontations were almost a comic sideshow in the lead-up to matches between the clubs with all the focus on their supposed animosity. In truth, for the rest of us, the constant harping on about it was more of a pain than whatever they inflicted on each other and an unnecessary distraction. Consecutive defeats saw the wheels slip off the Bulls wagon and we lost top spot, having held it for virtually the entire summer. In the heat, St Helens taught us a lesson, inflicting our first home league defeat for two years and putting a half century of points on us for the first time in the summer era. Straight after that Friday-night game, half the squad were packed off on a coach to London to compete in the Middlesex Sevens, rugby union's traditional season opener. Despite being selected, I was still feeling the psychological effects of the Test fallout and was desperate to refresh and refocus on the remainder of the regular season. I asked Brian if I could be excused from the trip, although the experience might have been interesting, and, much to Stuart Fielden's disgust, I was allowed to. Not only did the chosen few face a long, arduous journey through the early hours, dwelling on a poor performance, but the transport broke down and they were left stranded in the dark waiting for a replacement. I can't imagine how annoyed I would have been to have suffered that but I was full of admiration as I lay on the couch watching the boys teach all and sundry a lesson with their speed of support play, handling and aggressive defence to lift the trophy. I was proud of their efforts although some – even among our players and staff – wondered what was the point and value of the exercise. Looking at the bigger picture, it was an important coup for the code and its profile.

We lost heavily at Castleford the following weekend to set alarm bells ringing and I was sin-binned for the first time in my career, by Steve Ganson, for holding down at the tackle. I've always liked Steve but he does enjoy flourishing a card. We briefly regained top spot with a last-minute try at Headingley to win another thriller with Leeds. Mental resolve kept us in the match and I managed to break clear to set the position for Leon Pryce's late game-breaker, which was the personal boost I needed to get my head sorted. We bashed Wigan and then played in the last competitive game at Hull's old Boulevard ground, one of the most intimidating arenas in sport. Players used to enter the pitch through a cage and it felt at times like you were being thrown to the lions, not least because of the baying, often spitting, crowd in the infamous Threepenny Stand. I loved it there; it was my kind of ground, the sort of hostile, crackling environment that inspired me to try and shoot down the hecklers. Bradford finished second and went to St Helens for the match that ensured the easiest route to the Grand Final. Conditions were awful – cold wind and rain – and we sensed that it could be our night. That feeling was enhanced when Sean Long was forced to drop to the Saints bench after pulling a muscle in the warm-up. He came on to spark a home revival after we had blasted them in the first period and Paul Sculthorpe could have taken the match into extra time if he had been successful with a last-minute conversion. Some of the media were claiming that it was another Ian Millward ruse but if Longy could have been on there from the start he would have and Saints definitely missed his direction. Conditions dictated that all the tries came from kicks but we kept our heads to ensure a return trip to Old Trafford.

The immediate reward was a welcome four days off and we ditched the Harrogate routine while we waited to see who we would face as Nobby looked to keep us sharp and focused. Throughout training the week before the Grand Final, Brandon Costin was sensational; he must have won the Harry Sunderland trophy three times over and I told all my mates that he was set for a blinder and would be worth a punt as Man of the Match. I should have kept in mind what Scott Naylor had said to me before my first final because Brandon had a shocker and made some crucial errors. After losing to St Helens by two points in 1999, we went one better in 2002 and were defeated by a Sean Long drop goal, raising questions about our capability to beat them when it really mattered. The match will be best remembered for the late controversy that had Nobby calling referee Russell Smith gutless but I have always felt that we contributed too much to our own downfall to blame anyone else. Very early on Paul Wellens suffered a bad injury when he collided with Brandon. Wello is a tough guy, one of the most courageous around, but afterwards his face was a mess. We'd scored early on the back of that disruption and the first contentious decision came soon after – and I was at the centre of it. Paul Deacon put up a bomb, I challenged for it with Paul Newlove and when the ball came clear Mick Withers sent Deacs in. The move was referred to Gerry Kershaw, the video referee but at no time did I think he would rule a knock-on against me. I'd not felt the ball even brush me, I'd just challenged for it and was shocked to see the touchdown ruled out. Under today's interpretation, I'm sure we would have got a 'benefit of the doubt' call. People have pointed to that decision as being a sign of what was to follow but it was early in the game and we carved out enough chances after that to win without any last-gasp dramas.

What St Helens were so good at was hanging in there and staying on the ropes just long enough to come up with a sucker punch. Towards the end, before Sean Long's one-pointer proved to be the difference, there had been six other attempts. I was probably next in line but by the end I was suffering from cramp which happens quite a bit in football stadiums. Invariably we have to wear long studs rather than moulded ones because of the thicker grass and that really takes it out of you. The final act that night is still a talking point. Should Chris Joynt have been penalised for a voluntary tackle in the final ten seconds? Probably. Would Paul Deacon have kicked the winning goal? Possibly. The truth is, however, we should not have been relying on that. At the end Jimmy Lowes, in particular, was incandescent with Russell Smith and I'm sure would have lynched him if he hadn't been restrained by some of our other players. I didn't see their confrontation and I'm not sure if I would have held Jimmy back, he felt that strongly and wanted to make his point.

Behind his anger, as much as anything, was sadness. It was Brian McDermott's last match before retiring and such a genuine warrior, who meant so much to us as a group, should not have gone out in those circumstances. I was looking for him but he was so visibly upset that he was ending his career that way that I couldn't even begin to console him. It was the exact opposite of the joy I'd felt for Bernard Dwyer two years earlier. Even after Brian had got out of his kit for the last time, there was no change in his haunting look. You could tell that going through his mind was that this heart-breaking loss would be his final playing memory; there would be no opportunity for him to right that particular wrong. That wasn't the way Macca should have retired and I still feel for him to this day when I often think about it, because it was so unjust. Players in big games tend to speak quietly about landmarks like that, but you can read it in their eyes how much they want to succeed for their mates. When you're in such a pressur-ised team situation there's little merit in saying 'Let's do it for so-and-so'. It might make a good headline but it really isn't like that.

At least I had the diversion of a Test series with the Kiwis to consider. It was sponsored by the government's 'Don't Drink Drive' campaign which all the players had to buy into by signing contracts to uphold the message. This time, when the squad flew out for the usual preamble in Spain, we were more attuned to David Waite's methods and his mode of delivery. By the same token, he was astute enough to modify his in-depth analysis to get it over more effectively. We gave away a significant advantage with the choice of venue for the First Test which for some strange reason, the RFL took to Ewood Park, Blackburn. Historically, the first match always favours the home side as the tourists get acclimatised but we were as unfamiliar as they were to the ground, and it showed. I'm all for spreading the sport for the greater good but I'm not sure how taking it from a more traditional Test match stadium, that we felt comfortable in, a few miles down the road was supposed to help that aim. Even though we had the crowd behind us, it was more like a neutral venue. Likewise, the New Zealand squad benefited from being on tour and that opening international was their fifth game together. Mind you, we got stronger as a group after that hit out and they petered out so there is a balance needed. There was an added difficulty with the use of some newly developed rugby balls, which failed to perform in the wet. Most affected was Karl Pratt on his Great Britain debut who was mercilessly exposed on the wing by Stacey Jones' pinpoint kicks and Henry Fa'afili's spring-heeled jumps, which saw him grab a hat-trick. That was despite wearing ridiculous gloves, but then wingers have always been a different breed. Pratty was absolutely distraught after the match and there is not a lot a teammate can say or do in those situations, other than to let them know that you are there for them, if needed. I was back on the bench and, although we lost, it was one of my more memorable games in a Great Britain shirt. When I came on I felt good and relished the physical challenge of the big Kiwi boys. I made something like forty tackles in fifty minutes and helped send Leon over for a try just before half-time to nudge us ahead. It was the first time I had taken on Ali Lauitiiti; he was on fire and such a difficult man to hold or counter when he was getting those miracle balls out of tackles for which he was renowned. The match seemed to turn in the second half when Jerry Seuseu's 'Samoan Kiss' decked Stuart Fielden and gave them a big lift. It was a big clash between the pair who were the respective 'go forward' men and both in terrific form at the time. I scored our late consolation effort but there is always immense satisfaction in going over for your country and it was uplifting to make a contribution, especially after the mid-season Sydney debacle.

It is often said in sport that one man's misfortune is another's opportunity and, although we were all gutted when Keiron Cunningham dislocated his elbow, it meant that a man tiling his kitchen was hastily drafted into the side and I, for one, was made up to have Jimmy Lowes in the mix. We had an understanding and from a selfish point of view, I knew that I had a better chance of getting quality ball when I asked for it with him around calling the shots. No one wishes injury on a player as good as Keiron but Jimmy relished his surprise call-up. We were staying in a Marriott Hotel and sharing rooms but Jimmy ended up in a huge penthouse suite, on his own. Mind you, that was probably just to keep him out of the way of arguing with people.

Straight away, one of the main benefits was in team meetings where Andy Farrell tended to be the sole voice because he was such an imposing character. Jimmy was never short of an opinion, he really got into it in an effort to make the most of his belated chance and, because he was so well respected, others listened to him. There was the usual overreaction after we'd been defeated in the First Test on the back of what had happened in Australia, and I could understand that, but the main mood was one of frustration inside our camp. We retained most of our confidence and belief because we knew we'd played well and three mistakes out wide had all proved to be costly. Those errors had been the difference between the sides on the scoreboard. I was back in the run-on side for the Second Test at Huddersfield – where there was a full house – and for just over an hour it was an almost perfect performance from us. Jimmy was fired up and dominated but the fact that we faded out for a draw said a lot about our bench strength at the time; we just didn't have seventeen players who could compete at that level. Funnily enough, those who had been so quick to denigrate us the week before were now extolling that top-notch international rugby league was back but then there are no half measures in sport. With Great Britain, it is always either total despair or utter elation but the support was, as ever, magnificent and donning the red, white and blue in this country is always fantastic.

Afterwards it was announced that whoever won the final encounter would be awarded the newly commissioned Baskiville Trophy, which was a coup for us as we couldn't take the series outright. We'd actually come out on top for once administratively. Normally we'd become used to sitting in the hotel prior to a series and finding out that the Aussies had got their referee or the Kiwis were going to be given latitude on the way they wanted to play. We'd be expected to go out there and be strong despite the weak set-up behind us, but this time our suits had won. It was a great call to put the silver salver on the line in a deciding Test, although the best we could do was share the series. Whoever negotiated that had pulled a blinder but the New Zealand management also deserved great credit for agreeing to the principle that they had to win overall to take the spoils. It was a huge psychological boost for the British lads heading to the JJB Stadium, knowing that everything was up for grabs. I was on the bench again and did the first and last quarter in combination with Adrian Morley who had been a doubt all week with a virus and had to be nursed through. He was one of our chiefs and we needed him out there in some capacity. I also became a victim of Jerry Seuseu when he caught me with a knee. I was out for a couple of seconds but I managed to get back up and come round. I was seeing flashing stars, which generally means that you've got concussion and I couldn't remember what I was doing. I was led to the sideline but was desperate to get back on. I found myself sitting on the bench with Doctor Brookes and he was asking me: 'Where are we playing?' I honestly had no idea but my sole concern was to return to the action. I replied, 'You know where we're playing, what are you asking me for?' He followed up with, 'Who are we playing and what is the score?' I didn't have a clue but an overriding instinct to be on the field took over. I said, 'Doc, what the fuck are you asking me for? You know who it is and the big electronic scoreboard is over there, so just look.' I convinced him enough to let me out there again but it was a lesson in the art of deflection. International rugby is a lot harder when you're trying to find your feet from the minute you come on and you're not in tune with the tempo of the game and that was a major factor as to why my performances had been a bit up and down, like they had for Bradford during the regular season. By my standards, I didn't really have any consistency in what I was doing. The squad, though, had developed a great unity and became tighter together in the circumstances generated by being in camp. The guards and boundaries built up between us in opposition over a season had gradually come down. By the time we got to that last week, we were on the up having gone from defeat to a draw, then handed the chance of ultimate victory. The only downside with being cooped up in Manchester was that it really did rain all the time.

The Kiwis nearly caught us at the end of a terrific third game. Ali scored a try after a typically free-flowing move sprinkled with great offloads but their style was just starting to change a little bit because of the number of top-line players they have performing each week in the NRL. Their natural flamboyance has been given a tougher Aussie edge and attitude as a result. Some of their free spirit may have gone but they still hurt. Tackling them is painful, running into them is generally not to be recommended and once they get on a roll they all love to keep the ball alive; they've got some freak-ishly skilful players. Keith Senior had a massive game for us, like he has on so many occasions throughout his distinguished Great Britain career, and I managed to get back to stop Francis Meli late on to help seal victory. Early in my GB days, because Andy Farrell and Paul Sculthorpe were so domi-nant with the ball, I tended to do the dirty work in defence with the likes of Chris Joynt and Adrian Morley. It was a tremendous feeling to pick up my first international trophy, even if it was by default, and it tasted even sweeter bearing in mind what had happened in July when it all seemed to be over and I was at my lowest ebb.

Emotions had switched dramatically in the space of a couple of weeks. You can't have knee-jerk reactions in sport, you have to view things over time, but it was important for us as a group to show everyone that we weren't as bad as had been made out and that things were coming together on the international front. It had been a long and, at times, desperate two years since this crop had broken through in the World Cup but we now had some-thing to show for our efforts. The moment when we got presented with the Baskiville Shield and then paraded it around the JJB Stadium is something I will always savour because of what it had cost to get it. In the aftermath, there were so many mixed feelings about the season. It had started with joy in the World Club Challenge; desperation in Sydney followed; there was the heartbreak of a contentious Grand Final loss and then the euphoria of pick-ing up silverware with my country. When I win something there's always a feeling of 'what's next?' It makes me want more but when I lose I tend to dwell on things and brood over them. Performance-wise, 2002 wasn't a great year for me. On a personal satisfaction level and looking at how I'd contributed to the team, it was sketchy. The man in the mirror knew that, although the season had looked good on paper, I had been stalling a little bit. The big saving grace was that at least the two big wins had come against antipodean opposition – and I was no longer single. At the end of the year, Faye and I were married at Weetwood Hall in Leeds and honeymooned in Mexico. Nowadays every rugby league player seems to have their wedding in December. It's about the only month clear of playing commitments and has become an endless round of nuptial celebrations in recent years.

NINE

HAND OF FATE

Everything I have experienced in rugby league – the extreme range of emotions, successes, desperation, pain, glory, laughter, loneliness and comradeship – featured strongly in 2003. It was a defining time in so many ways for me; an entire career in a season. From very nearly losing a hand to being crowned 'Man of Steel' was only part of it, as domestic triumph vied with more international distress of the cruellest kind. And, as my prowess and reputation rose to new heights, I knew that I would be leaving the club that had set me on that rocky, fraught path.

We had a new dimension at the Bulls with the acquisition of Shontayne Hape and a guy with more to prove than most, Karl Pratt. I didn't know much about Shonny except that our other Kiwis confirmed he was a good player, although he arrived a bit green, just like Lesley. He soon showed what a talented centre he was, while Pratty brought enthusiasm and even more character to the side. He was great to have around the dressing room, a bit of a strange kid but then funny guys generally are. He was coming off his Test nightmare and, after his attitude was questioned, having been released by Leeds with a year of his contract still to run. Even though he knew he was Bradford-bound for a while before that, the insinuations hurt him. No one likes to be cut, even if they have already secured alternative employment. He was a Jack-the-Lad type – we always used to say he had some gypsy in him; he was always the first away from training, had several off-field problems but when he was at the club he was great. We had a whole bunch of weirdos at Bradford, especially when we were at our most successful, and Karl typified that, but Nobby's great strength was the way he managed to mould such a disparate, maverick, wild bunch into an effective team. It was something we used to sit and talk about, that none of us were normal but it was a set-up that really worked.

Pre-season was a very tough one built around the Ashes series at the end of the year. I was desperate to play in the Tests and give my best showing; that thought kept me going through the dark, dank December nights. Warm-weather work switched from Spain to Portugal for the first time for any team and, although the training facilities were second to none, the complex on the Algarve was shocking. The beds were narrow and if the person you shared a room with was in there at the same time, you couldn't fully get past each other. The food was appalling; we expended massive amounts of energy, were ravenous afterwards and then were faced with something that looked and tasted like a cat scraped off the road outside – it was dreadful. If that wasn't bad enough, while we were on our one night out, the patio doors to our rooms were jimmied open and everyone was robbed. Tevita, who didn't drink and had stayed back there, saw one of the thieves at work but just thought it was someone mucking about and we all got stung. As part of the week we reviewed the Grand Final and the hurt of losing by a drop goal. It's good to go over stuff like that to get your emotions set for the year. It also fine-tunes you to the mindset of how much it means to win, no matter how hard the task of watching those reruns. Again, it makes you realise how fine the line is between desolation and ultimate fulfilment.

Brian Noble gave me more of a free role for the season; I was given licence to roam to best effect rather than just stay raiding down the right, which was good. I'd started as a wide runner who occasionally got into the middle to help the team go forward but, more and more, I felt that I was better suited to getting in behind the rucks and taking the momentum on in midfield. I enjoyed being in the centre of the action and testing myself out against the other big men and Nobby recognised that. In any walk of life, if you relish what you are doing, you tend to do it to the best of your ability and that was one of the main reasons why I flourished that season. The return to Odsal was great and it was good to see the rejuvenated stadium after it had been spruced up in our absence. It was back to being a major venue for the modern era. I love playing there, always have done and always will. The place meant a lot to me when I was with the Bulls and going back now, because of what I achieved there, is still special. Before the season started, Leon Pryce appeared on wounding charges after an incident in a pub and although he was apprehensive that he could go down for it and do a bit of time, we managed to keep his spirits up by treating him exactly as he would have expected. That meant occasionally taking the piss while also being as supportive as possible. I always thought he had an arse like Grace Jones and reassured him by saying that he'd be in real trouble if he went to jail – and I was his mate! Joking aside, he was down about it and there was a lot of pressure on him, but he handled it quite well and eventually paid for what he had done with a spell of community service. Being behind bars wouldn't have taught him anything and I think the sentence he got was the right one.

On the other side of the coin, the whole squad received a massive boost when Jimmy Lowes decided to delay his planned retirement and signed up for one last hurrah. Selfishly, I was really buoyed by the news. When you play down the middle, you need a really good hooker and he was the finest in the business. He brought the best out of me, personally and professionally, and was just the kind of leader we needed around the place, especially as the club hadn't found anyone to replace him – which was a near impossible task anyway. We worked tremendously together, there was never an occasion when I did not get the ball from him when I shouted for it and, unlike some of the other pivots I've worked with, I can't remember ever receiving a bad pass from him. He set up so much and, if ever I could, I'd try to repay the favour for him. We wanted him out there for the full eighty minutes so I'd go in and do some tackling for him while he took a breather. As he got older, other sides used to target him on defence to wear him out because they knew of his value with the ball. He was an argumentative, fierce competitor; everything you wanted in a rugby league player. He was incredibly skilful and unbelievably dedicated; a lot of my training regime came from his example. He was always out running and doing extras non-stop – he understood that he needed to if he was to maintain his prowess in the key position he occupied. Like so many others in the Bradford side, he wasn't destined to be a superstar when he set out as a small scrum-half at Hunslet. He never played enough international football because of the presence of Keiron Cuningham but that didn't really bother him. Jimmy had more nicknames for himself than any other guy I've come across. Variously he's been 'The Keg', 'The Chemist' – because he used to get hold of vials of guarana and hand them out in the dressing room before matches – 'The Magnet' and 'The Postman'. He used to turn up for training and continually reinvent himself and, because he was the man, we used to end up calling him whatever he wanted.

Before the incident with my hand, the Bulls hadn't got off to the best of starts, losing the Grand Final rematch that traditionally opened the season convincingly to Saints. They blitzed us in the first half, especially with the powerful running of Darren Britt who was someone I'd always admired for the way he played the game; he was a big slab of a bloke. Barry Ward, on the other hand, somewhat less of an athlete, really annoyed me. Afterwards, there was the usual clueless scratching around for reasons behind the defeat and this time most commentators decided it was because we were an ageing side. The truth was that we were beaten by a motivated team which was better prepared for the start of the season but, yet again, how the campaign finished was all that mattered. Ultimately, that is what is remembered.

That seemed such a long way off when I was finally sent home a relieved man from the Bradford Royal Infirmary to recuperate after having my hand repaired. I hadn't had a proper break from the beginning of the 2000 season and I used that as a positive during the forced downtime. By the same token, I didn't want to lose the feeling of guilt about having let others down as a motivating spur. I've got a strong conscience; I'm not religious, but I like to try and do what I believe to be the right thing. I'd made a massive mistake, which I didn't want to lose sight of, and I needed to regain the respect of those who meant the most to me inside and outside the game.

In order to prove my fitness for the cup semi-final against Wigan on my return, I played in a midweek reserve game at home to Featherstone, which we won by 100 points, although I was the worst player on the pitch. Because of the strapping needed to cover my hand and the limited mobility of it, Lee Gilmour came up with the nickname of 'The Claw', but at least the protection got me back on the field. It was weird and strange running out in front of about ten people at Odsal and although the Fev lads were mainly aspiring amateurs, it appeared that their entire game plan was based around hammering me. Every time I got near the ball there seemed to be six or seven of them flying in trying to smash me and although they weren't the biggest, it was just what I needed to regain some confidence and game awareness. It's so physically demanding on your lungs to play at the top level, you can do as much training as you want but you need time out there in the middle to get the true feel of things.

On the back of that non-contest, though, Nobby restored me to the first-team line-up for the Sunday semi, the added incentive for me – not that I needed one – was that Leeds had qualified for the decider in Cardiff the day before and I was desperate to face them. At the same time as watching them defeat St Helens in a classic on television, I was mentally preparing myself not to let my own team down. I knew I could go hard and push through the pain of being tired and out of breath with my heart-rate racing and I was visualising overcoming the obstacles to try and make a telling contribution. I always like to get my hands on the ball early in a big game and within the first minute against the Warriors I was held up over the try line; that restored a lot of self-belief. Greg Mackey had taught me at Wollongong that it was important to get blowing straight away when you're coming back after injury and to make your first physical contact good, whether tackling or driving the ball forward strongly.

It was tight in the first half but we always knew we were going to win because Wigan were down on numbers and had a young team out. A well-rehearsed move between me, Robbie Paul and Jimmy Lowes sent in Lee Radford and turned things in the second half, which saw us pull away – that was a great feeling. Towards the end, just as I was starting to feel content at being back, I got a bad two-and-a-half-inch gash across my knee which was about an inch deep from someone's bladed boot and I had to come off. It was a nasty one and I wondered about my karma but I knew it wouldn't stop me playing in the final. Nobby went out of his way to praise me afterwards for my performance and it meant a lot, but he was smart and he knew how to work me to keep me simmering. He understood that what was important to me was to be right by people, I owed him big time and tried everything I could in my performance to repay him, and he returned the compliment.

There was less than a fortnight to prepare for the Challenge Cup final but that suited me because it meant an instant focus, although I missed the intervening league game with Hull because of the knee which, with what was also going on with my hand, became quite badly infected. I had to have another course of antibiotics the night before the cup final and there was almost constant discomfort from my hand, but there was no way I was going to miss out on Cardiff. During the week leading up to it, I spent a lot of time thinking myself fit and how I was going to get over my disadvantages and turn them into positives. My resolve was heightened when we lost Stuart Fielden, who was injured at Hull, and we were gutted for him. He was a dominant force for us at the time and immediately a lot of people, including some notable ex-players, were saying that we couldn't win it without him, which was a further incentive and gave the rest of the pack a real rev up. We went into the game as underdogs anyway, despite our record against Leeds, as they were unbeaten from the beginning of the season. Conversely, we had a core of players with a lot of big-game experience which they lacked. Unusually, I was nervous before the match, but a lot of factors were riding on it: it was Leeds, I was worried whether I would last the pace of a final and there were still doubts about whether the knee had fully healed and if my hand would hold out. I'd prepared well, though, and I thought the omens were on my side because the night before, in the hotel, a few of us were playing the card game 'crash' and I won each of the three rubbers. It was only a tenner a time but I felt my luck was in, even more so when I was given a room to myself.

That allowed me to prepare better and in my own way; I slept well, unlike Mick Withers who was ill overnight and had to drop out of the Bradford side. That meant a late call-up for Scott Naylor and mixed feelings for me. I was made up for my best mate who had been gutted to have initially been left out, but Mick and I also got on really well. Scott was approaching the end of his time with the Bulls – and in all likelihood at the biggest occasions – while, as it proved, Mick had several more golden moments at the top ahead of him. It was difficult weighing up the conflicting emotions but not a distraction. On the morning of the game I woke up feeling ten-feet tall and full of positive nervous energy. I just knew we were going to win. I'm not sure whether Matt Adamson in the opposing ranks was quite so confident. He had suffered a bad facial injury in the lead-up but declared himself fit and we were determined to test it as much as possible. It wasn't so much that he was foolhardy to play, more that the way the contest got built up in the Rhinos camp was solely to do with his bravery and courage rather than what their side was capable of. That self-centredness also took the focus off our achievements and we weren't going to show him any sympathy or go soft on him, as Leon proved soon after the kick-off when he caught him square on the jaw.

The noise in the Millennium Stadium when the sides came out was incredible; you couldn't even hear your teammates and being the first final played out under a roof condensed the atmosphere ten times over. I was pumped up even during the pre-match obligations and determined to make an instant, physical impression. I felt strong and near-invincible after all the time off, during which I'd realised how much the constant rugby had worn me out. Keith Senior was the victim of my full force a couple of times in the opening stages. However, that did reopen the knee wound;

1. A letter from school friend Andy Lightfoot sends me down to Stanningley ARLFC and the start of the journey. I'm in the back row, third from left.

2. Early rewards for the boys; playing in a team has instant appeal.

3. An early action shot as the scrawny kid shows his appetite for work.

4. *Above:* An early example of my shyness in front of an audience, with Dad on the microphone behind me.

5. *Left:* A prized possession, my Canterbury Bulldogs shirt; in a strange twist of fate, around twenty years later I nearly joined them.

6. Running out for the 'Books' at Wollongong University as I served my apprenticeship overseas.

7. The Bull begins to rage! I make the Super League 'Dream Team' for the first time in 2000. The selection included: Kris Radlinksi, Jason Robinson, Steve Renouf (all Wigan); Michael Eagar (Castleford); Graham Mackay (Leeds); Tommy Martyn, Sean Long (both St Helens); Stuart Fielden (Bradford); Keiron Cunningham (St Helens); Terry O'Connor (Wigan); Jamie Peacock (Bradford); Denis Betts, Andy Farrell (both Wigan).

8. Dirt tracker to Rolls-Royce – in awe playing for England in the 2000 World Cup.

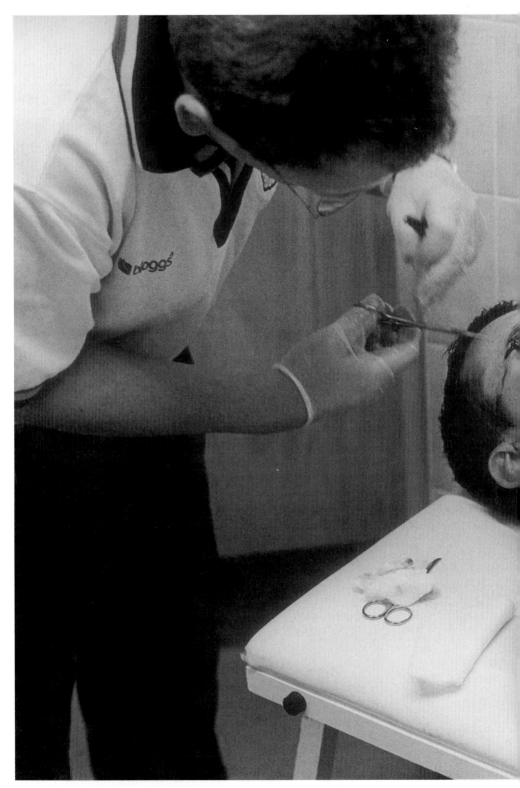

9. The scars of battle – stitching the wounds after the 2001 Grand Final. (Ian Beesley)

10. *Left:* Trying to evade future Bradford teammate Logan Swann. Victory at the JJB Stadium in 2002 meant Great Britain claimed the Baskiville Shield, despite sharing the series.

11. *Below:* Robbie Paul stands by as I prepare to hand off Ryan Bailey in an epic Challenge Cup final at the Millennium Stadium in 2003.

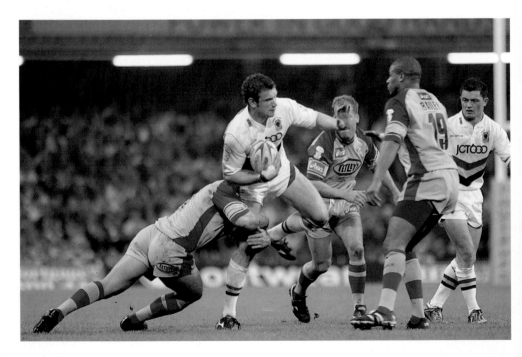

12. *Above:* In the dressing room at Cardiff after we'd beaten Leeds in the 2003 Challenge Cup decider. It was the culmination of one of my favourite ever games.

13. *Right:* Sharing the moment with Mum and Dad.

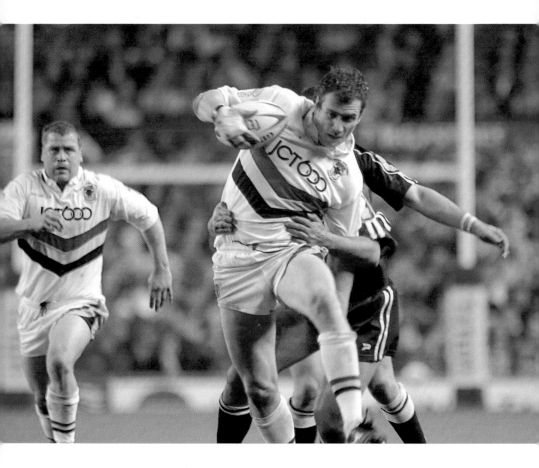

14. *Above:* Taking on the Wigan defence in the 2003 Grand Final despite the troublesome hand. Jimmy Lowes – as ever – waits in support on his fairytale farewell.

15. *Right:* Captain's prize – holding the World Club Challenge Trophy aloft after Bradford beat Penrith at Huddersfield in 2004.

16. Bradford's astonishing run to ultimate glory in 2005 was fashioned on the back of incredible team spirit; Leon Pryce arranged a 'Superheroes, Priests and Army' fancy-dress outing.

17. *Above:* Claiming a try for Bradford in my last Odsal appearance for the Bulls during the huge play-off win against Hull in 2005.

18. *Left:* After my final performance for the Bulls, I take in the moment with Lewis at Old Trafford as I try to hide the agony of that most 'personal' of injuries.

19. *Left:* The new boy attempting to make an impression – training with Leeds at the start of 2006, I endeavour to beat Ryan Bailey during a drill at our Kirkstall base.

20. *Below:* The greatest derby in rugby league, only this time wearing the Rhinos colours against Bradford in July 2006, with Sam Burgess, behind me, on debut for the Bulls.

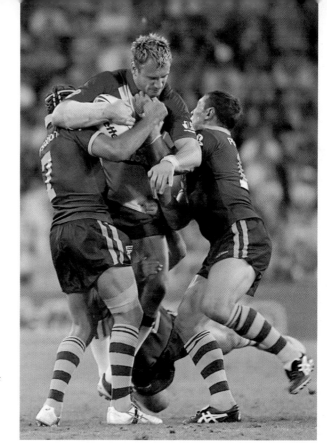

21. Caught in a green-and-gold sandwich as we go out of the Tri-Nations in Brisbane during 2006; my efforts in the series helped win me the 'International Forward of the Year' accolade.

22. Trying to set a skipper's example during our sensational victory in Sydney; I catch Willie Mason after he had laid out Stuart Fielden.

23. *Above:* Taking on Willie Talau at Knowsley Road in the 2007 play-offs. Saints won one of the most brutal clashes of the Super League era that night; from that defeat, though, we knew we had their measure.

24. *Below:* Faye and Lewis – supporters supreme.

25. My sixth 'Dream Team' selection in eight years, a joint record, and an indication of the consistency I strive for.

26. *Above:* Taking on iron man Jason Cayless at Old Trafford as the Rhinos produce one of the all-time great performances to claim the championship crown in 2007.

27. *Left:* Walking across the hallowed Headingley Carnegie turf with the top prize – complete with regular shoes! – at the homecoming in 2007.

28. *Below:* Also at the Headingley Carnegie homecoming; Lewis adjusts my tie for the cameras.

29. *Above:* Skittling
the Kiwis in the
opening Gillette
Fusion Test of 2007 at
the Galpharm Stadium,
Huddersfield. (Andrew
Varley)

30. *Right:* I
thoroughly enjoy
playing alongside
Gareth Ellis for club
and country – he'll be
a sure-fire hit in the
NRL in 2009.

31. Probably my last appearance in a Great Britain shirt as we win a series for the first time in a generation – Adrian Morley, deservedly, helps me to collect the prize.

the pad protecting it was useless but although it stung now and again, involvement in the action blocked everything else out. I was underneath Gary Connolly when he went over for a Leeds try and although there was some debate about whether he got the ball down legally, I had no doubt that he had – it was clever play from him. I heard several fans say it was a double movement but I like to see the advantage given to the attacking team anyway.

In encounters like that, with so much at stake and where both sides are so highly charged and well matched, you sometimes have to look for an 'X' factor to make the difference. I read somewhere during the build-up that Leeds had Darren Robinson, a sports psychologist, working for them, and he was in the tunnel area as we ran off at half-time. I can vividly recall him looking us up and down as we passed him, presumably studying our body language for signs to report back on. That really wound me up. I was thinking, 'You little man, who the fuck are you looking at? You have no idea what we are going to come out and do in the second half!' When we got in the dressing room, a lot of the other Bradford boys had felt the same. They had seen him making notes as they went by him and that geed us all up to open the second half with a blitz. I spoke a bit at half-time about 'who does this guy think he is?' and about 'proving him wrong' about how fatigued he thought we were, so there was double satisfaction when I scored just after the interval. That showed him! It was a classic example of reverse psychology. The momentum swung our way very early in the second half because of that try. Jimmy was smart at dummy-half, he shaped to go one way, switched to the blind side and gave me a perfect short pass which I steamed onto and managed to take some defenders over the line with me. A few of my Leeds-supporting mates later questioned whether I had got the ball down but they knew I was an honest lad and I definitely had. I was pissed off that the decision even went to the video referee, I glared straight into the eye of Russell Smith who was asking for clarification upstairs and said to him very slowly and deliberately, 'It's a try'. In the act of setting it up though, Jimmy injured his back and had to go off, which was a real blow.

Another key incident after that was a collision between Mark Calderwood and Lesley Vainikolo after Leeds had kicked from the base of a scrum for their speedy winger. Nobby had made us well aware of the move in training and how we had to cover against it, and as soon as the scrum broke I set off to get back and help out. Les may have given Calders a nudge that warranted a penalty but play was waved on and I was just really pleased to

have got back behind them to mop up by kicking the ball dead. Showing
that desire for the team gave me more personal satisfaction than the touchdown. The atmosphere got extremely tense and quite eerie in the last
quarter, during which there was no score. Often, at times during games, the
Bradford fans used to go a bit quiet when we were struggling and behind
the eight ball, even though that was when we needed them the most. We
were stuck defending on our own line for all we were worth but we just
were not going to let Leeds in.

Kevin Sinfield thought we were finally ready to crack when, with a few
minutes left, he elected not to go for goal, which would have brought the
sides level, but to run a penalty chance the Rhinos had been awarded. All the
debate afterwards was around whether that decision was the right one but
he knew his own mind and it's hard to criticise someone for that. Both sides
were shattered and, even though I was a bit surprised he didn't take what was
on offer, he obviously thought that we would collapse having to defend one
more set. As it turned out, we had three more to keep out and I'm not sure in
all the endless discussion about whether he had missed a golden opportunity,
we got enough credit for surviving. Not that victory was clear cut, as towards
the end there was the bizarre sight of our boys leaping up and down because
we thought we'd won as the stadium clock had gone down to zero and
someone had let a claxon horn off. Members of the ground staff were running on to start building the presentation stage but Leeds rightly continued
to attack as the official final hooter hadn't sounded. Russell Smith shouted,
'Play on, play on', and we had to get ready to go again; it would have been
desperate if we had lost under those circumstances.

Even though we played ten minutes of additional time for all the
video-refereeing decisions, things were going well for us; we had a real in-
the-trenches mentality and I felt that I could have defended all night if
necessary. We were working so hard for each other, soaking up the Leeds
attacks, that it was incredibly enjoyable being out there. Victory didn't make
up for losing the Grand Final by the closest of margins only a few months
before – you can never revisit history and that cup decider was a different
chapter – but it remains one of my all-time favourite games. I could never
have imagined, sitting disconsolately in my kitchen surrounded by a pool of
blood, that a couple of months later I would be using that same hand to lift
a trophy against my home-town club and having played the best I ever had
in a final. The feeling didn't get much better. I missed the Lance Todd trophy for Man of the Match by one vote. When I finish my career, if I haven't

achieved it, I might look back on that and wonder but Gary Connolly deserved it, even if he was on the losing side. He came up with some big plays and I don't begrudge him, not least because of everything he did in the sport, as well as that game. When he was called up to collect it, he was absolutely distraught and got some ridiculous criticism in certain quarters for seeming almost disdainful. He knew it was likely to have been his last shot at a major occasion, where he had narrowly lost out while performing magnificently. That must have been so hard to take for someone who is such a huge competitor and anyone who couldn't see that doesn't understand sport and the emotion it generates, especially in a high-collision arena.

The compliments about my performance were flowing afterwards, especially from Brian Noble and, unusually, Bulls chairman, Chris Caisley. He rarely spoke in such a way and it obviously showed how much it meant to him to beat Leeds. Annoyingly, I had to wait behind in the dressing room afterwards to have seven stitches put right inside my knee, which delayed me joining the celebrations. The last thing I needed after a bruising encounter like that was a big needle in the middle of the cut to numb it and I was eventually the last one out. Saturday night, I was shattered but I made up for it on the bus journey home, even though I could feel infection setting in. The ride back was one of the best drinks I have ever enjoyed with any team; I've rarely felt so close to a group of guys and because it was such a long way home, it was a good session. I couldn't imagine how the Leeds lads must have felt doing the same journey. That's the polarity in finals; it's always either black or white.

That result set a bandwagon rolling for the rest of the Super League season; our weekly form had been a bit patchy up until then but we put together a string of impressive results on the back of the renewed confidence gained in Cardiff. There was a real feeling that we could achieve the double which was endorsed by the then-Huddersfield coach Tony Smith, later my boss at Leeds and at international level. It was in that encounter against the Giants that I scored my longest-ever try in terms of ground covered – I have occassionaly reminded Tony of that since. It was from just over halfway and I outsprinted winger Lee Greenwood although, to be honest, I don't think he wanted to tackle me and he let me go on purpose. I couldn't believe how far I'd run when I finally touched the ball down and glanced back up the pitch. Normally when I made a break I got a nosebleed and looked for someone to pass to but on that occasion I backed myself and managed to make it to the posts.

The important win after that was at home to Leeds in front of 22,000 fans, which saw us go top of the table for the first time that season. There had been a lot of talk coming out of their camp that they had been robbed at the cup final by referee Russell Smith and were going to lodge a formal complaint. So, it was important for us to beat them well, to show that he wasn't a factor but the way we had defended was. Emotions run high straight after a high-profile game that goes to the wire, with silverware at stake. Journalists love it because after that often come the best quotes and headlines. The Rhinos had provided them while we just celebrated.

As things started to come together on the field, Faye and I moved house to Guiseley, a more salubrious area of West Leeds and a couple of streets down from where Brian Noble was living – obviously to keep myself in his mind's eye and, therefore, the team. Soon after settling in, on a summer's afternoon following training, there was a knock on the door and a rather posh lady stood there. I said, 'Yeah, love?' She asked me, 'Have you got two peacocks in your back garden?' I looked at her and replied, 'Are you taking the piss out of me?' That took her back somewhat. She said, 'Oh no, not at all.' I told her that was my name. She explained that two of the birds had got loose from a house a couple of miles away and they had been seen on the estate heading towards us. I said I'd go and have a look and, sure enough, when I wandered out there, the pair of them were on our lawn. I had to ring the RSPCA and there was another surreal conversion as Mr Peacock reported the whereabouts of two of his namesakes. They were on the run for a couple of weeks before their eventual capture; no one could catch them and at one point they even attacked Brian's missus. I often wondered if he thought I'd sent them round to do the business as a warning against dropping me.

Our thirteen-match unbeaten run came to a somewhat surprise end on a stinking-hot afternoon at Odsal against London Broncos, when their scrum-half Denis Moran scored a memorable hat-trick after, literally, just stepping off a plane from Australia. He had returned home for a few days because of a family bereavement and it was some feat even though some of the officials must have thought he was still back in Oz, he was that far offside from kicks for two of his touchdowns. Nevertheless, the men from the capital deserved to win. The second sin-binning of my career came against Hull, after an altercation with their hooker Dean Triester at the KC Stadium. Like the time before, Steve Ganson was the man in the middle and although he isn't frightened to reach into his pocket, I like him; he's good craic and not frightened to put his arse on the line, which I admire.

The season then took an odd turn when we lost a near-unprecedented three games on the trot at home, the strangest being the second match when we capitulated to St Helens 35-0. Oddly, and not for the first time, it was one of my better performances – certainly against Saints – but it was a somewhat hollow feeling to receive the Man of the Match award for the Bulls. It poured down and everything they tried, in spite of the conditions, stuck for them and they continued their hoodoo over us that year; we couldn't seem to beat them. We couldn't seem to lose against Leeds, yet they had no problem with St Helens and Ian Millward's side knew how to overcome us – it was pretty strange all round. Late on in that Saints match, Sean Long dropped a goal even though victory had been assured long before then. He was taking the mickey, undoubtedly, but that's exactly what a cheeky half-back should have been doing against their nearest rivals – attempting to gain any psychological advantage he could. It still makes me laugh thinking about it now. Of much greater concern was Robbie Paul suffering a broken arm. He was covering full-back at the time, because Mick Withers was injured, and playing really well. It was early on in the match and we knew it was a bad one because of the way he was holding it; he was a big loss for us.

The following week Karl Pratt was ruled out for the remainder of the season with the shoulder injury that eventually ended his career and Stu Fielden was crocked again after he had just made his comeback. That mounting injury toll looked as though it would seriously undermine our title bid. Indeed, the thought around the rugby league world was that winning the Challenge Cup had taken too much out of us and we couldn't add the championship crown. That, and the individual talent in the squad, served only to fuel our desire.

A break from the Super League programme signalled the death knell of the 'Origin' concept in Britain when Yorkshire thrashed Lancashire – who again had all the star names. White Rose spirit, as so often in the past, rose to the occasion; we won 56-6 and the clash had run its course as an intermediate representative tier. Fair enough, the RFL had tried it – although not really backed it – and the players had put in as much as they could do given the preparation time available. On the back of that match David Waite announced his Great Britain squad for the Ashes clashes and made a point at the press conference of calling me the best forward in the domestic game which was a real personal boost. Things felt like they were going right; even in training I was at the front of everything and I had a real buzz about me.

I'd hardly had a drink after the hand incident, the Challenge Cup win aside; I was really looking after myself and everything was snowballing positively. So it was with the team too, and a big midweek revenge win in London, when Leon ripped the Broncos to bits, took us back to the summit. We felt we owed them one and it was satisfying to deliver in such emphatic style. With the nominated captains falling to injury almost by the week, I had the honour of skippering the side for the first time in my career against Huddersfield at Odsal – although I must have been about fifty-sixth in line. I really enjoyed it, we won and I took the time to tell a few people afterwards that I was statistically the best leader the club had ever had, not that anyone was listening.

The big game towards the finish of the regular rounds was at Leeds when we narrowly took the spoils after I helped send Mike Forshaw in for the winning try towards the end. It was a sensational contest on a very warm late-summer night with the famous Headingley venue packed and as colourful as I'd ever seen it. In my team role you rarely get to be in a position to set up a clinching score, that's normally the job of a half-back or centre, but we'd done some specific targeting work in training and I shouted to Paul Deacon for the ball. I broke through but didn't have the speed to go all the way. Gary Connolly tackled me but I managed to get a crap ball out to Forsh who did brilliantly to take it and go over. It was an immensely satisfying feeling, especially as it was against the Rhinos and in a game that meant such a lot to our respective finishing positions. It remains another of my favourite encounters. My form was such that I even managed two tries in a match back down in the capital, a feat I hadn't managed since breaking into the side; mind you, both were from no more than ten metres out, which was more like my range.

We secured the Minor Premiership with victory in another fantastic contest against Leeds, this time at Odsal; Paul Deacon dropped a late goal to win it. Every clash with them was magnificent to play in and, as an advert for the code, exactly what derbies should be about; namely a competitive rivalry and tradition that has continued to grow, especially having now seen it from both sides. We were presented with the shield for topping the league the following week at home to Castleford, although the impact was a little lessened because they beat us. It should really have been given to us straight after the Leeds game when the euphoria was at its highest but, no doubt, the Bulls management wanted to make sure they pulled in a crowd the following week and held it back.

In the qualifying match for the Grand Final, we faced Leeds yet again. Of the 300-odd Super League games I've played in, it seems that about fifty of them have been Leeds–Bradford encounters and we managed to continue our unbeaten run against them. Mick Withers was back after a long spell out, which gave us a real lift. He was a proven, big-game player and safe as houses at the back, which bred even greater confidence in the guys in front of him. I took a hit from someone during the game and although I wasn't knocked out, when I got up to play the ball, for a split second before my head cleared, I thought, 'Why am I here? I should be at home reading a magazine.' As he's done throughout his career, Leon turned the outcome, coming off the bench to grab the vital try at the most opportune time. He might not be liked by all fans and players but I thoroughly enjoyed playing alongside him. To qualify for a third consecutive Grand Final was immense and the product of two complementary driving forces: the desire to be the first side to do the treble and to exorcise the disappointment of losing in such desperate circumstances the year before. We'd had a tough, interrupted year but earned the week's rest, which was important.

In the run-up to the Old Trafford showdown, the seasonal prizes were given out and I was fortunate enough to be showered with them, including four at the Bulls' club night. I even won Sky's '80 Second Challenge', thrown out to test players representing all the Super League clubs about their knowledge of the sport on *Boots 'N' All*, even though I had to take the cup home in a carrier bag. It was a better-looking trophy than some of the other more prestigious ones to be honest and I did practise by getting the lads to fire questions at me before my attempt. That was my competitive streak coming to the fore; I wanted to give it my best shot and managed to come up with enough right answers to claim the silverware.

Again, looking back at the events of early March with my hand, I had proved the old adage that 'it's not about when a man falls, but how many times and how he gets back up again.' I'd built on my intense disappointment and proved to those around me and myself that I could recover to take my career to a new, higher level. No one outside the inner sanctum knew what had gone on or could appreciate the motivating desire. It's nice to win some personal awards because it means your team must be going well, but I do find it all a bit embarrassing, especially when I have to get up there to accept them. I'd rather just be notified in the post or have the accolades wrapped and sent round.

The 'Man of Steel' awards on the Monday before the Grand Final are the culmination of a very long day. We'd trained in the morning, gone to Old

Trafford for the traditional previewing open-press afternoon for the game, travelled back to get suited and booted and then whisked off to the presentations in the evening. Faye had been to Las Vegas for a friend's wedding but only been there two days before flying back to support me, which meant a great deal. It was the first time I had been invited and I was overawed by it all. The trophy that meant the most for me was the 'Players' Player of the Year'; it's probably the smallest on the mantelpiece but it is personally the most gratifying. The greatest judges of your worth are your peers and to win the one that was voted for by all the other fellow professionals from across the sport felt fantastic. It means you've obviously left an impression and whoever I've cast a vote for has been the bloke who's earned my respect the most, not necessarily been the flashest. Being basically shy, accepting the tributes is pretty awful. I'm uneasy about having praise lavished upon me which is obviously what happens on those occasions. It doesn't lessen the gratitude but it makes me genuinely uncomfortable; I don't know if that's in my upbringing or just a personal thing. When you are then thrust upon a stage, there is an initial buzz when seeing your name engraved but a part of me wants to be anywhere else at the time, especially as it's actions, rather than words, that define what you have done.

When they announced that I'd also won the 'Man of Steel' award, I was in a state of shock when recalled onto the stage. My only regret, which remains with me, was that in the moment I forgot to thank Jimmy Lowes. The whole presentation was a bit surreal. Sky, who normally hosted the event and provided the highlights, were in dispute with the Rugby Football League about the terms of a new contract and the rights to Super League, so the BBC supplied the footage and it was dire. All they showed as the highlights of my year was me walking up and down the pitch at Odsal on a camcorder, none of the usual high-impact close-up hits, flashing colour and appropriate soundtrack. Fortunately Sky's version was shown in the lead-up to the Grand Final and that was great but I was annoyed, as well as anxious when I went up there and I missed out mentioning the man who was one of the main reasons why I was nominated and the player I had become. I'd voted for Wigan's Craig Smith as Players' Player – I had to keep it in the forwards' union – I'd admired what he'd done in a side that had struggled with injuries but had still made it through to the last night. BBC commentator Dave Woods, who was the compere, told me to lift the main trophy aloft after I had accepted it and, being naïve, I did and felt a right burk. I did get £5,000 as well, which never goes amiss, and before I had even sat down, Jimmy was already donating it to the players' end of season 'Mad Monday' pool. Funnily enough, he didn't put his hand in his pocket throughout that long celebration when it came around.

Brian Noble, who at last picked up the 'Coach of the Year' gong and who had stood by me so strongly said that I'd carried the side physically and emotionally during the year, which was a magnificent compliment but I was looked after by him and Jimmy if the truth is told. You can't buy that kind of loyalty. The teammates of the 'Man of Steel' implicitly share in that award, they know they have a vested interest in it but I said that I wasn't going to put any of the silverware on display at home until we had won the Grand Final. Ironically, though, as my individual stock reached its highest level, my days at Bradford became numbered. I deliberately mentioned in the Press interviews at the 'Man of Steel' dinner that I wouldn't mind having a crack in the Australian club game when my existing deal expired in 2005. I'd gone up several playing levels since my previous contract had been agreed at Odsal, including becoming a Great Britain regular – an honour which is only afforded to around twenty players a year – and had now been recognised by my fellow professionals and the voting panel as being the best. On the basis of that, I sought what I thought was a justifiable renegotiation. In an ideal world, you wouldn't even have to use an agent, although if you've got a good one who looks after a few players, at least you know your correct market value. I'm a bit old-fashioned in that respect. I've never wanted more than I was worth; I wasn't going to rip the club off and hoped they would operate the same way, appreciate my merit and we would strike a deal that was satisfactory, right and fair to both parties. It's never quite like that in the real world, though, and Bradford weren't even willing to look at it. Just as they were getting the maximum out of me, I knew that there was no long-term future there. My heart and soul was in that club, I'd given my absolute all, repaid the faith shown in me with every ounce of strength and minute of time but there seemed to be no loyalty coming back the other way and that really hurt. Aside from the brevity of a rugby player's career, what infuriated me more than anything was that they were not being just.

I couldn't see myself playing with any other Super League outfit at the time and had spoken to Matt Elliott at Canberra on a few occasions since he'd left Bradford and he was keen to get me out there. Likewise, through Danny Gartner, I spoke to and met Canterbury more than once and further down the line, in 2005, when my deal with Bradford was about to expire, a guy from Penrith turned up and knocked on my door and asked if I wanted to sign for them. You don't need extra motivation to perform against the

Aussies, who were on their way over, but the thought that I could be putting myself in the shop window for a deal to be playing alongside them was an added spur.

Before that, though, there was the matter of another Grand Final. It was my third in a row and going into it on the back of losing one, the will to win was greater than ever. We were on the verge of something really special having already taken out the Challenge Cup and League Leaders' Shield. There was talk among the boys about what it would mean being part of a side that could achieve a unique treble. Interest had been building year on year in the event and Old Trafford witnessed its first sell-out. One of the best parts is waiting in the tunnel getting ready to walk into that throng and then entering to an absolute crescendo of noise. There's no hanging about or ceremony beforehand, it's straight into battle, which is great. Robbie, a real big game player, was back after three months out and Brian Noble again demonstrated his loyalty to his chief lieutenants by drafting him in. Wigan were the first side to qualify for the ultimate decider from outside the top two. General consensus was split: either they would be fatigued from their greater exertions to get to Old Trafford or buoyed by the momentum of a long, confidence-restoring unbeaten run. We weren't expecting them to oblige as they had in 2001 and let us wrap matters up by the break. They came out with vigour and emotion and because of the week off we had to build up a head of steam as the contest developed to quell that. We stuck with them in the early stages but we also knew they would tire and we did eventually wear them down; it was a big side against a young one and experience counted.

We were again the victims of a dubious video-refereeing call, this time against Lesley, but we remained positive throughout on the back of some typically uncompromising defence. A new hero was unearthed in Stuart Reardon, who took his chance after the injuries to Mick Withers and Robbie. He had been on the fringes for a while at Bradford and worked hard to make the most of his opportunity. We were good mates and had a lot in common, not least that he had also come into the game late, and his terrific try eventually settled the outcome. He always had talent, it was about him applying himself and the Harry Sunderland Trophy he picked up as the game's best showed just how much he had done that. It was good to see another local lad coming through as well. He was particularly close friends with Leon; they were both from West Bowling and the Bulls crowd related to that. Leon was castigated for a high tackle on Brian Carney which saw the dangerous Wigan winger – who had done so much to get his side to Old Trafford – taken off but it was more of a head slam into the turf which did not contravene any rule; it was just part of the game then. Leon did a great job when he came off the bench, firstly by taking out one of their best strike players – Carney had destroyed Leeds the week before – and then with an act for which he became notorious in 2007, when he showed a surprising degree of 'ball control'. The victim of the 'testicular tug' was Andy Farrell – it was later shown on *Soccer AM* – and Faz's head went after that; he was more concerned with getting retribution than playing the game.

The match was summed up by the reaction of the two hookers in the aftermath. Jimmy Lowes scripted his own make-believe ending with the final try to close his career and Terry Newton was desolate, in tears after losing another Grand Final. Their conflicting emotions were the perfect illustration of sport. There were a lot of young, local lads in the Wigan team then and Tez was the leader of them. He was very influential and it really hurt him; losing with his home-town club was hard to take, especially as they were coming off a seemingly fated winning streak. We were made up for Jimmy; not many get to pick the perfect way to go out, but a champion bloke retired acknowledged as a champion player. That made everything so much sweeter for all of us. We were saying farewell to the heart of that Bulls pack with Mike Forshaw and Danny Gartner also leaving, and it was particularly poignant for me as they were all role models. There was real sentiment in the dressing room afterwards, not just because we were drawing a line under that team but we were also losing some close friends. When you first get into professional sport and at the end of every season players move on, you tend to think, 'I'm losing all my mates'. As you get more into it you realise that's just how it works. People grow old or move on; you keep in touch but you don't get to have the same really close ties with them as you do in combat. For that valued trio to go out on such a high was very special, especially for DG and Jimmy because it was the last game they ever played. It also meant that Stuey Fielden and I were going to have to step up and try to fill that senior role.

My frame of mind could hardly have been better going into the Ashes Tests, although I was feeling the effects of punishing myself to get back after suffering the hand scare. It really had taken its toll on me; I was weary. There was some talk that the Aussies were a weakened outfit, although they had banged on for long enough about how they could field four sides of equal strength, so we weren't buying into that too much, although there were a few stellar names missing. They were picking guys in form but we did feel we had a genuine chance to turn them over in a series for the first time in thirty-odd years. That, though, brings its own extra pressures and expectations. I had put in a big season for the Bulls, especially mentally, and sometimes it is difficult to get up again, coming off the back of a Grand Final. You certainly don't want to be chasing peak physical condition in Test matches and the potential exhaustion factor was why I was rested against New Zealand 'A'; it would have been a game of little benefit to me. The surprise selection in David Waite's last British squad was Warrington prop Paul Wood – who had to be convinced his call-up was not a wind-up. I didn't really know him that well until we all got together and he is a top fella. It was gutting for all of us that having been given his stage, he was badly injured in the warm-up match with the Kiwis and missed the main fare. It was good to have a bolter in the squad to freshen things up and it also gave hope to a lot of the other young talent coming through on the fringes that, no matter which club they were with, it was how they were performing that counted – that was another key element of David Waite's philosophy.

It was back to Spain with the squad, mainly to recharge the batteries after so many tough domestic games and with another trio of the most demanding matches on the horizon. With the length of season we have, making an impact and playing well in those punishing clashes, in such a short space of time and with the ferocity rising every week, does take a hell of a lot out of you, especially in a psychological sense. No sooner have you built up for a massive high and started to naturally come down from it than you're needing to gear up again. Each time the summit is slightly higher – and this was probably the cruellest Test series ever to be on the wrong end of. It was desperate to come so close but end up empty handed. The Kangaroos are in the history books as having whitewashed us but they only led for something like eleven minutes over the entire three-match series, they stole every game at the death. The difference again was principally down to the respective bench strengths, which is not to bag any of our guys but we needed a slightly larger pool of players that could cope at that level. If we'd had that, then I'm absolutely convinced we would have won all of the encounters. The narrowness of the margin should always be remembered. There was so little between us; it was unbelievably close.

All of the media focus going into the First Test seemed to be on Adrian Morley who had conquered the NRL. He'd done a massive job out there, winning and then reaching another Grand Final and proving all the doubters wrong. He'd even been voted the 'Player of the Year' at Sydney Roosters which was a massive feat with the calibre of player they had there. He gets naturally fired up anyway but when you add in his massive passion to play for Great Britain it was no surprise he was jumping out of his skin to get at the Aussies. He desperately wanted to be first among them and to make the initial contact a statement for the whole series. I was lined up next to him as we kicked off at Wigan and as we set off I was thinking, 'Hell, he *is* sprinting here' as I tried to keep up with him. Then it happened, he reached Robbie Kearns and 'boompf'. When you're going in at that speed and trying to hit someone that big, if you're slightly off, it is going to look bad. Especially when the referee in that situation is the worst person you can have in Steve Ganson. He was never going to be shy about sending someone off, even if we had only been going seven seconds or so. For me, the more sensible solution would have been to stick Moz in the sin bin for ten minutes to cool down, especially as his 'victim' milked it for all it was worth. It seemed even harsher when Adrian didn't cop a ban when he visited the disciplinary early the following week.

It changed our psyche for the next seventy-nine minutes, especially among the pack. We knew we would have to get through on desire and belief in each other to cover and scramble, which overrode any other game plan. All the systems are replaced by bravado and guts to make those desperate try-saving tackles and to still take it to them despite having a column of your infantry down. There probably was an impact on us and our recovery later down the line, especially with the other Tests coming up at such short intervals, but all I could think was: 'It's on here, we're going to have to perform.' Put simply, everyone did. That's what made losing with five minutes to go so much of a heartbreaker; you'd rather get hammered and save the mental turmoil. We couldn't have given more or played better with twelve men but we were just out on our feet in those closing stages, absolutely shattered, and it took the ultimate toll. Even though our resources were limited, Barrie McDermott was only used for about five minutes off the bench but presumably David Waite couldn't afford for another man to be dismissed. Normally the First Test is the best chance to register a win, even though the Aussies had had very good preparation coming into the game. We just had to look at the numerous positives to come out of our battling display. We rallied round to try and help Moz the best we could but he was distraught. I was sharing rooms with him in camp but straight afterwards he went home to spend some time with his family and the friends closest to him in Salford. It was a good move to get away from the inevitable spotlight. At about two in the morning the phone rang and when I answered, half asleep, someone said: 'Who's that?' I replied, slightly irritated, 'It's JP, who the fuck is that?' The caller, who sounded a bit worse for wear, said 'it's BG'. 'Who's that?' I said, starting to get really annoyed. 'It's Bobbie Goulding, is Moz there?' I told him he'd slipped off home and Bobbie – who's a real character - just said, 'Okay then, well send him my best wishes' and put the phone down. It may have been exasperating to have been disturbed but it summed up the spirit and goodwill that exists between the rugby league family.

In between the First and Second Tests we had a practice run-through against the England 'A' lads at Odsal, which was refereed by Colin Morris. Barely a couple of minutes into the 'game' he blew his whistle, motioned Moz over and sent him off. It was the perfect way to ease the mood and everyone, especially the recipient, saw the funny side. In the Second Test at Hull, we were absolutely outstanding in the first half, building a big lead, with everything going to plan. Again, we didn't have the nous to shut the game down and as the Kangaroos started to rally – as we knew they would – we froze. We'd been 20-8 up and in the closing stages found ourselves a point behind after they conjured a couple of superb scores, and we were getting increasingly desperate. I went to rip the ball off Willie Mason to try and get us one final shot but the referee wrongly penalised me because he thought Paul Sculthorpe had also been involved in the tackle and it wasn't a legal one-on-one steal. We'd had nothing off Tim Mander all afternoon; the penalty count was four times in favour of his countrymen but Craig Fitzgibbon kicked the goal and won the game. I loved to watch Fitzy play-ing for the Roosters and in Origin clashes, the work he gets through is phenomenal; he would truly add quality to Super League. He's from the Wollongong area and is prepared to graft until he bleeds. We've had some terrific battles and built up a mutual respect but he's got all the strings to his bow and it makes you jealous sometimes. In that Test, he'd also made a sensational tackle tracking back on Brian Carney, which probably swung the match and the Ashes. Fitzy was at the top of his form.

When his winning kick went over, it was one of the worst feelings I have ever had on a rugby field, I thought I'd let the whole country down and it was my fault that we'd lost. David Waite was annoyed that we'd deserted the game plan – especially the highly effective kicking game of the first half that had seemingly put us in total control. My job had just been to keep carting the ball up, but there was some truth in that we'd blown it. You could see the desperation in the Aussies' faces, they knew how hard they'd been made to work for victory but for them it just seemed like losing wasn't an option. Back at the hotel I was numb; it meant so much to beat the Kangaroos but now the series was gone. It was a truly awful sensation, perhaps even worse than losing in the Sydney Test when we'd been justifiably steamrollered. There was a feeling of such emptiness and questions surfaced about where we could look to now. A real opportunity to finally turn them over had been snatched away from us, twice, despite the heroics that had put us in winning positions. Brett Kimmorley had run the show for the Green and Golds as they constantly fought back and it was the first time I had faced him or seen him at work close-up. He was tremendous, the difference throughout the three matches and watching him expertly direct his forwards to where they needed to be at the absolute height of the action was a real lesson. I would have loved to have played alongside him.

The final game of the year was at Huddersfield and the only call was to make sure that we were not going to be whitewashed. The week was pretty relaxed and spent building everyone back up – only for our hopes to be dashed at the death again by two moments of genius from Darren Lockyer. We couldn't believe that lightning had not only struck twice, but now a third time on the bounce. To go from such highs with Bradford to three successive losses in the most devastating fashion was near unbearable. You don't appreciate the skill, vision and awareness of the opposition when you're fighting with every available muscle; when Lockyer broke away for what was the equalising try I was thinking 'You twat' – reflection is for after the battle – then panic set in. Momentum shifts spread like wildfire, no matter what you do to try and prevent them, and Lockyer then came up with an even more astonishing play for Luke Ricketson to snatch the win with seconds left. We could seek solace by justifiably pointing to our overall improvement under the Waite regime. The change had been immense from 2001, and we had gone from just being in games to genuinely frightening the very best inside two years. David had engendered a real sense of belief that we could win; that had not been the case for a generation. We hadn't got the results but we knew we were getting there with a bunch of young-sters who had no inhibitions. After the last Test, which marked the season's end, we felt entitled to really unwind and having not been to bed all night, I was trying to kiss David at eight the following morning and begging him to stay on. It was cringingly embarrassing but I hadn't really let myself go for ages and therefore I was steaming, and it all came out. I'm sure the other boys who had emerged under him felt the same and, although he said he would, he was just humouring me. We were pretty certain that Brian Noble would be taking over, he had been groomed for the role but Ellery Hanley's name was again thrown into the mix by the Press. Although he would have been a great choice, Nobby's club record meant that you really couldn't look past him – unless the powers that be insisted that the post had to be full-time and he didn't fancy it on those terms – but that was for the future.

When the world ratings came out, I had gone up to third-best second-rower, which – considering how it had nearly all come to an end after my altercation with the glass door – was very satisfying. In so many ways my entire story was summed up by that season; coming from not being able to do anything to taking a place at the top table. Even though I was sick of the sight of the Aussies, I chose to have a three-week holiday over there to recover from the extreme exploits of the season and see what the craic was. I hooked up with a few mates like Jenno, Matt and Danny and bumped into Brian Noble. Discussions were still ongoing about whether I would be staying at Bradford and I mentioned to him that the club had not done the right thing by me. They had the reigning 'Man of Steel' but were paying wages way beneath that status and wouldn't negotiate. I told him of my hurt and that I was off and he suggested that things would be sorted once the existing contract was up but, as it turned out, they never were. Being in that environment further opened my eyes to the profile of the sport and its players over there, and what Moz had achieved seriously whetted my appetite. I like the lifestyle, if not the occasional heat, and knew that there were some incredibly hard decisions in front of me. There is a tinge of regret that I never did test myself in the Aussie club competition – I'll never know if I could have made it – but the missed opportunity was probably a legacy of coming to the top ranks late in my career. I didn't cement a first-team slot until I was twenty-one and didn't pull an above average wage until five years later, so I honestly couldn't afford to look at the NRL if I was to do the right thing by my family. I would have loved to have given it a shot, especially after the 2003 Ashes series because I was confident that I could have held my own and been tough enough to make an impression in that company. I'd have backed myself to do okay, but it was not to be. Instead, I became even more determined to show the Aussies what I could do, while wearing a Great Britain shirt.

TEN

THE BEST TEAMS WON

Bradford signed the international man of mystery in 2004 when Toa Kohe-Love arrived from Hull. He was a great bloke but no one knew where he was coming from or what he was about. That reputation was enhanced when he only played a game and a half for the Bulls before suffering a serious injury which saddened us all. He'd been a great servant in Super League and this was his big chance; we were looking forward to having him around and it was a real shame that he missed the year with bad knee ligament damage. He was in that tough Scott Naylor mould and opponents knew they'd be sore after facing him. Fellow Kiwi Logan Swann also joined us and he was only around for the season, having his best game on debut. I can't speak highly enough of him; he added to the training ethic at the club and was really underrated at the Bulls because he was another to struggle with injuries. He was one of those guys who got through a heap of work that wasn't noticed unless you played with him. People tended to get on his back and by the time it came to renewing his initial one-year option, a certain key person within the Bulls didn't rate him. They were not part of the dressing room inner sanctum and didn't realise how highly we regarded and respected him. He remains one of my favourites to have played alongside even though it was for such a short time. The offer that Warrington made him was probably too good for anyone to turn down – they could see his value – especially for a guy who was so tight with his money. He spent most of his time away from the ground scouring the second-hand shops. He once bragged about how proud he was to have found a crockery set that only cost him ten pence per cup. Otherwise he was gone for hours with the accounts lady in the office, working out how he could save twenty pence in tax. He drove a 'G'-registered Mini Metro that cost a hundred quid; nothing could part him from his cash. By the end of the campaign, injury free and with his future settled, he was excellent and showed what he was all about.

Bizarrely, Brian McDermott finally got his deserved testimonial game – a year after he had left – against Castleford. It was part of our pre-season schedule as we prepared to face Penrith Panthers in the World Club Challenge. I ended up captaining the side, after Paul Deacon had been forced off just before half-time with a scratched retina, and it was an honour to be nominally in charge as we paid tribute to a magnificent servant, who was another vital influence on my career. That put me in the frame to lead the boys in the match that would determine the best club side on the planet. Against the Tigers, Paul Johnson posted four tries on his debut and he was another guy I had got on really well with when in camp with Great Britain. With having such a prestigious early date on the calendar, Brian Noble flogged us even more than normal in those first weeks back. I'm convinced that nowadays a lot of the boys who opt for post-season internationals with the likes of Scotland or Samoa partly do it so that they can avoid some of that initial gruelling work, their international commitments giving them greater leeway on when they return to club action.

Following another friendly, at Wakefield, where I maintained my exemplary record as skipper, Nobby gave me the armband for the Penrith clash saying that I led by example and, 'had moments of verbal expertise in the dressing room', which I took to be a compliment. I might not do the best interviews but when I say something, I mean it and speak from the heart. One of my strengths is reading what others are feeling and I can capture a mood and emotion on the back of that – which is probably why I'm pretty good at poker – I can sense a vibe and articulate it. I also look outside my sport for insight and I've been told that drawing on those influences has had real meaning for some of the players. Lance Armstrong is one who has been an inspirational figure for me and I've keenly analysed how he overcame all his challenges. I was especially taken by his notion that going up hills, the most arduous part of cycling, was countered in his mind by him convincing himself that there was no such thing as gravity and so he would not be beaten by them. That same single-mindedness to overcome adversity was evident when he faced allegations of being a drugs cheat while also battling serious illness. At Bradford, you'd often hear whispers that we were supposedly on the juice but those who generally resorted to such comments were invariably bitter about being left behind or beaten. When you're young, stuff like that doesn't bother you but as you get older it becomes a little bit more annoying because of the sacrifices you know you've made. Likewise, when I'm struggling out there on the field, I refer back to some of the pioneering people who have climbed Everest, had no right to survive and should statistically have died in the undertaking. That puts the physical hardships I'm going through playing sport and how far I can push myself into some kind of perspective. I truly believe that there are few limits to human endurance. They are the kind of heroic deeds I like to look to and, where necessary, call upon for the group.

For those of us who had lost so distressingly to the Kangaroos in the Ashes Series, playing an Aussie club side first up in the new campaign could have been the perfect antidote but we had other reasons for wanting to succeed, most of which centred around Mick Withers. He was incredibly fired up because he was playing his home-town club who had deemed him not good enough and cut him as an aspiring junior. We fed off his hurt as he produced a Man of the Match performance and claimed retribution. Having come over here rather than playing in the NRL, this was his one shot at them to prove they were wrong and he took it magnificently. He had lined up alongside some of those in the Penrith side in his formative years and disliked them because when he went back there they showed him little or no regard. For the rest of us, we knew that we had to be at our best to claim the crown because – and full credit to John Lang and Shane Richardson – the Panthers had arranged to come over ten days before, organised a proper acclimatision and preparation programme and had a near full-strength team. They were taking the contest seriously and if we won it would be a rightly acclaimed victory, as the losers would have no excuses to fall back on. That was a major motivating factor for us, along with the chance of holding all four available trophies.

We were the underdogs, though, not least because we'd lost our first-choice half-backs – Robbie and Deacs – to injury, which was a big blow. Their replacements, Leon Pryce and Karl Pratt, although very different in style, added something extra. Leon was looking to claim the stand-off berth and this was his first major opportunity to prove that he was worthy of the role. He had decided that he'd got to a point in his career where he didn't want to be continually coming off the bench or to be regarded simply as a utility player. It was time for him to show what he could do in his preferred position, and he did. Our chances were thought to have lessened with Jimmy Lowes having retired. The line of thought was that our chief organiser was missing. Youngster Aaron Smith came into the hooking role and had a great game in the most intense of environments. He was a fine prospect from the Hunslet nursery and although he was a quiet lad, he was tough. In some ways he had a thankless task and eventually left the Bulls before really making his mark. I was up against an internationally renowned back row of two Kiwis and an Aussie, including one of the biggest opponents I have ever faced in Tony Puletua – a massive challenge in itself.

The tone of the match, played at Huddersfield, was set by the first carry from the kick-off. I'd never seen Paul Anderson take up a ball so hard in his life; he ran straight at Craig Gower who landed somewhere near Heathrow Airport – he absolutely splattered him. We knew then that we could take them on effectively up the middle. I managed to make the first clean break and we established a good lead by the interval, especially considering the cold conditions. That was when the experiences of the recent Tests kicked in because at half-time Nobby, and those of us who had played in them, stressed that we could not afford to sit back and think we had won against opponents who were conditioned to play to the death and for pride. Three scores up meant little and we knew that we had to post points again to put them away. For once, however, in Anglo-Aussie clashes, it was us that went over late on to secure victory. It was important for me, with uncertainty surrounding where my long-term future lay, to leave a reminder with the NRL champion side of what I was all about. That made it even sweeter going up to collect the trophy, especially as the result further restored merit in the game over here. Great Britain had regained some respect the previous autumn from the way we had applied ourselves in brutal contests, despite suffering a whitewash. That series had meant more than when we had lost 2-1 in 2001 but been blitzed in the second and third Tests. The Australian game knew things were changing for the better in our hemisphere; that was one of the reasons why Penrith had left nothing to chance, unlike Newcastle when they had come over a couple of years before, and to convincingly come out on top against them was a real fillip.

We couldn't have made a better start to the Super League season either as Lesley Vainikolo crossed for five tries on the opening night against Wigan at Odsal. It was an astonishing feat and an array of touchdowns that illustrated his full repertoire of skills. Straight after the match I was driven down to London to appear on *Soccer AM* the following morning. I was the first rugby league player to go on the cult show, although I think they were after Paul

Sculthorpe first up. He wasn't too keen but I'd mentioned to him that I was a big fan and he duly passed my number on. It was a great experience and a lot of fun although I did learn a salutary lesson. I received great applause when I came into the studio but it was obvious that some of the people based in the south didn't have a clue who I was. Being a football fan, Helen Chamberlain could not get over my physique or the footage from the game the night before. Most of the sports people you speak to who are aware of rugby league have a massive amount of admiration for the game and how hard it is. There is a large following among the betting people in football; the Friday night Super League encounter is a big event for them and they like to follow it. I talked through the game against Wigan with Tim Lovejoy and he asked me at the end of the interview who I thought were our major rivals for the crown. I mentioned the usual suspects, Leeds, Saints and Wigan and he said, 'What? Wigan, after what you've just done to them?' In what I thought at the time was just a throwaway remark I countered, 'Oh, alright then, not the Warriors.' We all went to the pub afterwards and it was a great experience which I'd love to do again. They've rung me a few times since but I've always had something else already arranged that clashed with it.

Within about three weeks of holding all four trophies, one of them had gone when we lost heavily to St Helens in the Challenge Cup. They blitzed us, Lee Gilmour scoring a sensational try to show us just what we'd let go. There was so much talent at Bradford in his position that he needed to look elsewhere and judging by the number of trophies he's won at Saints since, it was a good move for him. He wanted to play the full eighty minutes, felt he wasn't getting his chance at the Bulls and some teams do get broken up on the back of success, plus that's also the beauty of the salary cap. The next time we saw Ian Millward's men they'd gone from the sublime to the ridiculous, turning up at Easter with an almost total reserve side as he rested his main men for their upcoming cup final. That led on to the exposé of Sean Long and Martin Gleeson having bet on the outcome of the encounter and that their side would lose – which they did, heavily. I couldn't really see what all the fuss was about and certainly thought the respective three- and four-month bans they received were draconian. Bookies are fine when the odds are in their favour, they don't think twice about exploiting or bankrupting possibly vulnerable punters but if the tables are turned on them, they squeal. I know both the lads well and if they were guilty of anything, it was stupidity or naïvety – to put the bets on in their own names was not the cleverest thing to do. The rumours still persist that there were other, high-profile people involved in the game who also made quite a killing on that coup but escaped punishment. The most disappointing aspect was that Bradford and their fans were again the victims of a Saints ploy but it misfired on them by busting their season open. They may have ultimately won the cup but their league form tailed away and the seeds of Millward's ultimate downfall could be traced back to that match, which was some kind of poetic justice. For the sport, it was a shame that a paper like the *Daily Mail* – who broke the story and gave it such back page prominence – rarely offered any meaningful insight or positive headlines and coverage otherwise. I suppose scandal sells. After that game, we were more concerned with the serious knee injury that Tevita Vaikona suffered, which effectively ended his Bradford career. That was a huge loss for us. 'TV' brought a whole new dimension to the side; he was the best big winger you could have. Blockbusting Lesley Vainikolo has been a sensation but he would be the first to admit that his soulmate revolutionised wing play by actively getting in the mix. He'd do twenty-odd carries a match for the team to take the pressure off his forwards and could also finish as well. He scored some freakish tries out wide from a range of distances.

In May, after a couple of patchy performances, we went on the road to play London. We travelled down the night before and Brian Noble called a team meeting when we got there to gee us up for the game. We sat in a horseshoe shape and he started to go round pointing at everyone outlining what he expected of them. He began with Stu Fielden and told him: 'Tomorrow, you can beat your opposite number; you're the best prop in the world – outstanding.' Then it was Les's turn and Nobby continued: 'You're the finest winger in the competition, go out there and prove it.' For Joe Vagana it was: 'No one can stop you when you carry the ball'; Stuart Reardon was told, 'You're on fire' and to Leon Pryce Nobby said: 'You can break a game open at any time.' Then he got to Lee Radford and, without breaking his stream of consciousness, he said: 'Lee, you just try your best, son.' The whole room burst out laughing.

Bradford's home matches that weren't on television were again staged at 6 p.m. on a Sunday. Few of the players, particularly those who had families, liked that scheduling because it tended to wreck their social life. I wasn't too badly affected because it was just me and Faye and I could see the logic that it was in some ways a good way for the fans to end their weekend. For the performers, however, it was something of a nightmare. We'd have to spend the waiting time watching the other sides on the box and we were just itching to get out there and play our part. It wasn't the greatest decision, especially as the pubs generally shut at ten-thirty so there was little time to celebrate or drown sorrows afterwards.

A much better call was confirmation of the anticipated elevation of Brian Noble to the role of Great Britain coach, albeit in a part-time capacity as he retained his Bradford commitment. He was the ideal candidate and I was delighted for him. Taking on the national coaching mantle could be covered in that fashion but the RFL struggled to replace everything else that David Waite had done with regard to his day-to-day, immensely detailed player monitoring and performance-analysis programmes.

At Widnes, I took a heavy whack on the nose that needed a few stitches before I could go back on. The only surprise was that it had taken so long for someone to find such a large target. My form was okay but we only just won there and our vulnerability was shown with a subsequent defeat away at St Helens, and a mid-season loss at home to Leeds. Against Saints, Jason Hooper scored a hat-trick; we could tell it wasn't going to be our day by the manner of one of his tries. We packed down for a scrum in their quarter and decided to try and shove them off the ball to win back possession. Instead, it squirted out at a strange angle, which we didn't have covered; he picked it up in the clear and raced eighty metres to claim the touchdown. The Rhinos' win put them five points ahead at the top and they were smashing everyone at the time thanks to the influence of their new coach, Tony Smith. Not only did he revive their fortunes but you could see that he was doing something revolutionary over there. Leeds were miles ahead of their rivals that year and having not been able to buy a win over us the season before, they had now completed an unprecedented summer double, which clearly heartened them. With our title credentials waning, Brian Noble called an open team meeting where everyone was encouraged to have their say as to where and how they thought we could get things back on track. Les piped up that he thought we weren't fit enough and that we needed everyone training harder, together and more often. That sounded great coming from a winger and those of us who knew we would be punished the most under such a regime glared in his direction. Nobby took the suggestion on board and it was then we found out that, unbeknown to us, Les had been given a fortnight's compassionate leave to go to a funeral in New Zealand and set it all up so that he wouldn't have to do it.

Towards the end of June, we went to Dublin to help a charitable foundation and set up links with the fledgling Irish Rugby League. The trip, which was one of the worst organised, turned out to be something of a disaster, not least because it spawned a hideous green away kit the following season. We left straight after our match with Huddersfield to get the (very) early ferry across on Monday morning. We hooked up with Dublin University on our arrival and were told that we were going to a barbeque which we were ready for. Everyone was ravenous with it being the day after a game and desperately wanted to replenish their energy levels. The coach dropped us off near a park and we were led on a walk through it, looking round and wondering where the food was. Our guide turned off into a housing estate and we started thinking, 'there's something not quite right here'. Then a call went out from the front: 'Okay, we're here.' Thirty of us, all starving, rocked up in the back garden of a corner-plot semi-detached house, which belonged to someone who was connected to the university. He'd put his four patio chairs out, had brought his computer chair down from the study and his wife was running round, with a baby in her arms, trying to keep the tiny grill stocked. That wasn't the most encouraging start and things got little better. We had an unbelievable police escort – I'd never known one like it – for over an hour to get to a monastery to do a training session with a Gaelic football side, who weren't there when we arrived. The England football team were playing against Croatia in the European Championships and we were pretty keen to see it. The match had already started when the other mob finally arrived, although there were only five or six of them, so the majority of us opted to stay on the bus and watch the soccer instead. We ate in the monastery and Brian and Chris Caisley had a falling out about who was going to represent the club at a reception at the British embassy. In the end we renamed the whole trip 'Pratty's stag do'.

Around that time, rumours started to surface about Iestyn Harris' return to the code and how it would be with the Bulls rather than Leeds, who had originally loaned him out to rugby union – and also the money he was being offered to do so. Some were reporting it to be a package that amounted to as much as £800,000. There was no doubt that we needed impetus and he was exactly the right sort of player to provide it, which brought an excitement to our ranks, except maybe for Leon, as it was likely to jeopardise the position he so coveted. Apart from that, Iestyn's eventual arrival at Bradford was far from disruptive, his talents improved us towards the end of that season and it was good for the code to tempt him back. We trained hard anyway but he helped build on that by introducing some new ideas from outside. Personally, his recruitment left a sour taste, which was nothing against him. I'd been told that there was no more money left for anyone and then miraculously some had been found. Even though the club tried to make out it had come from a sponsor, I knew that I had been lied to, which I certainly didn't appreciate and the breakdown in trust proved terminal. At no time did I ever hold that against Iestyn; good luck to him, he fully deserved what he could negotiate, but his arrival and the manner of it made my up my mind about whether or not to leave.

Back on the pitch, I went on a mini try-scoring spree, although my four-pointer against Wakefield was lost in headlines centring on a brawl which saw Karl Pratt dismissed on Iestyn's debut. Although I found the whitewash again at Wigan, the *Soccer AM* jibe came back to haunt me. I took the first carry of the night and got hammered and then another later in the same set, which I like to do, and got hammered again. The next time I got the ball, I was hammered once more and I started thinking, 'It's going to be a long night tonight.' Their coach Denis Betts later explained it was deliberate retribution for my comments. It showed how desperate the times were at the JJB if they were taking flippant asides I'd made on television as a gee-up; however, I was sore for a while afterwards. That was a game where all the plaudits deservedly went to Andy Farrell. He'd moved up to prop by then and took to the role very well at the end of his thirteen-a-side days. The transition was good for him; it seemed to suit him having the ball in his hands earlier in the play and taking defences on up the middle as his primary duty.

Brian Noble was incredibly disappointed at how we fell away late on at Hull after that, as the odds began to plummet on the chances of us holding on to any of our hard-earned silverware. In the run-up to the third meeting with Leeds, the talk was again that they had put in a six-figure bid for my services. I don't think they did because they knew that at the end of the following season I would be out of contract anyway and would be available without them having to pay a transfer fee. Publicity was again behind it and I did get the impression that I was being used as a pawn in a war of words between Rhinos chief executive Gary Hetherington and Bulls chairman Chris Caisley, with the backdrop being their ongoing dispute over Iestyn. It was food and drink for the papers but it didn't bother me.

Towards the end of the season, Brian was back to using me in concerted bursts, almost as an auxiliary prop, partly because the team's form, as well as my own, wasn't particularly great. We were struggling emotionally and motivationally; the nucleus of the side was growing old and there were one or two new faces trying to fit in. Being unfamiliar with what was needed in my new role, I was running out of gas quicker and even though I was beginning to relish it, what was expected of me took some adapting to. The year before, Mike Forshaw, whose opinions I valued, mentioned to me that I'd make a good front-rower one day. Although some of our aura had gone – we'd also become a massive feather in the opposition cap after our success in 2003 – our accumulated experience on the playing and coaching staff saw us mount a late run to claim second place on the league ladder going into the play-offs. The runners-up spot was effectively secured, and our confidence was boosted when we beat Hull in a match which saw Jason Smith and Stuart Fielden continue their ongoing personal duel. We'd been spluttering like an old car at times but that performance got us motoring again. Jason liked to wind Stu up and he was always one to take the bait. Instead of just cocking his fist, as Stuey was wont to do, he actually caught Jason with a beauty, which went down well with the rest of us. An injury-time success at Warrington, where Iestyn – who by now was settling in well – scored a tremendous try to get us level against his old club, had those same critics who'd written off our chances sitting up again and mentioning our play-off mentality. It was a result that also made the other clubs look warily over their shoulders; they knew we were contenders.

A further galvanising factor was trying to make sure that Lesley ended up as the top try scorer in the competition, having vied with Danny McGuire for the honour throughout the campaign. It may have been a bit of a sideshow but it pulled us closer together as a group, especially as it again encapsulated the fervent rivalry between Bradford and Leeds at the time. We'd do anything to get one over on them and vice versa. Against St Helens, Shontayne gave away a personal score by passing to Les, even though he was already over the try line and that was an indication of how we were try-ing to help each other out, rather than go for personal glory. The two of them were like Laurel and Hardy anyway, they were very close. Sean Long, somewhat ironically, made his return after the betting ban in that match at the place where it had all blown up and he was vilified. Various items got thrown at him as he made his way on and off the pitch, which was shock-ing. Shouting at him was one thing but most of the people who resorted to chucking things wouldn't dare front him up face to face, which was pathetic. He gets booed everywhere now; that's just the way it goes for him.

Our one really good performance of the season came in the qualifying semi-final for reaching Old Trafford at Headingley. John Ledger, the rugby league correspondent of the *Yorkshire Post* helped us out in the preparation for that game. Someone pinned up an article of his on the dressing room wall which rated the respective teams going into that clash. He publicly demeaned a few of our guys and that stung them. Leeds had totally reversed previous form against us during the year but not many of their relatively young side, which had deservedly finished top, had play-off experience, whereas we did in abundance. Our preparation in the run-up had an extra zip, it was incredibly determined and focused and there was a sense that we were going to produce something special. We peaked for that encounter; Shonny got us off to the perfect start with a couple of early tries, and then some superb scrambling defence halted the Rhinos' response. I had a decent game and we finished strongly for a memorable win that delighted our fans. By now, as a group, we'd become attuned to getting to and preparing for the end-of-season finale.

Some of the boys, especially the overseas guys, always went for a meal together and played some cards the night before but I generally preferred to do my own build-up and, anyway, I had other things on my mind. Faye was about to deliver our first child and as it was a breach birth, we knew she would have to have a caesarean around the time of the Grand Final. We were offered two dates, the Monday or Friday leading up to Old Trafford and went for the earlier of the two. I spent most of the time surrounding the game in and out of hospital after our son Lewis had been successfully born but it was the best possible distraction.

Knowing exactly what to expect from the occasion, we were fast and physical come the kick-off, which knocked Leeds – who had qualified after beating Wigan – out of their stride a little. They looked a little bit too pumped up and sometimes a game can go past you when that happens. They kicked a lot to and behind Lesley to help get themselves back into the game, with Mark Calderwood chasing like Asafa Powell to try and deny him space and time. Les couldn't get the head of steam he wanted and always seemed to be sprinting in the wrong direction in cover; his energy went and he started to get fed up with constantly having Calders, quite literally, on his back. Without having Tevita as an alternative outlet, a key element of our initial go forward was blunted. It was also apparent in that game just how much we'd missed the influence of Jimmy Lowes. We'd struggled at hooker all year; it was never settled who our best dummy-half was. Bradford had gone in for Shane Millard who'd proved himself on both sides of the world but didn't get him and that was unfortunate. We'd tried a few players filling in there, including Karl Pratt, Robbie Paul – who never liked it – and even Paul Deacon, but it was too specialist a role for a stopgap. It's the mainstay of the side; the most influential position on the field and, invariably, the key character off it. If we needed a further illustration, Matt Diskin showed us what we were missing with a Man of the Match performance for Leeds. He did me at marker for his try, which he never ceases to mention, although whenever I come across a picture of me trampling over him I capture it on my mobile and send it to him. I like reminding him that although that may have been his day, I was generally on top. He was the best player on the night and had a great year, which was so cruelly ended when he did finally make his deserved Great Britain debut in the Tri-Nations and his knee went within minutes of going on the field. The way he has come back from that since is a massive credit to him.

Ultimately goal kicks were the difference in the Grand Final but Leeds deserved their victory; we weren't the best team throughout the campaign and we'd done well to even get to the last night. Even so, it proved to be a game too far. A lot of focus was on Robbie dropping the ball under little duress late on that set the position for Danny McGuire's winning try but that was just an accumulation of pressure, not the reason we lost and Robbie was able to handle that. In truth, we should have been able to defend the set from the scrum but we weren't good enough to do it. It was Leeds' first title triumph for over a generation and despite having been a fan, and knowing how much it meant to the club and their supporters, even in the cold light of day I couldn't share in that joy. Because of our less-than-impressive form during the year, we had honestly never thought that we were going to win Super League, so defeat at the final hurdle was not quite as devastating, especially when compared to 1999 and 2002. Then we had been robbed of our due reward in such cruel circumstances; those defeats had really hurt. I may have been defeated but I'd gained a son so I could hardly call myself a loser, there were more important considerations that gave me a wider sense of perspective. Lewis's arrival changed the way I thought about a lot of things; even going into that game just knowing I was a dad. I realised he wasn't watching but it was special to think that he might be witnessing my deeds some day.

Neither the Bradford players nor Brian Noble had too much time to dwell on the outcome as we were in camp for the start of the reconstituted Tri-Nations competition. Before we played our first game, the 'Golden Boot' was awarded to the world's best player at a glittering ceremony at the Royal Armouries in Leeds and the Australian media were incensed when

Andy Farrell was the recipient. Only a small party went representing GB and when word got back that Faz had won, we were buoyed by the news. Apart from the fact that he deserved it, we felt that it was about time the efforts of our boys were recognised on a wider stage. Wayne Bennett, the Australian coaching guru, endorsed the choice and was heavily critical of his country's journalists but it was no contest as to who knew best there. Clare Balding was one of the hosts that night and I like watching her when she's on the BBC because you can see her genuine enthusiasm for a sport that, at the time, was new to her. She clearly likes, admires and respects it, and, even if she didn't fully understand the nuances, showed a genuine willingness to want to learn more. It was great to see that someone open-minded from outside was enjoying being a part of the rugby league family and could convey that feeling to the watching audience.

The concept of putting the three top nations together over a run of matches, some eighteen months after the possibility of international rugby being dead, excited us immensely even though we knew it would be an enormous challenge. Just to go from a half-arsed Ashes series, when players didn't want to really come over, to a full-blown spectacular featuring the best in the world was an amazing prospect. I've never met its architect, Wayne Bennett, face to face – and I'd love to – but I can't thank him enough for rescuing and giving true worth to representative rugby league. It means so much to me and clearly the players of all the competing nations and having his weight behind it was the clincher. We always knew that playing five such matches in consecutive weeks would be difficult for us; we don't have much say or pull when it comes to doing things in our favour internationally, but we were hugely supportive of the general idea. Going into it I thought we had a lot more proven, big-game guys to call on such as Faz, Scully, Longy, Iestyn, Moz, Stuey, myself and all the Leeds boys who'd performed so brilliantly throughout the year. I reckoned that we would go well. The make-up of the squad was the culmination of a lot of development work, which had gone on throughout the Super League era and we were confident of finally making a mark.

The first match between Australia and New Zealand had been a draw over there at the same time as our Grand Final, which confirmed our belief that we could really achieve something and that the field was wide open. We watched the return fixture between the two at Loftus Road with interest. It was a smart move to take the game to the part of London most favoured by Antipodeans and the sell-out atmosphere sounded great.

We made our bow at another unfamiliar venue when the City of Manchester Stadium staged rugby league for the first time. I could see the idea behind kicking-off our involvement with a bang at a big, accessible venue, and it was a great place to play, but again it was a bit like surrendering our home advantage. That, though, was the least of my concerns in the run-up. Sean O'Loughlin had been due to make his debut but he was ruled out after he was hit by a virus, brought in by Paul Johnson. Paul suffered terribly and was really sick; he also managed to pass it on to me. We trained in camp until the Thursday morning before being allowed home for a night to rest up. By the time I settled on the sofa, I was starting to resemble something out of *The Exorcist*, shaking uncontrollably and throwing up everywhere; I couldn't hold anything down. On the Friday morning GB doctor Chris Brookes came round and set up a drip in my front room with plasma and water in it because I couldn't eat. I'd lost a lot of weight, about five or six kilograms, and still felt like shit on the Saturday morning but it was the Aussies, so I had to be there, and he came round to set another drip up. I got to the hotel and I really wasn't well but I was totally focused and switched on mentally and you can push yourself beyond normal boundaries if you want something that badly. I talked myself into it by being loud in the dressing room, mainly for the benefit of getting myself up but also to help boost the lads. I was switched on to playing well and did, thanks to the way Brooksy looked after me – including having another drip ready at half-time. Then there was Nobby's total faith in me, yet again. He knew that some players can't play when they're sick but somehow I can, it's something I've always been able to do and their nursing helped me through.

We weren't too bothered about having to play under slightly unfamiliar international rulings or with an unknown referee in New Zealander Glen Black; we just got on with it. I had a hand in the opening try with a long run but that was down to smart play from Paul Sculthorpe. I was about to just hit the ball up and he shouted: 'No, come with me on the inside.' He then gave me a pass at the perfect time and I went straight through Craig Gower; Scully had spotted a weakness. As soon as I got into open space I thought I'd better get rid of the ball and nearly cocked up before getting it away to Terry Newton and he sent Martin Gleeson over for a fantastic try. Brian Carney then added a wonderful solo effort and, once again, we were dominating the game until about five minutes from time. We created enough chances to secure a win but, as was becoming such a familiar tale against the Kangaroos, were guilty of not converting them. There was also some great, desperate defence from the Aussies; I have to grudgingly give them that. Willie Mason had kept them in it with a crucial try just before half-time; he was so hard to stop, especially as he had come on as sub as we tired. He give them some real impact. I was substituted with about ten minutes to go and by then I had physically gone, I was absolutely shattered and could only watch again in horror as the Green and Golds pulled out the winning score with seconds remaining. That was principally down to the effort of Nathan Hindmarsh, who hauled himself into a position to charge down Andy Farrell's drop-goal attempt that would have broken the dead-lock in our favour. Nathan and I came through at roughly the same time on the international scene and were similar types of players; rangy, wide-running back-rowers. We've both changed a lot since those days and he's become the dustman, the one who cleans up after everybody at Parramatta and, to a certain extent, with New South Wales and Australia. Whenever there is a mistake or a loose ball, or a tackle that needs making, he is there.

In the dressing room afterwards I felt like death but the overall mood was high. We took more confidence out of that defeat than we had done the previous year. We had come up against their full-strength team and had been on top for long stretches. Although it was soul-destroying to lose, we knew that if could have stayed switched on for the last of the eighty minutes then we would have earned at least a point and that our optimism beforehand would have looked justified. Victory meant that the Aussies were through to the final and they immediately split up into groups and went on some R&R in various European haunts with their days off, which significantly refreshed them.

The following week at the Galpharm Stadium, we took our renewed belief into the match against the Kiwis and came up with a good win, although the first half belonged to Sonny Bill Williams, who was absolutely fantastic. He is a genuine rare talent and someone I'd pay to go and watch because he does things that no other player can. I just hope he's over his horrific run of injuries. When we came off at half-time everyone was no doubt thinking 'here we go again' but we showed immense character to blitz them at the start of the second half. Two of our tries went to Stuart Reardon and it was great to see him given his chance on the international stage while Danny McGuire was the man of that match; his defence-split-ting runs tore the New Zealanders to pieces. He bamboozled them and Stu showed some real class to finish off his approach work. Then it was Australia again at Wigan and, at last, after so many near misses, a vital victory.

We built on the second half of the Kiwi clash and, although the Aussies had no need to win, that didn't come into it; they are as passionate about playing for their country as anyone else. It mattered to them, especially because they knew that if we won, it was us they would be facing in the final, so psychological points were up for grabs. We revelled at one of our favourite venues and even when the Kangaroos got it back to 18-12, for once we didn't fear a late comeback. There was a genuine feeling amongst us that we were taking the glory and they were not going to snatch it at the death this time. Nothing is quite like beating them and my contribution was again mainly a defensive one; there was a real satisfaction in topping the tackle count. That was my niche role in the side, to take over from the likes of Chris Joynt and Mike Forshaw who had undertaken that task with such distinction. You've got to be a bit like a chameleon at times in team sport and change to suit what is required in any particular set-up. In this series my job revolved around tackling in order to keep the guys like Scully and Faz fresher, thus allowing them to make their mark on attack. When Keith Senior went in for the try that settled matters, I couldn't help but notice the look on the faces of the Aussies. Their mass disappointment showed just how much the loss meant to them, overriding the media talk beforehand that they had nothing to play for. It felt so good to reverse those expressions after the totally downcast ones we'd worn in the previous four meetings with them.

Even though we'd qualified for the decider, there were few celebrations; we were acutely aware of the need to complete the job. We genuinely felt that the win had given us the momentum, a sensation that was enhanced when we headed the final group table. It was vital for the credibility of the new competition that we made the final to silence the sceptics and it meant that Elland Road would almost certainly be a sell-out. I was rested for the last round-robin game at Hull against the Kiwis that secured our top billing.

Being a Leeds United fan, playing on their home ground for the first time, having been to matches there as a boy, was an extra buzz. All my mates were in the crowd and because we'd got better as the tournament unfolded, almost everyone going to the game felt that it was our year. Perhaps because we were slight favourites and with rugby league generally on so much of a high, we tended to focus too much in training on gimmicks and, as a result, didn't prepare thoroughly enough. It was not a case of us being over confident. We were concentrating too much on perfecting chip kicks which might win us a tight game rather than the hard work that would get us into the position to try those sorts of moves. We might have needed a game-breaking play off the back of a scrum at some stage but we had players who could manufacture something like that, and we took our eyes off working together as a team and the pack being a unit. Reiterating the graft we had put in and the need to take any opportunity on offer would have been a better exercise. Putting Danny Maggs on the bench was also a strange decision, he had already shown that he could worry the very best; I still don't understand tactically why Brian did that. It didn't affect the balance of the team, although it might have made us a bit more predictable without him, and it may have unsettled Danny.

We knew nothing of Shane Webke's knee collapsing on the morning of the game and him having to have a late fitness test but word had got back that there were nerves in the Aussie camp. There was fear at possibly being the first Kangaroo side for a long while to go back home defeated. As it turned out, that proved to be their inspiration and they produced an astonishing opening half that was near perfection. In contrast, everything we tried went wrong and the more we endeavoured to stop it, the greater they capitalised; it was like trying to put out bush fires, we just couldn't do it. They married their incredible focus to fantastically high skill levels and ruthless execution; every conjured pass went to hand, each half break was turned into a clean one and they were flooding through in support. We were like King Canute, we just couldn't turn back the tide. Looking back now, and no matter how much it pains, you have to admire a performance like that under such pressure and it spoke volumes for the personnel they had in their team. Darren Lockyer was astonishing and set an incredible captain's lead. He was inspirational, at the heart of everything and he soon had everyone firing around him; his was a truly exceptional performance.

I was substituted after twenty minutes, which was disappointing because I thought I was one of the guys who was still taking it to them, and doing alright when I had the ball in hand. They were so dominant when they were attacking that we were blowing out our arses when we did finally get possession but I wanted to stay out there to try and stem the damage. I was putting my hand up to carry the ball when we were all knackered and thought I was making a difference but Nobby must have felt otherwise. You've just got to roll with those things; Sean Long was brought off around the same time and he was quite upset about it. Because everyone had believed the hype about our chances, we were – perhaps understandably – booed off at half-time after conceding virtually a point a minute. It was an instinctive reaction; the crowd were as shell-shocked as we were. We did show some of our true character, both as blokes and as a team, to hold it together in the second half, even though the game was done. Our efforts reflected the characteristics of the nation, of digging in and refusing to lie down. There was some truth in what was said by the Great Britain management afterwards, that one bad half should not overshadow four and a bit very good performances, but that was also a touch of damage limitation. We'd probably played as well as any GB squad had in the previous thirty years over the course of the tournament but ultimately when the trophy was up for grabs we just hadn't performed. It was the strongest possible message about what being a professional meant.

The only real upside for us was that it was the start of international rugby league moving successfully into the modern era. The trial tri-series concept had caught on, the series made a profit and it was a genuine rebirth that was taken seriously. Regardless of the final outcome, it had been a great competition to be a part of and having to play five matches of that standard in a row had proved to be too much for us, just. Once again, the amount of high-intensity battle exposed the depth of our squad but it was just what the sport needed. It was immediately obvious that the standard was going to improve throughout the three nations.

On a personal level, I felt similar to how I did after the 2002 Sydney debacle. The manner of the defeat in the final stayed with me for quite a while. I was plagued by 'what ifs' and because it was the last match of the year, there was no way of immediately putting things right and that scarred me. I was going to bed at night thinking about how we had wasted such a tremendous opportunity and felt the same unresolved feelings the next morning, wondering whether such a spectacular chance would ever come round again or if we had completely blown it. I kept turning over what we could have done differently, and for a while afterwards suffered bouts of insomnia. It wasn't depression in the same way that it had been before, more of a struggle to come up with answers to explain what had happened but none were forthcoming; it was a difficult time.

That wasn't particularly helped when the first stories started to appear that I'd signed for Leeds. Although I hadn't, I was seriously thinking about playing for them. Tony Smith's immediate influence had seen them play an exciting brand of rugby that was changing the face of the code. They also had a lot of local lads coming through who were leading the vanguard. Suddenly, they were the team that everyone wanted to play for, all the positives were pointing towards them. I'd supported them from the start and you could see they were on the verge of truly exciting times again at Headingley. I was casting an eye in their direction and seriously considering that I'd like to be a part of it.

Even though I knew I would be leaving Bradford, I was still an advocate for them. I'd been speaking to Gareth Ellis while we were together with Great Britain and the Bulls were in for his signature as his contract was up at Wakefield. I was trying to convince him that they were a great set-up and I think he was keen to join after listening to me extol the club's virtues. That just showed how much the place still meant to me, although, ironically, we ended up being teammates together in blue and amber.

ELEVEN

'UNBREAKABULL', 'FORMIDABULL', SENSATIONAL

Halfway through my swansong season at Bradford we were in almost total disarray, which made our ultimate achievement of lifting the Super League title all the more astonishing and remarkable. Dressing rooms are all about dynamics and human interaction but they can only be at their most productive when those within them feel settled. At the start of the 2005 season the bulk of our squad was anything but, and that uncertainty and disruption began to rub off on the coaching staff. We'd been a dominant side, built on the back of stability and great friendship and yet the core of it – young, British and having grown together – were on the verge of leaving. As well as myself, Leon Pryce, Stuart Reardon, Lee Radford and Rob Parker – one of rugby league's true funny men – were facing massive career choices. Brian Noble was juggling a club that looked like it would need to undergo a huge transformation – while still having to produce the week-to-week goods – with his growing responsibilities as the national coach.

Nobby has been great for me and his best asset is the way he manages his players, although not necessarily the younger ones. He knew how to handle the pros and, no matter what the circumstances, he ensured that they would be ready and able to perform whenever they took the field. His record in getting teams to peak at the right time and reach finals speaks for itself. He has a great sense of humour and is a smart bloke, you can tell that when you hear him on television. Occasionally he'll come across a phrase or an idea and store it for later use and he's not frightened to look at how others do things; he incorporates their methods and adapts them to his advantage, or to best suit the people he's working with. He is a magnificent match-day motivator who is prepared to put himself among the muck and bullets with his players and a lot of coaches nowadays don't do that so much. He's happy to have a beer with his players and even put himself up as a figure of fun among the group if he believes it's for the welfare of the team. That was one of the main reasons he was so good at manipulating and getting the best out of some really strong personalities in and around the Bradford team over the years. Not everyone would agree with him on certain issues but he was nearly always spot on at finding the right words, especially before a game or at half-time. I used to enjoy listening to them and got something out of virtually every one; he could hit just the right tone and he was a fine judge of the collective mood. He looked after players and, more importantly, treated them with respect and not like school children. But the start of 2005 was tough for him. He never lost the faith of those in the dressing room but there were murmurings around the squad and it seemed as though his relationship with Chris Caisley – not least over player negotiations – was becoming increasingly fragile. On one occasion, as things wouldn't seem to come together on the field, some of the squad were grumbling about him in the toilet after training – a common occurrence in any workplace – when he emerged rather sheepishly from one of the cubicles and I know that discussion hurt him.

That was where we needed Robbie Paul, who was, as it turned out, also in his last campaign as a Bull. Brian had made me skipper and Robbie club captain, which suited our respective attributes. I could get on with trying to set a lead on the field, which was my forte and he was brilliant at handling the media and public relations side of things. The decision to strip him of the on-field duties really upset Robbie but he took it in the right way and was immediately supportive of me without a hint of bitterness. Robbie is the only bloke in the world I know who never gets fazed by anything. Brian and I once talked about it being an unwritten rule of the sport that you can't embarrass Robbie Paul. His self confidence is admirable but sometimes what gets overlooked is how good a player he was for us. In 2003, when he spent a lot of the season at full-back until he broke his arm, he was by far and away the best player at the club. People who come across his tremendous assurance might assume he's self-obsessed but the truth is the exact opposite; he is the ultimate team man. As captain he was absolutely selfless, he'd do anything for those alongside him; play in any position, wouldn't moan, rally round a pal – the kind of things that those outside such a tight-knit group don't often see or fully appreciate. The real shame was, as

Leon pointed out at the time, that Robbie went out with a bit of a whimper at Odsal when he moved to Huddersfield. He got quietly shunted out the door while the focus was on others who were leaving and that wasn't the way he should have been treated. He was the fulcrum at Bradford, with some supreme performances on the field and their positive image off it, and a huge part of the ongoing success. RP became the modern, public face of a brand that was so meticulously built and was exactly the kind of chirpy character every dressing-room environment needs, especially when training regimes are so tough. He was always prepared to take the piss out of himself and could be a parody of his image at times but when tough things needed to be said, he was also the man. In 2005, when the team seemed to be going off the rails, he responded to the challenge, responsibly represented how the players felt to the management and had no qualms about saying what had to be said to Nobby. Despite his stature, it takes a big bloke to do that. Watching him showed me a key quality required for being a good, respected captain: to be forthright and intelligently speak your mind.

We had every excuse to let the season peter out, especially after some poor early performances, but the longer it went on, the more we resolved not to exit on anything other than a high. It wasn't so much a firm pledge or some kind of destiny, more a growing, instinctive understanding that if we were going – after everything we had been through together – then it would be on as big a stage as possible. That built a momentum and passion within the squad that ultimately proved to be irresistible, even though we were forced to play virtual knock-out rugby for the final two months of the season. The first choice for a number of those who eventually departed was to stay, but once a few had announced that they would be going, that seemed to make the decision easier for the rest; they realised that Odsal might not be the place it was – spiritually, at least. Once futures had been resolved, it cleared the decks for a single, hugely unifying focus and everything then clicked into place.

Things went wrong from the start that year, with the supposed acquisition of Gareth Ellis being very poorly handled. A number of Bradford players were rumoured to be going to Wakefield as makeweights in the deal, the most likely candidates mentioned were Jamie Langley and Stuart Reardon. These guys were really liked and valued around the place and although now having lined up with Gaz I consider him one of the top three teammates I've ever played with, at the time I was thinking: 'This fella's not worth those two.' It was an indication of the disharmony that was to follow.

Another massive blow came when Shontayne Hape was ruled out for six months with knee ligament damage suffered in the Tri-Nations and then we had to cope with Ryan Hudson's drugs ban after he tested positive for steroids. He joined us from Castleford in pre-season and seemed to be the established hooker we needed to finally take on the Jimmy Lowes role. Raz was fitting in really well and training the house down, and we couldn't believe it when the reasons behind why that was started to come out. A lot of our pre-season work had been structured around him operating in that pivotal dummy-half role and to lose a leader so close to the start of the campaign set us back further. Ryan's misdemeanours came out while we were in camp in Albufera, Portugal, where another new recruit, Brisbane's Brad Myers was given an insight into the humour of his new colleagues. On a night out, we filled a shot glass up with Tabasco sauce without telling him what it was and he drank it all, in one. His eyes immediately began watering and he was spluttering for the next couple of hours, barely able to speak. All he kept repeating was, 'Why have you done it to me?' over and over again to which I think he got the sympathetic reply: 'Unlucky, ginger nuts.' He looked a treat when we wore our new lime-green away shirt, his red hair standing out even more and making him look like a set of traffic lights.

Perhaps unsurprisingly, in view of the disruptions, our initial results were poor, with a home defeat against an enthusiastic Wakefield – I had to go off with cramp in both legs because of the heavy ground – and away at Widnes. The Wildcats deserved their victory but we were expected to hit back against the Vikings. We dropped a lot of ball in the first forty and it got quite heated at half-time. I adopted a bit of a forward's mentality and fired into the backs telling them to do their job. Nobby told me that I was out of order and we were a team. He was right but you can't help yourself sometimes. That made it 'shit or bust' for us away at Wigan and in the pre-match build-up, by way of motivation, I produced a letter I'd been sent from a retired teacher, Ruth Catton, who'd written to offer her support in our darkest times. The captain had changed, we'd lost our first two matches against sides we'd been expected to beat and the rumours were still circulating about where a number of us would be playing long term. It felt that the flak was coming from everywhere, particularly at me – not that a skipper has that much influence over results – but her letter to say that she was still behind us was massively welcome. Sometimes the loudest voices are the most negative ones who drown out those who are truly supportive and she showed that there were still people out there rooting for and believing in us. We really needed to hear that. We resolved, there and then, to play for those who did care and triumphed by a point at the JJB. It was probably one of my best performances in a Bradford shirt – and in front of a watching Tony Smith. We fell behind but there was a desperation and collective force within us that we weren't going to lose. They were exactly the qualities we drew on later in the season.

Simmering in the background were the final throes of me trying to renegotiate a better deal with the club. They made an offer, and what finally tipped the scales for me to leave was the comment made to my representative by Chris Caisley when I turned it down. He reportedly said, 'He can get fucked then, we'll just bring an Aussie over.' Crass disrespect like that really helps make your mind up. About a week later, I first met Leeds on a dark, cold March night up at Tony Smith's farmhouse on the outskirts of Huddersfield, with Gary Hetherington also present, and we had a very productive chat. The thought of going to play for the side that had been our bitterest rivals left me in a state of utter turmoil inside. Even though I knew I was doing the right thing, there was still a sense of it being dishonourable. I analysed whether it could be that the Headingley grass was just appearing greener; but then Bradford hadn't been right by me and I was sure that I didn't owe them anything. If I'd been without morals or conscience, those conundrums would have been so much easier to resolve. I had to do a lot of soul-searching, look deep inside myself at what was most important to me and at the same time captain a losing team that was on the verge of drowning. Undoubtedly, my family suffered. My head was constantly spinning, weighing up the pros and cons, and there is only so much energy that you can put into each pot. Something else had to give way and I was poor with my nearest and dearest that season.

Easter put us back in a hole as first up Leeds spanked us at home. We were in the contest for the first quarter but they then ran away with it. That really hurt us all and then we had to back up away at Saints. Although we worked tirelessly, we were beaten again. I was in tears afterwards through exhaustion and emotion, especially as late in the game, while trying to come up with an offload to win it, Saints had snapped up the ball and gone the length of the field – their speciality – to post the winning points. I cared so much about Nobby, who was under increasing pressure, the players and the club and I was at a loss to know what to do to turn things around. After I'd got showered and we started talking about the game, the sense of frustration was almost overwhelming. We were trying so hard but nothing was coming off; the anguish was almost total. Brian was at his best around that time. He took me for a couple of pints at our local pub, the, Thornhill Arms, and said: 'We'll get things right and back together again.' He was very reassuring but there was no immediate improvement and we went down again, at Warrington. We thought we were ready to come out and play well but made a shocking start and suffered our third successive defeat despite nearly getting back into the game.

Some kind of perspective was regained by the death of Bradford legend Trevor Foster. He was a magnificent player, helped revive the club after it folded in the early sixties and, as the official timekeeper, was on every team bus with us up to the time he passed away. When you read about some of the things he'd achieved in his career, you couldn't help but be inspired. However, more than just being a great player, he was a tremendous person to have around the place. I was honoured and humbled to be asked to be one of his pall-bearers as his boots were unlaced for the last time. It wasn't just a sad loss for the Bradford club and the city in which he left such a mark, but also to the whole of the sport. His influence is still deeply missed. Our clash at home to Huddersfield was turned into a memorial tribute and fortunately we were able to do him proud with a big win. That match also signalled my full-time move to prop and effectively the start of a second career. I'd dabbled in the role but now enjoyed the greater physicality and confrontation of testing myself to the limit against the big guys. I think it also helps a team having one of your leaders in the middle and an example can be laid from there. Like those I'd admired the most on my way up, I would never ask any player to do something I wouldn't, and you can prove what you stand for and are about by setting that kind of a lead, literally, from the front.

Those qualities must have appealed to Brian, who transferred his belief in me at club level to the international arena, when he named me as vice-captain to Paul Sculthorpe for Great Britain when the Tri-Nations training squad was announced. I was hoping for the chance and it was a fantastic boost, although things still were not going right for the Bulls as we crashed out of the Challenge Cup at Hull. John Kear had his side primed for that trophy and they blew us away early on, although we fought back pretty well to make it tense at the finish. The architect of their success was Paul Cooke, who had been left out of the GB ranks and that was one of the dangers of a club coach also having a national responsibility. We were often coming up against talented guys who had a point to prove to Brian. Our

squad was looking increasingly threadbare and the first of three vital signings that helped turn things around came in the shape of Canterbury centre
Ben Harris who, although young, had already won a Grand Final. He was
a great capture, especially tightening us up defensively and was a really nice
kid who I've a lot of time for. He got stuck in and grafted rather than being
a flashy try-scorer and we needed him. Not that you'd have noticed his
influence straight away though, as we suffered consecutive home defeats in
mid-season that looked like they would signal the end of our Super League
hopes. We led easily against Warrington before conceding thirty-six points
in as many minutes. Then followed our worst hour, but also the nearest we
came to a turning point. St Helens inflicted a record 66-4 defeat on us at
home and even though Leon got sent off for a foul on Jamie Lyon, Saints
– under their excellent coach Daniel Anderson – were by then on fire. We
were just embarrassing and any pretensions we might have had were put
well and truly into the sharpest relief, we were so far off the pace. I'd been
humiliated with Great Britain in Sydney, but realistically, everything had
conspired against us in that game. This was mortifying, a new low.

We needed to turn things around quickly and get some key players back.
Lesley Vainikolo, who had been out for over a month with knee damage – something he really suffered with – was sent on a two-week rehab
course to Lilleshall but we told everyone he'd been dispatched to fat camp.
Importantly, assistant coach Steve McNamara began to take more of a leading role and became increasingly influential within the squad as he found
his feet. We welcomed and responded to his input and fresh outlook and
he became a vital component in our renaissance. Almost immediately after
the Saints debacle there was a different feeling about the boys. During the
nextweek there was a renewed vigour and concentration in training and
our team meetings were incredibly channelled. In the dressing room at the
Galpharm Stadium, before facing Huddersfield, you could hear a pin drop,
such was the focus and I knew we were going to play well. I tried to tap
into that before we went out and told the team that, if necessary, I was
coming off on a stretcher rather than lose. That might have sounded melo-
dramatic but you could see that all of them were ready to work themselves
to a standstill and we fed off that force to register a much-needed win.

The *Telegraph and Argus* ran a two-page feature in the aftermath of that
game about where all the Bulls players who were out of contract at the end
of the season were likely to be plying their trade. For me, they reckoned
that the NRL was still the most likely destination although I was probably

testing my market value and they linked me with Warrington as well. I was in contact with George Peponis at Canterbury, where Danny Gartner's dad Clive was an influential figure, and he put them on to me. It would have been a difficult move with such a young family but I would have loved the chance. They are renowned as a no-nonsense, incredibly tough side that are notoriously hard to beat and, funnily enough, one of the earliest rugby pictures taken of me at home shows me wearing a Bulldogs shirt. I did also meet with Wolves coach Paul Cullen and their major shareholder Simon Moran, and I was immediately impressed with their enthusiasm and plans to transform the club into a major force. Their vibe felt similar to what I'd experienced at Bradford in 1999 and I emerged with great respect for them both. In the end, as lifelong Warrington fans, they understood and appreciated my desire to fulfil my boyhood ambition and play for the club I had followed as a youngster. I've been in contact with pop impresario Simon a few times since and he's been really good with me, including getting front-row tickets to see The Killers and access to the backstage party afterwards.

I got into trouble after we'd drawn at home to Widnes and was disciplined by the Rugby Football League for calling referee Steve Ganson 'a joke' and his touch judges 'cowards in a man's game' in my post-match interview. I defended the charge myself, was given a £500 fine and costs against, appealed the ruling and at the beginning of 2006 had it overturned. We weren't given a penalty until the seventieth minute and at one stage had been 19-0 down with our fans ferociously booing and leaving in droves. Stories abounded that Steve had been denied a car-parking place by a Bradford steward when he arrived, which he was less than happy about. During the game, Rob Parker said to him: 'You can't penalise me for offside when I'm standing right next you.' He responded: 'Yes I can, watch.' He promptly marched us back again. That was part of my defence, but when the official video tape arrived back from the RFL, which should have included his comments as the officials are all wired up, it had mysteriously lost its sound. I was caught in my fury by a journalist straight after the game and I regretted using the words I did. I would never blame the men in the middle for our deficiencies, and I appreciate how hard a job they have to do but there were some mitigating circumstances that afternoon for my outburst.

Our second important signing was Ian Henderson who, although born over here, had played all his rugby in Australia after his family had emigrated when he was a kid, and he arrived from Parramatta. He was the recognised acting half-back and organiser we were desperate for, despite being an arrogant little man. On his first night we all went out for a drink and I had to straighten him out when he started telling everyone that he was the best hooker in the competition and was going to play for Great Britain. We nearly settled our differing views on that outside and had to be split up, which was some introduction to his new teammates but he was a tough competitor, a good player and could back it up. It took him a few games to get used to us but we were a different outfit with him in it.

We went to Leeds at the beginning of July and beforehand I stressed that we needed to show that we could still do it on the big stage. Although we lost, the feeling afterwards was that we had started to get our mojo back – I'd even managed a try. Having been in the contest, we went 36-14 down with about a quarter of an hour to go and, behind the posts, I said to the guys: 'We don't deserve this, the amount of graft we're putting in and certainly not to be jeered'. I urged them to go out and get their just desserts and we ended on top, scoring two late, morale-boosting tries. That rewarded the extra training a lot of us were putting in; we were doing loads of work after hours in an effort to turn results around.

Even harder than what had taken place on the field, was meeting Brian Noble the next day to tell him that I had made my mind up and that I wouldn't be staying. The walk seemed to take forever from the car to his office and I just didn't want to go in there. He was doing the video review of the previous night's match in his office at the time, which was on behind him. He said to me: 'You're signing for these bastards?' It was the only time I have ever lied to him. I mumbled, 'No, it'll probably be Australia.' He looked at me and I glanced back at him but he knew that I wasn't telling the truth and I knew it. I felt like I was deserting the guy who had brought me up, but at the back of my mind was the feeling that I had been badly let down by the club. It was one of the most difficult conversations I have ever had. Even when so many things seemed to be going wrong, Brian hadn't shied away from relating to his players. Later on I went to meet Chris Caisley to inform him where I'd be going and, to be fair, even though we didn't have a relationship, he was very good in that meeting. Some of the rumours I had heard about him and his way with people didn't seem to ring as true afterwards. He asked what Bradford could do to make me stay and when he realised that it was all a bit too late, he accepted that my decision was part of life and business, even though I could see that he was pissed off. From that moment on he has always been right with me and it just proved that you do need to be face to face with some people to fully understand them. I told him that he should interact and be more hands-on with the players because then they would appreciate better where he was coming from, rather than seeing him once in a blue moon. In the end, however, he also relinquished his role.

It would be naïve to think that all the players didn't talk to each other about their impending futures, however guarded they had to be. I first mentioned I was going to Lee Radford, who'd become a rock in the team by then, the successor to the likes of Danny Gartner, Mike Forshaw and Brad Mackay. He'd really established himself in that unstinting, unglamorous role that all successful sides need and teammates love playing alongside. I was close to him because we were similar kinds of people and he was really annoyed with me. He could see the reasoning behind it and I told him that it was just the way sport was – as he was soon to find out – and asked him not to tell anyone. Within a fortnight, everyone in the squad knew, although it had not been publicly announced, and Stu Reardon and Leon Pryce started putting pictures up of me above my spot in the dressing room. It started on a relatively small scale, they'd found one of Tony Smith shaking hands with Dave Furner when he joined Leeds and substituted my head on top of it. The next day a couple more were up there; then there was one with my face morphed onto Wayne McDonald's body and a similarly doctored pic- ture of Peter Crouch cut out of a newspaper. They kept going and, by the end, the montage compilation covered something like three metres by two. Eventually, I had to go and take it down. That pair were also leaving but it seemed to be solely me who was getting the hammer. I mentioned to Leon that he was having a laugh. I was joining my boyhood club and he was leav- ing his to go to one of Bradford's biggest rivals, St Helens, but was getting off scot-free. Everything got deflected onto me but it was in good fun and I was happy to shoulder the ridicule in the end.

All of a sudden, within a month, futures were settled and out in the open, everyone knew where they stood and with the edge of secrecy and uncer- tainty lifted, we were able to move on and concentrate on how best to leave a mark. Our last defeat had come on a red-hot afternoon at Wakefield where, once again, there was commitment to the cause but no reward. That was summed up when I chased back the length of the field to try and deny Colum Halpenny. I got to him just as he reached the try line but I couldn't prevent him getting the ball down and it wiped me out for a while afterwards. The revival began at home to Leigh when Shonny made a welcome return and immediately Les became a much more potent threat.

There was probably no better centre and wing pairing in the world. We thrashed Widnes and our half-backs Iestyn and Deacs were really starting to fire. They were getting on well and Iestyn's input was important, he was always one to be encouraging others to do more after our formal training commitments were over.

Literally and figuratively, the biggest presence among the squad was Kiwi prop Joe Vagana, who is the best import in the Super League era. He has become something of a godfather at Bradford. Nobby told us that the club were laying out big money to entice him over in the first place but he has repaid every bit of it and some. Even though he is now in his mid-thirties, he is still doing the business. He added a fear factor when he arrived, opponents were scared of him, they remembered his fight in the 2000 World Cup and he brought a reputation with him. He's certainly got some menace in him while, off the field, he's perfected the art of cheating at cards. One of his greatest assets was involving all the potential factions that make up a side and he excelled at integrating the British players and the overseas contingent. He has totally bought into being in England, the same as Mick Withers did, and that was another vital factor as we started to dig ourselves out of our hole. The pair of them made sure that whatever else was going on, there would be a sense of togetherness. I used to spend a lot of any game shouting at Joe to help him get through periods when he was tired but he never let the side down; if you needed him to do a drive to get things rolling, he'd be there and do it every time.

There was a three-day Great Britain training exercise with the Royal Marines in Bath in the middle of everything and I felt weird talking to the Leeds players, especially when the Bradford boys were giving me some right stick about who I should go and sit with. The link-up was a great idea; we did lots of different stuff including a blind abseil. Mike Forshaw and Jamie Thackray got the shakes and at one point we all thought that they would never get down. By then Paul Sculthorpe's season was over as his injury curse struck again. I got to hear about that when a journalist rang to tell me while I was playing a game of poker with some of the Bradford squad after training one day and I was in shock for a while with the realisation that I could be in line to take over. I'd taken his call in the toilet and it was one of those 'wow', sit-down moments. I was dazed and couldn't concentrate for an hour or so, and lost most of my chips as my rivals took some easy pickings. I was gutted for Scully, that his nightmare was continuing. I knew that we needed him out there if we were going to have a better chance in the Tri-Nations but the feeling that I might be going to lead my nation into battle was immense and nearly overwhelming. There are more people who have stood on the moon than skippered Great Britain in a Test series, so I knew that I was on the verge of being incredibly privileged. The only problem was that Brian Noble didn't immediately confirm who Paul's successor was going to be. I think he might have had the hump with me about leaving Bradford, and understandably so.

My 200th career appearance was, ironically, at Leeds and although nothing had officially been announced – it couldn't be until 1 September when contract renegotiation deadlines formally expired – I had the surreal experience of the Leeds fans in the South Stand cheering me and being greeted by stony silence from the Bulls followers, even though I had a decent game and we won convincingly. On 31 August, Bradford officially confirmed that I would be leaving and the following day the Rhinos announced that I had signed for them on a four-year deal. The whole thing was artificial and odd and in any other business the anti-tampering law would not be enforceable. I was giving up a benefit but it was a dream deal for professional reasons. I was joining a young, stable team that clearly, with the players in it, had the potential to be the best in the competition. They were being coached by someone innovative who was doing things a little bit differently and every whisper seemed good about the Headingley set-up. I'd discussed things with Faye and took a little bit of advice from Dad but ultimately, as they were my boots, I had to be totally convinced that whatever I decided to do I would be comfortable living by. A big factor for me was that Brian McDermott was there and I spoke to him a lot during the year; he was my link. He'd shown me that such a move could be done. He was 'Mister Bradford' but he'd successfully made the transition to the Leeds coaching staff, although initially he'd found it strange and difficult. He said it was great there and his presence was a major reason why I also wanted to be a part of it. I'd always dreamt of running out in front of the South Stand, wearing the home colours, and now I had my chance. I'd been offered more money elsewhere, but that was never an issue once Leeds had declared their interest in me playing for my home-city club.

Brian Noble relented and named me as the GB captain, with Irishman Brian Carney as the new vice-captain. He brought a different perspective and outgoing personality to the dressing room, having come late to the code from Gaelic football, and was a good choice. The way he adapted from hardly playing the game until his late twenties to becoming the best winger in the NRL during his season at Newcastle Knights in 2006 is a huge testament to him. His is not my kind of humour, though I can see why others think he is funny, but I respect him more for the way he played the game. That's the bit I admire most, not his off-field antics; sometimes if you are known too much for that it overshadows your contribution where it really matters – and he could really produce the goods.

As the winning habit returned at club level, Leon was instrumental in arranging for us to go out as a group in fancy dress, in an effort to reinforce our team spirit and cement us as a band of brothers for the run-in. There were three designated types of costume and we were split into teams: army, priests and superheroes. We were due to meet at The George near Odsal stadium and about ten of us caught the bus dressed as either Batman – like me – or Robin, which raised some funny looks. Nobby rang me and I told him the arrangements and he agreed to come down and have a few beers with us. He seemed really keen and said he'd be there. About twenty minutes or so later, after we'd all gathered and got the first round in, he rang me again in a bit of a panic asking where the hell we all were. I told him we were in The George and he said: 'So am I, dressed as a knight in full Longshanks gear, chainmail and with an authentic sword in hand and there's none of you here, only football hooligans.' I think he thought it might have all been a set-up until he realised he was in a pub of the same name in nearby Wibsey! That day brought us even closer together as a team and we were getting tighter anyway, having embarked upon our unbeaten run.

All the ingredients you need to win a Grand Final were beginning to come together: the social side, a genuine sprit, a reason to want to win, some skilful players and a spot-on coaching staff. We were on a bandwagon. And then there was Moz. We already had a big pack but, with Sydney Roosters out of the running in Australia, one of the world's best and most intimidating forwards arrived on a short-term loan. By then we'd made a simple commitment in the remaining games to continually run harder at teams and we got the massive lift of having one of the game's best battering rams joining us. You could see what Adrian Morley meant to everyone the minute he walked into the dressing room for the first time at training. Some said it wasn't ethical but Warrington had done the same with Andrew Johns and they were the rules at the time. Nobby had a good relationship with Moz and with his Great Britain hat on would have seen the value of keeping him fit before the Tri-Nations. That was part of the attraction for all parties. It was fantastic for me to get the chance to play alongside him at club level and see him at work every day, rather than just in the frenzied international arena.

In the run up to the play-offs, Les set a new Super League record with six tries in a match as we took Hull apart. I was jeered, called Judas, and when I scored there was barely a cheer. Some had even gone to the lengths of preparing placards showing me with a noose around my neck. To do something premeditated like that is pure vindictiveness. It may have illustrated a passion about the team and how much it meant, but resorting to such actions was hardly channelling that fervour in the right way. It's not a spur of the moment thing like booing and it hurt, as did the poison letters I'd also started receiving and which were desperately unfair on Faye. The most vociferous condemnation of such actions came from Chris Caisley, who stated that it was completely disrespectful considering the effort I'd always put in. He didn't have to say that but felt strongly about it and it helped calm things down. I was hugely grateful that the club's figurehead supported me and he also pointed out that my move was not to spite Bradford. Who would want to deny someone the right and chance to fulfil a vision they had from when they were five years old? But that's sport. As in 2003, I monopolised the Bulls awards night at the Cedar Court hotel but each trophy that came my way met with a muted ripple of applause, at best. I thought I'd played well during the year and that in such trying circumstances it was one of my best seasons; I was immensely gratified that the coaches and players considered so too.

In the last game of the regular season we gave Saints a jolt as they picked up the League Leaders' Shield. Leon produced a wonder try to seal victory with a glorious sidestep, which stunned the Knowsley Road crowd. The roll had started and, more importantly, that victory meant that we finished third. No side had won from there but Wigan had made a Grand Final from outside the top two and we had the experience necessary to make history. We were becoming increasingly confident and just started to get a feeling that it could be our year. There was also a growing sense that the sides we were coming up against also felt that force weighing against them. My only problem was that I'd injured my knee at Saints and at first it felt serious. I went down in a tackle and got a sharp pain through it and when I tried to stand up my knee buckled under me, which wasn't a good sign. I started to panic like an idiot and couldn't believe that we'd got so far but I might not be able to take it any further. My first thought was that I would be out for months but after about a minute I could put some weight back on the joint and it started to get easier. It turned out to be a medial ligament strain, which still hurt like hell but wasn't too serious. I don't believe in fate – that implies not having to work to achieve – but maybe some force was looking out for me there.

London were first up in the play-offs, at Odsal, and it was tight for the first forty minutes. In the dressing room at half-time, I remember thinking that there was no way on earth such a game would be my last in a Bradford shirt – which meant everything to me – and with that group of mates. At the start of the second half I took that determination onto the pitch and scored a decent try, brushing off a couple of tacklers on my way to the line and we kicked on from there. It may even have been a turning point for the Bradford crowd. They could clearly see how much it meant to me to go out in the best possible way and their cheers of acclaim were back with that touchdown. Giving my all was never going to be an issue, no matter where I was going; that was indisputable. It was further illustrated when Hull were our next visitors and we trounced them 71-0. Stephen Kearney's early sending-off and their falling away in form might have had a bearing on the margin but that Bradford team was never going to play together in that historic bowl again and we were not going to be beaten that night, no matter who we'd faced. The wave of raw emotion going into the game was like a protective shield round us. I managed to set up the first try and score the second and we unleashed our full attacking repertoire to devastating and appropriate effect. To qualify for the Grand Final we had to go back and win at Saints. They were a broken side and – although they gave it a massive go – became the first team to top the table but not qualify for the decider. Terry Newton had ended the seasons of Sean Long and Lee Gilmour in a tempestuous game with Wigan – Darren Albert was also out – and that was a huge factor in them running out of numbers and steam. They probably peaked too early in the campaign and Tez certainly didn't help their cause; I asked him later on if I needed to thank him for contributing to my Grand Final winner's ring. We needed a late try from Shonny to finally secure victory but the feeling of elation in getting to Old Trafford the tough way was the greatest I'd experienced up to that point. We were battered and bruised having come through so much must-win rugby, but we'd got there.

We only had a week to prepare and I missed the first two days of training in the lead-up because my knee was still very sore, even though I'd have played on one leg if necessary. When you've taken part in so many games, you need different reasons to motivate yourself and I used the thought that it was going to be my last appearance as a Bull to make sure I was going to give everything. For once, I joined the traditional pre-Grand Final meal at an Italian restaurant in Bradford because I wanted to prolong being in the company of such a special group of guys. The game itself against Leeds, of all teams, was an ugly one but we turned the previous year's tactics on them and did the job. I was incredibly pumped up in the tunnel beforehand and from the kick-off I was the first downfield by a mile and hit Chris McKenna. Then I went after and smashed Richie Mathers and was soon lining up Marcus Bai for similar treatment. In the collision, his head somehow caught me in the most sensitive of areas. I didn't feel anything for a couple of seconds, it was weird – but then I was hit with the worst, sickening pain. I started to retch as I was running back into the defensive line and was winded at the same time. I could hardly run and Steve Mac came on to find out the trouble. I told him I'd been hit in the knackers and his advice was to try and run it off. I was still taking on the Rhinos tacklers for the next five or so minutes but I was in agony; I'd been caught plum on my plums.

At half-time I thought I'd pulled my groin because I'd tightened right up into my stomach area but I had to give it a big start to the second half as the game was still very much in the balance and I knew I had limited time out there. Nobby wisely spelled us all anyway because we were weary from battling through the previous twelve weeks. Les barrelled in from close range to score the try that won the game, although the score that put us on our way was down to more opportunistic magic from Leon and I couldn't have been happier for him. I knew how much that one meant to him. My form in the closing third of the year, in particular, had won some rave reviews and I had even received a nomination for 'Man of Steel'. But, for my money it should have gone to Leon, not Jamie Lyon. He, as much as anyone, wanted to sign off in the best possible manner, being a proud Bradford lad, and he was sensational. He knew it was time for him to move on and that realisation still hurt but he was fantastic in the big games and he was constantly pulling out massive plays for us.

I couldn't have written my own script better, despite the pain. I'd gone from captaining the Bulls in a record home defeat, being booed off for leaving to join the Rhinos, to my final act of lifting the Super League trophy. I owed Bradford massively; the players, coaches and back-room staff helped make me the person I am today. To go out holding silverware aloft for them was the ultimate. I wasn't even bothered that they gave me a microphone and I had to address the fans; by then I was a mixture of elation and anguish.

I wanted to do the lap of honour as quickly as I could and then get back inside. Afterwards, back at Bradford in the Coral Stand, while the general celebrations went on, I was confined to the toilet where I sat, sweating, in complete agony for about twenty minutes trying not to pass out. I was desperate to join my mates and to celebrate; we were leaving in the best possible manner but I just wanted to go home. I could barely stand, even though I knew Faye deserved to be part of the post-match revelry with the other families and friends who'd sacrificed so much.

I made up for it the next day when the players got together for a long, farewell drink that included the official homecoming, but when I'd woken up that morning, I could barely move. We'd arranged to meet in Robbie's pub and I was sitting in the corner with the club doctor Roger Brown examining my balls to see if there was a rupture. There was no way on earth I was going to hospital that day and missing our final session together, so he gave me some strong painkillers, the alcohol began to flow and the rest is a bit of a blur. We arrived at Odsal on the team bus and, before we were intro-duced to the adoring crowd, we assembled in the office at the top of the bowl. We would have been a pretty intimidating gang to come across if you didn't know us, as it proved for one middle-aged journalist who popped his head round the door to enquire if he could ask a couple of quick questions. Les decided to welcome him by putting in a massive shoulder tackle and the guy hit the ground with such a force that all the glasses on the nearby tables shot up into the air; he must have felt like he'd been mugged and for a minute we thought the Volcano had killed him. Lee Radford had t-shirts made up for all of us to wear – mine of course had Peter Crouch on it – and that was indicative of the kind of spirit we'd created towards the end. I can't remember what I said to the crowd that afternoon because I was drunk. I know it wasn't much but I wish we could have feted Robbie more. It was never mentioned that he was off and he was such a special part of the club. He never got the leaving do he should have because he just quietly slipped away. That's not normally his style but, as ever, he did what was best for the team. When it's your last opportunity to do something together as a group, that makes it extra-special. It's probably the wrong analogy but it was as though that particular team had been diagnosed with a terminal illness, so we were determined to enjoy and appreciate each other all the more because every time we did something it could have been the last – there were no second chances. If there was an underlying reason as to how we went from also-rans to champions, that was it.

The following day, I was in so much pain that I couldn't even roll over in bed. I could barely drive but I got myself down to the hospital. By then I was convinced that because of the swelling, which was the size of a melon, I was going to lose a testicle and I was on heavy painkillers. While I was in agony at the Bradford Royal Infirmary, waiting to see the medical staff, I was besieged by some Bradford fans for my autograph. I was honoured and flattered, although the casualty department hardly seemed like the time or the place. As a postscript, in 2006, Bradford were docked two points for breaching the salary cap during the previous season but for me that didn't taint anything. You can blame administrators but you can never take things away from the efforts of the players and coaching staff and what we achieved that year. No one has the right to tarnish it and I don't know if such a feat will ever be done again.

I was delayed by a day from joining the Great Britain boys in La Manga while I waited for the all-clear on my injury. I'd already spoken to the senior guys in the squad; Keiron Cunningham, Moz, Keith Senior and a couple of others, about a collective responsibility, which was not easy bearing in mind the intensity with which we'd confronted each other during the year. I told them I needed their help and experience of playing at that level, which in many cases was in excess of mine, and that I might not always have the best thing to say at the right time. It would need their input and that we should all try and set the right standard rather than having one figurehead. That was a conscious decision to change the leadership style there had been under Andy Farrell and institute something more similar to what we'd done at Bradford that year. I've always admired Faz for everything he's achieved throughout his distinguished playing career but at Great Britain level he was too much of a dominant personality in the lead-up to matches. Sometimes with him, people felt intimidated because he had such a presence and too many were frightened to say their piece or stand up and make a valid point around him. He had a tremendous commitment to everything he did, second to none, and I've tried to emulate that. That was why I knew he was going to be a success at rugby union. Very few could have gone from such a glittering Super League career to a completely different sport and playing role and achieve international recognition. He was studying tapes for months before his move so that he would be prepared and that's the reason he's been at the top for so long. Nevertheless, I wanted to draw on the help of others rather than be the lone voice that the squad would soon become sick of and which wouldn't have as much impact and influence.

On the Monday night before I was allowed to depart for Spain, I was genuinely worried that I might not get there at all. Fortunately, a scan revealed that I had severe bruising rather than a split or twist, which meant that there was still a blood supply to the injury and it would heal. That was a huge relief, although I ended up playing the first two Tests wearing a construction like a cricket box to protect myself from further damage. Once I'd got the all-clear, there was no way that I wouldn't be leading out the side.

The Aussies and Kiwis came over here level after each winning away, which indicated how close the series was expected to be. Ironically, bearing in mind how things went, the New Zealanders – who we were up against first – arrived complaining that their squad was understrength. That was something we were to hear again in 2007, albeit under different circumstances, and it seems to be part of their mentality when they get a couple of guys missing. Going into the third match, at Loftus Road, I didn't think that our preparation was good enough. We hadn't really focused enough on the game plan we needed to implement against them, it all became a little bit rushed and that showed in our disappointing performance. We concentrated too much on fitness or relaxing rather than working on how to start well and nullify their threat. Beginning at an unfamiliar venue wasn't ideal either and yet another example of giving away our home advantage to a side that had played there before.

Everything about getting to the point of playing seemed hurried but nothing detracted from leading the team out. You don't realise how special a feeling it is until you do it and get the sense of the footsteps you are following in and the honour associated with the role. I tend to visualise scenarios before a match anyway but captaining my country was something I had thought about constantly since being appointed. I was desperate not to let the jersey or the legendary players who had worn it before down, whether in my personal performance or as part of a team which we hoped could do itself justice. Queens Park Rangers' ground was a strange place, well away from the core of the sport, but I still genuinely felt as though I was representing the whole of the rugby league family as I strode to the halfway line. Not just the professional or even the amateur playing ranks, but also the mass of volunteers who clean out the dressing rooms and take on so many other essential jobs to make the game happen; the admin staff, reporters – everyone who has a vested interest in the code. It is a massive but immensely enjoyable responsibility to feel that you are at the pinnacle of your sport and an ambassador for the whole fraternity. I didn't say anything in particular beforehand, but getting changed and standing around waiting for the call to leave the dressing rooms felt like an eternity; I was just happy to finally get out there. There were no flashbacks about how far I had come or time for self-congratulation there was solely game focus on the Kiwis. Having struggled with the injury beforehand, my main thought was to not let that affect how I wanted to play. I know I'm not the best singer but I always try to belt out the national anthem with real passion and it annoys me when I see British teams that are motionless when it's played before their contests. My wailing shout was as loud and as poor as ever but it evoked a deep-seated emotional bond and even now, hearing it strike up still makes the hairs stand up on the back of my neck.

I was at prop for the first time in a Great Britain shirt but hopes of a winning start to my reign were shattered by Stacey Jones. We let in some soft tries, our intensity was down and we failed to really put them under pressure. Brian Carney had a nightmare and was lambasted afterwards for conceding a couple of touchdowns when he fumbled kicks. What was so incredibly disappointing at the press conference on the Monday afterwards was that he was the only guy that the journalists wanted to swarm round and interview and yet in the same room was Paul Johnson – who had scored a hat-trick and was the first British forward to achieve the feat in almost a century. If that isn't focusing on the negative – which is so often a trait in sports reporting here – then I don't know what is. Opposing me, Ruben Wiki set a world record for the number of Test appearances. He is a true, legendary warrior, a yardstick for front-rowers and an inspirational leader who would never back down. He must be phenomenal to play alongside and is renowned for his unrelenting attitude to training. The way he has transformed himself from a centre to become one of the best props in the world, and is still going at the top, is a benchmark for everybody in the game.

The following week we faced the Aussies at Wigan in the wet and cold and encountered a familiar scenario when we conceded two tries very late on to suffer defeat by a margin we didn't deserve. The line between success and failure at that level was becoming so fine, Ben Cooper's long-range interception showed that, but we fought back incredibly well, trailed by only two points for virtually the whole of the second half and had chances to win. They still had the more destructive game-breakers and in this series full-back Anthony Minichello came to the fore. He was amazingly dependable at the back and made few mistakes and was so hard to nail down on the kick chase. To concede consecutive defeats as captain was a huge personal blow.

New Zealand at Huddersfield became a must-win game and there was a lot of pressure outside and even within the camp. We'd lost heavily in the final the year before but now we were in severe danger of not even making it and the knives had been quickly sharpened, with some questioning our ability. That brought the best out of us and we produced our finest performance to date in the competition to take the Kiwis apart, which was exactly what Nigel Vagana tried to do to Paul Deacon's face early on. It was a disgraceful tackle, one of the worst I'd seen, which caught Deacs at his most vulnerable. We didn't realise how serious it was at the time, nor did we know of the dressing-room dramas that had seen the medical staff worried for his welfare, but when he came in on the Monday his head was yellow and swollen up to the size of a football. Until that incident, he'd had his most influential game in a Great Britain shirt, after a couple of false starts, but he didn't moan about it and just got on with things despite the obvious pain. It summed up his bravery. Brian Carney made his critics eat their words with two sensational, trademark tries. It was a terrific response to come back from his hammering in the capital – which had seen us virtually shield him from the Press thereafter – to destroy the same opponents a fortnight later. Unfortunately, after scoring the second he turned round and limped straight down the tunnel but then his hamstrings did seem to be made out of chocolate; he was always pulling them. Overall our performance was terrific and to register a first win under my stewardship in such an emphatic fashion did wonders; it was a tremendous feeling.

The magnitude of our victory meant that any of the three nations could make the final, provided that we beat the Kangaroos in Hull. That is exactly what the concept was about; uncertainty of outcome and no dead rubbers. The only problem was that so many of our players were battle weary after such a long, draining and demanding Super League season – especially the Bradford guys. Between matches we couldn't do a lot other than look after ourselves and try to restore some energy. Because we'd been training together for three weeks by then, we knew the systems and game plans. Mentally we were fine, pulling on the GB jersey saw to that, but we didn't know how much we had left in our reserve tanks. We were in the game with the Aussies up until half-time, even though we knew we hadn't played well and dropped a lot of ball. I got frustrated that Nobby brought me off, I felt that as captain in such a do-or-die encounter I needed to be out there and I thought I'd been doing a pretty decent job. When you've got such a highly competitive nature, and even though you know decisions have to be made for the good of the team, it can be frustrating. It's not seeking selfish personal glory, just a desire to be in there trying to lead your mates out of trouble. Trent Barrett – despite a unique double sin-binning in a Test match – took control after the break, Brent Tate scored an astonishing eighty-metre solo try and that put it to bed for them.

By the time we trudged off the field with our season ended, I was gone; shattered in all departments. All I wanted to do was get home to Faye and Lewis because I'd had to concentrate so hard on rugby with all the challenges I faced. I'd come out on the right side of most of them and it was my most memorable season to date, but I'd paid the price elsewhere. That was why I watched the Tri-Nations final at home, although it was taking place only a good stone's throw away at Elland Road. Faye would have killed me otherwise and I couldn't have blamed her. It was a majestic performance from New Zealand that had me leaping off the settee and one which proved to the watching public what we had already known, that the Aussies weren't invincible. They knew that too, but somehow they had always seemed to have what it took to win finals. Stacey flew back round the world to mastermind the Kiwis' unbelievable win and Brian McClennan did a fantastic job to pick up his troops after we had beaten them so convincingly and they had been on the verge of going home. To not only defeat the Aussies but to nil them on the back of that was an astonishing display and a measure of his coaching ability. I was buzzing watching it, not least because Shontayne had a fantastic game at loose-forward in the black and white. He could accommodate any role asked of him and the more times he had his hands on the ball the better. It was also significant that so many of their players were attached to Super League clubs. I was excited Ali Lauitiiti was involved and that I would be lining up alongside him the following season. I was also incredibly jealous at not being a part of it. Great Britain's results had again been disappointing but what meant the most, and what I clung on to, was being the captain. I was named in the 'World XIII' for the first time in the aftermath and it was a huge honour to be recognised in such a fashion. On the Monday after we'd been knocked out, the players, staff and management had a meeting where everyone realised that something needed to change and that we all had to have a long, hard look at what we needed to be doing if we were to be consistently competitive at that level, especially as the road was going to be longer and harder once the competition moved to the southern hemisphere.

Before I could even take proper stock, there was a photo shoot at Headingley of me holding up a Rhinos shirt for the first time. It was the No.10, whose previous incumbent – South Stand hero Barrie McDermott – had just retired; only mine was a couple of sizes smaller. I knew he'd done a great job for the club in that position and I was looking to at least emulate that, rather than seeing it as adding to the weight of expectation. I felt like I was in limbo in the time off before officially joining the Leeds pre-season regime. I'd built a truly lifelong, special bond with the guys I was leaving at Bradford and it had all been so rosy at the end. Nevertheless, I was gone from all that camaraderie and the characteristics I'd liked about those blokes. Sitting at home there was a stark realisation that I had to put all that behind me now and move on; to swap a BD postcode for an LS one. It was almost like going up to big school while at the same time suffering the bereavement of a very close relative.

The transition would have been so much harder without Faye. I'll be forever grateful for how supportive she was, especially as a mother with a young son to look after. Weighing up moving clubs is incredibly daunting and the thought of changing everything about the way you've played the game takes total concentration, almost to the exclusion of everything and everybody else in your life, which you start to take for granted. It was all such an exhausting experience and immediate family were put on the backburner, which is something I'll always regret. I made a pledge at the end of 2005 that I'd never sacrifice or neglect their needs again; it was totally out of order. I got a fairytale ending with the Bulls but it cost in other ways. Perhaps my kick in the balls in the Grand Final, at the height of my domestic triumph, was both literal and metaphorical – some kind of an appropriate remainder of the pain I had caused them. They had to take a back seat that year while I was tormented on a number of fronts; it was a difficult time for all of us.

I wore my new Leeds training gear for lounging about in at home, just to get used to it, the Bradford kit having become so familiar – almost as a second skin – and that helped spur me on for the next challenge. One of the main reasons I chose the Rhinos was to work with Tony Smith who had a reputation for breaking players' games down and concentrating on what coaches refer to as 'the little things' that ultimately, in pressure situations, make the difference between success and failure. He wanted to teach me about what he thought a prop's role was and I was keen to listen and remodel my game. If he wanted me to go out for fifty minutes and make forty tackles to help out the others rather than run the big plays, then I was happy with that.

The most embarrassing aspect of entering a new and unfamiliar environment, especially where everybody recognises you, is not knowing the names of some of the younger players and the staff who work around the place; you feel unintentionally rude. I just tried to concentrate on being my normal self. Richie Mathers was particularly helpful putting me at ease straight away, especially on the social side and so was Matthew Diskin. Even though we both came from Stanningley and quickly became firm allies, I didn't know Jamie Jones-Buchanan that well beforehand. We'd led separate lives and, having only come across each other on fiercely opposing sides in matches, we'd only really been nodding acquaintances until then. I had to go on the Headingley pitch at the traditional Boxing Day game to be formally introduced to the fans and briefly interviewed, which was all a bit embarrassing. Before starting official pre-season training soon after that, I'd done a lot on my own because I passionately wanted to make an impression when I got to the Rhinos' Kirkstall base. There were no trumpets or fanfares when I arrived, and nor should there have been, I was just allocated my space and we were into it. There was no time for niceties either and the first few hours left me feeling physically sick because the initial regime is so demanding, no matter how many times you've done it before.

TWELVE

FRUSTRATION AT HOME

The majesty of the venue could be one of the reasons why Leeds have historically come undone or struggled in some big games at home. The renamed Headingley Carnegie Stadium, one of the most famous, unique and iconic set-ups in the sporting world, has occasionally worked against the club. As I can testify, the opposition tend to naturally raise their game because of the opulent surroundings and, if they are from Yorkshire in particular, there is still a lingering feeling that the visitors want to put one over on the 'big club' that overshadows them and has, in the past, bought up their best players or coaches. Leon definitely felt that; being a proud Bradford-born lad, he loved nothing more than putting one over on the Rhinos, preferably on their own midden and the same applied to Brian Noble. With the quality and intensity of Super League these days, it is virtually impossible to get up for every game but one thing you can guarantee is that professional rugby players will still rise to the occasion at Headingley. I was about to experience what that meant from the other side and it was another aspect of the somewhat daunting new challenge I was eagerly, and somewhat nervously, anticipating as the physical conditioning broke me in.

Almost as soon as I arrived at Leeds, there were all sorts of rumours circulating that because I was the incumbent Great Britain captain and had occupied the role at Bradford, there would be friction and tension with Rhinos skipper Kevin Sinfield, who is younger than me. That, though, was never the case or even an issue but an example of the constant hype for news and consequent gossip that surrounds the largest club in the sport.

Sinny has done just as much as I have in the game and I have nothing but admiration for him. He is a natural leader who has spent his life in blue and amber and absolutely the correct choice as the team's spokesman. Almost immediately, things clicked between us and he actively encouraged input, like I had when taking over the GB reins. We sometimes have different ways of doing things and are contrasting characters but our outlooks are complementary and the balance works. I think he would freely admit that. Right from the start he was great with me and if I've ever wanted a platform to make a point he's encouraged it. It would have been understandable that he might have felt pressure with my arrival but I've no expectation to ever be captain at Leeds while he is playing. I'd be embarrassed if it happened because I massively respect the way he reads the game and what he does for the club, his views on the way the sport should be played and how much he means to the other guys at Headingley. Such a strong foundation is not something you'd want to upset, especially if team goals are to be achieved.

There has to be different people around a workplace to really get that vital spark. Everyone told me how hard it would be, not just to leave Bradford after nine successful seasons but to go to their biggest rivals; especially a side who we had spent so long trying to dissect for their weaknesses. I preferred to look at the positives the move offered; one of the main reasons I signed was because I liked the way Leeds were playing and the philosophy behind it. They were a young, exciting, predominantly locally produced squad, whereas the Bulls at the end of 2005 were an ageing team and I was losing my mates anyway. I felt my playing style would suit the mix at the Rhinos and we could learn from each other; that was an exciting proposition. I was eager and anxious, I knew it would take time to settle in and get to know my new teammates properly, because I came with a perception and standing but was something of an unknown quantity. They weren't sure what I was really about, what kind of personality I was and there was a cautiousness to speak to me as a mate to begin with, presumably because they felt that they couldn't take the mickey out of someone who had just led their country. That was a shame because dressing-room banter is at the very soul of team sport and to start with they wouldn't take me on. Once the verbal jousting starts, that's when you know you are settled and they quickly got to realise that I was up for anything being said about or to me. There was no pedestal or bullet-proof vest; I don't have any airs and graces and I wanted to be among everyone sharing the craic. There's nothing better than sitting around the dressing room with a bunch of teenagers and lads in their early twenties having a go – it's what keeps me young and in touch with other things that are going on in their lives. I knew how strong the amateur rugby league scene was in the city, from where the bulk had been recruited; I had the same kind of background and was looking forward to exerting some influence on their development. I'd never really had that at Bradford and it's one of the most enjoyable aspects of now wearing blue and amber.

There were also some adjustments to be made working under Tony Smith. His attention to detail and communication skills are exceptional but there was less direct input from the players compared to what I had been used to at the Bulls. I was a bit wary of him early on, I like to be vocal in training but I held back on that and learned to temper my natural desire to pass an opinion. I wasn't sure whether he was like his elder brother Brian, who I'd briefly come across when I joined the Bulls, who was very austere. I soon found out that he wasn't and was open to a laugh and a joke, even among the serious business of creating the right training attitude, which made things a lot easier. My eyes were opened just by being in new sur-roundings and coming across different methods. It was important to me that Tony added a year to his contract just after I arrived because he was one of the main reasons I'd chosen to make the move. I'd heard great things about him from the Leeds players; Brian McDermott spoke very highly of him and when I met him I'd been very impressed. I might have been fulfilling a childhood ambition but I also wanted to improve as a rugby player and I saw him as the best person to elicit that. The link with Brian Mac was vital; I wasn't going totally into the unknown and I knew he would be in my corner. I'd always wanted to work with him again, not least because he is such a funny bloke but switched on when it came down to business.

There were fewer barriers to break down or relationships to establish with some of the senior guys who I'd competed against regularly or appeared with in internationals. I also finally got to play alongside Shane Millard and he was as tough and as good a bloke off the field as he was on it. Mark O'Neill arrived as an Aussie Grand Final winner with Wests Tigers and I learned a hell of a lot from him. 'Buckets' had a tremendous knowledge of the game and incredible skill levels. The sadness was that we didn't get more matches out of him; he was a very smart footballer who thought deeply and cared about the sport but he was desperately unlucky with injury. The Boxing Day game summed that up; he created a try with a miracle offload after just five minutes to show what he could do and damaged his shoulder in the process. That match normally accounts for one overseas player a year;

their bodies aren't used to the climate and they are barely here for a fortnight before being pitched into a competitive scenario.

The possibility of playing Down Under in the Tri-Nations at the end of
2006 was a massive incentive for every elite British player going into the
campaign. I had vivid memories of watching some of Great Britain's finest
moments over there on television: Mike Gregory's long-range try in 1988,
Henderson Gill's boogie, Graham Steadman's touchdown in the corner in
Melbourne four years later, and I wanted to be part of that folklore and test
myself again in the Aussies' backyard. Pre-season, in January, we went to
Cumbria for a couple of days and concentrated heavily on defence. I'd been
used to a week in the sun with the Bulls and found myself in a freezing
youth hostel sleeping in bunk beds instead, which was something of a rude
awakening. We went on a bike ride over the fells and were all wearing tights
to keep out the cold. After about a minute of pedalling, mine caught on the
saddle and ripped a big hole around the area I wanted protecting the most.
We were too far away from the base to go back and I didn't want to be seen
by new teammates as being soft or a whinger so I soldiered on for over an
hour feeling ever more exposed and attacked by the frost as I went up the
hills. By the time we got back my balls had shrunk to the point of almost
disappearing completely and everything was chafed and numb. It took me a
couple of hours to find them again.

By then, the Leeds ranks had been reduced when Danny Ward was sacked,
which tellingly left us even lighter up front – a position where we did not
have a lot of cover. It hurt us, especially with everyone else signed up by
then; he was a quality player and whatever his misdemeanours were, it was
none of my business. It was strange coming across Nathan McAvoy again,
albeit only for a few months, when Leeds offered him a trial. I was pleased
and surprised to see him but he had the right attitude.

I finally got to make my bow in a Leeds shirt in a friendly against
Harlequins at the end of January. I've never been too fussed about such fixtures but I was incredibly up for that one because I was desperately eager to
make an impression. So much of the attention was focused on me; I managed to make the first tackle and even posted a try soon after having one
disallowed so it was a pretty decent outing. That was only an appetiser for
the real fare, which was the start of Super League a fortnight later and again
a home fixture, against Huddersfield. I was massively looking forward to the
game now the cobwebs had been blown away and the new shirt christened.
The state of the Headingley field – shared with the rugby union side, Leeds

Carnegie – was poor, as it often is at that time of the year despite the efforts of the ground staff. It doesn't play to our strengths; we are a top-of-the-ground, running side. For me, though, the strangest thing was coming up against Robbie Paul. I'm not sure whether Tony was testing me in the week leading up to the clash but he was less than complimentary about my old mate in the video analysis prior to the game. I found it hard, at first, to listen to people dissing guys I had played over 200 games with and witnessed their capabilities first hand. That was a stark realisation that I had moved on and he was now the opposition. We got away with a win and made an impressive start to the season playing some very good rugby. At Wigan, in front of the Sky cameras, we came back from sixteen points down in the first half and I was credited with helping start the revival. I like to be involved in a fightback – I think that was one of the reasons why Smithy wanted me – and Sinny scored a terrific winning try to show just what a class player he is. We lost narrowly in a rugged, low-scoring clash at Saints in a throwback to winter rugby. Paul Sculthorpe and James Graham were cited and subsequently banned, leading some to say we had been robbed, but that's the way the rules are. Referees aren't going to be able to see everything with the speed the game is played and that's what the on-report system is for. We had no complaints.

At the beginning of March – following on from our get-together after being knocked out of the Tri-Nations the previous late autumn, when some truths had been told – Great Britain team manager Phil Clarke resigned after five years in charge. He was scathing in his criticism of the Rugby Football League and their commitment to international rugby, claiming that we were no nearer to beating the southern hemisphere big guns than we had been for the last fifteen years. His outburst wasn't altogether a surprise. He was always very thorough and smart when he was in the post and wanted to do things properly, especially by way of player preparation, but he was increasingly frustrated that the powers that be didn't seem to be able to make that happen. He wanted to get that point out into the open and by virtue of his position and standing in the media, he could do it vociferously, even if it meant sacrificing his role within the national set-up as a result. He'd been a real help to me as captain. I'd been a little in awe of him at first, having watched him play at the highest level, but he gave me some great advice and a few pointers from his experience of being a Sky pundit about how to do interviews and that was an immense help. It comes across so much better for the watching audience, especially the casual viewer who might not instantly recognise the face in front of them, if they feel that the person on there knows what he is talking about. Adrian Morley is one of the best around at one-on-ones in front of the camera now because of the experience, exposure and training he gained when playing club rugby over in Australia. If we are serious about spreading the sport to its widest-possible audience, then the players are the best marketing tool and should be encouraged and used as such.

The Leeds players were pissed off with Castleford when our scheduled Friday night home game with them was put back by a couple of days because of a small, frost-encrusted section of ground in front of the South Stand. The Tigers just wanted more preparation time and that ruined our weekend and we made them pay when they did run out on the Sunday afternoon. I had my first trip to the south of France when we went across to face Super League new boys Catalans Dragons. That was something different, which enhanced the competition and was an expedition we were all looking forward to. The only downside was that, being early March, it was freezing – only about five degrees centigrade – and I had only packed a pair of shorts. We hammered them that night but it was the start of an overall revival in French rugby league, which is to be welcomed and, as a club, they have gone from strength to strength under wily Mick Potter. It was good to catch up with David Waite again and nice to get away among the lads for a couple of days, but I tore my knee ligament and had to come off during the match which soured things a little. Nor did the journey back improve my mood. It was snowing quite heavily as we came in to land at Leeds-Bradford airport and over the Tannoy the pilot said: 'Tell you what, we'll give it a go at landing.' For someone who's not that comfortable on a plane, that was the last thing I wanted to hear. I looked at some of the boys with raised eyebrows; it wasn't as if he was reverse parking a car and if he got it slightly wrong he could have another go. I was hardly instilled with confidence, but he did his stuff.

We thrashed Harlequins playing some great rugby to complete the month, with Danny McGuire again at the heart of it. To some extent, we peaked too early that season. That was probably a reaction to the bulk of the side having lost in the Grand Final; we'd come out strong and fired-up but tried too hard to begin with. We were entertaining, doing well as team and I thought my form was up there individually, but we didn't have the strength in depth to sustain it. One of my goals had been to make an instant impression but that ultimately took its toll; in hindsight it probably wasn't the best thing to do as I suffered burnout when it really mattered. I was learning a lot from Tony and Brian and enjoying my rugby alongside some of the highest-calibre young performers around. I thought I was adding to the intensity at training and in preparation for matches and was keen to pass on some of the tricks of the trade to the likes of Nick Scruton and Ryan Bailey if they ever asked me.

At Hull, Sinny got stretchered off – which was the overriding concern – and I took over the captaincy. That meant I was out there for a long part of the game and I came up with one of my best performances trying to drive the side forward to help overcome the loss. Taking the armband for my home-city club, albeit in the wrong circumstances, was an honour but not a huge deal as I knew I was just keeping it warm. Naturally, the first game I ran on as captain of the Rhinos was my initial meeting with Bradford since the move, at Headingley Carnegie, and I was shit. It was all too much for me; I was physically sick with anticipation in the dressing room beforehand, which was not like me at all. I got myself too pumped up to put in a monumental performance against them and I ended up running out of energy very quickly as a result. Straightaway, after five minutes, I was struggling for breath. I felt as though I was taking on all of them, trying to bash each and every one, while they were all looking to give it to me. It was a difficult game for me and I was glad to get it out of the way. In the manner of clashes between the two sides, Bradford took it with the last move of the game when Brett Ferres crashed over. I was pleased for him. I like him and he never really got a chance to shine there – that was probably his best moment in a Bulls shirt – but we were dumb as a team at shutting out games. I'd come from an environment where, probably because we were an older bunch, we knew how to do that but it was still relatively new to the Rhinos and we struggled with it. In many ways, learning from such games in 2006 contributed directly to how we finished the following season.

I got my first senior try for Leeds against Castleford on their return to Headingley Carnegie. It was from a few metres out and not particularly memorable or significant, but at least I remembered to acknowledge the fans. The very first time I ran out in a Leeds shirt they'd chanted my name but I didn't know that the convention was to clap them back and when I didn't react to them, I was jeered. I waited a couple of seconds after they had started the cheers following the touchdown and made sure that they could see I had returned the compliment. There were signs of what was to come when we were taken to the cleaners at Warrington on May Day, again in front of the television cameras. We knew we had some deficiencies and that we weren't the complete side that year and the Wolves ruthlessly exposed that. The following week, against Hull, we lost Richie Mathers permanently, which really hurt us. He was the glue that held the team together in many ways, on and off the field, with his genuine passion for the shirt and natural enthusiasm. He suffered a season-ending knee injury which left us further exposed without a recognised custodian – and full-back is such a crucial position which bolts the spine of a side. He was playing really well at the time and that type of long-term injury took him out of the picture a little socially, which didn't help us either. While he was recovering, it was announced that his Leeds days were over and he would be joining the new Gold Coast Titans in Australia. It was absolutely the correct decision; the challenge was there, he was young enough to take it and he did the right thing to at least give it a go. Soon after that, Chev Walker announced that he would be moving on and the young, home-grown team I'd joined seemed to be starting to break up. There was a slightly similar feeling to what I'd experienced at Bradford in 2005 – that the blokes I knew and got on well with were starting to disappear.

Any lingering thoughts or doubts about whether I had made the right move were dispelled when I made my return to Bradford and we romped to a 30-0 win in a terrific performance. It was a great feeling, although I wasn't one to rub it in – that's not the right way to behave – but it proved to be our last convincing display of the season. Remembering to go into the visiting dressing was an ordeal. Every time I come off at half-time there, because I'm tired, I nearly always walk past it because it's the first one after coming off the pitch. My mind and body was so attuned to the walk to the home shed that it was almost an automatic response when I jogged down the tunnel. I'm sure Steve McNamara, who was by then in charge at the Bulls, wouldn't have appreciated the intrusion. There was some good-natured booing from the Bradford crowd, as I'd expected, but the manner of our win tended to silence that by the end.

The whole of the Leeds club, especially the players, were rocked at the beginning of June but not by anything that was happening on the field. Tony Smith was rushed into hospital and it quickly became clear that his condition was grave. We couldn't believe it; we realised it had to be serious for someone as dedicated as him to miss work and it was shocking news. I jokingly texted him saying that he was really in Tenerife having a week's holiday but the seriousness of the reply illustrated how ill he was. Brian

McDermott took over for a couple of games and I played well in them. I desperately wanted to do it for my mate; I could see how nervous he was at the first team talk he gave. Leeds is a big club to get a hold of, especially as his first match in charge was a home, televised Challenge Cup quarter-final against Harlequins. There was then a further twist. Thankfully, Tony returned, not only to continue coaching but, far more importantly, his life-threatening condition was controllable under medication. That was great to hear but then Brian Mac was virtually in tears telling us that he had to leave. I was pleased for Macca, I knew taking over at Quins would be a good move for him and a great opportunity. All assistant coaches with ambition get to a point when they need to move on and takeover as the main man but, selfishly, I was gutted and disappointed. He was one of the reasons for me being there and an integral part of the Rhinos staff that we needed; a number of us felt that.

When our results started to dip soon after, a lot of fans equated Brian's departure as the cause but that was far too simplistic. It was a factor, undoubtedly, but it was a more visible reason than a lack of genuine strength in depth and so easier to latch on to and lay blame at. Two new players had come in: I'd played against Clinton Toopi internationally, but when he arrived he was a bit down on confidence. He grew as a character as he began to find his feet; he's someone I particularly admire and I grew close to him. We were lacking up front and Jamie Thackray – as much as he is an oddball and an enigma – added something in that department. He was another local lad coming home and had a genuine desire to make it at Leeds. A run of five defeats ripped the heart out of the season and all the players and coaching staff could have handled them better. We took the stick rather than the carrot option too easily; we started to do extra fitness sessions to halt the slide and they broke me. I couldn't handle them and, as an older player working in the toughest arena, the additional work during the week really hurt me. The spirit and confidence gradually drained away from the side and the losses sapped our energy, as did the way the senior players like myself and Tony were constantly copping it from all sides.

There was nothing in any of the matches we lost and if we'd come through that period scraping wins rather than suffering narrow defeats, we could have gone on and taken the title but instead we handed the initiative to St Helens. The unwanted nap began at Castleford, where we lost by a point and I had a run-in with referee Karl Kirkpatrick. He was always too arrogant; if you want to be treated with respect, you've got to show it to others and he just thought it was due to him. In such an honourable sport as rugby league, that is not going to happen. I was captain again because Kevin was out injured and we were eight points down in the second half when Karl said to me: 'Jamie, why are all your players telling me that I'm doing shit and giving me abuse? Why are they saying to me that I can't referee?' I told him it was because he was having an absolute shocker and he replied, 'Right then mate, we'll see!' From then on we didn't get a single penalty. I learnt from that not to speak my mind to a humourless official. Defeat in a top-quality encounter at home to Saints in a pulsating theatre, made even more dramatic by a backdrop of thunder and lightning, was hard to take. What stood out for me in that game, however, were the talents of Gaz Ellis. I knew he was a good player before I teamed up with him but seeing him close up, I quickly realised that he was a great and he took it to another level that night. Those five lost games probably cost him the 'Man of Steel' that year because you need to come from a successful club to win it. He was the candidate, as far as I was concerned, that best exemplified what the award stood for. Paul Wellens, who won it, was a worthy recipient but a back, while Gaz was in there amongst it at the coal face and, for me, that's what that particular accolade signifies. The atmosphere that night was absolutely fantastic and literally highly charged throughout the game. The South Stand regulars were in full voice, backing us constantly, and made a great noise; it was like a cauldron and I loved it.

With losses mounting and our position slipping in Super League, focus shifted to the Challenge Cup semi-final and a match we were clear favourites to win, against Huddersfield at the Grattan Stadium, as Odsal was now to be called. It was one of the lowest days in my club career. I was excited at being one step away from a major final with Leeds, but things started to go wrong when we got to the ground far too early. We were waiting around for a long while, although we were ready to play and started well. My first couple of carries were big and strong, and I was in the mix in the tackles but then I tried an offload and the Giants had obviously done their homework and had someone positioned in behind me to snap it up. Then I dropped a ball I normally wouldn't have and my mood began to darken. The harder I tried, the worse things seemed to get. I wasn't going to go into hiding or stop grafting just because it wasn't going my way but another offload went to ground soon after and possession was again lost. I came back on in the second half but my frustration mounted as I desperately tried to get us back in the contest. I didn't help by giving away a penalty for whacking Eorl

Crabtree around the head and then another for foul play. I normally played well in the big games and knew what was required in them but I'd let the team down and I was absolutely filthy with myself at the end. Jon Sharp got his team up for the battle perfectly that afternoon. We were as enthusiastic as Huddersfield but their attitude was better. Every one of their players performed well, even Michael De Vere – who possibly had his one good game for them – and they fully deserved to win. A lot of our season was judged on that performance but I had to accept that. I'd been brought to the club to win those sorts of matches and, even though there was no lack of effort, we hadn't. It was one of those desperate days although, on the back of what I'd learned in 2005, I was determined not to take my bitter disappointment home. There is more to life than rugby and I can't take my career concerns out on Faye and those closest to me; that's not fair. You deal with the desolation inside, regroup and get on with life. It angers me when I hear about people who take their work attitude home, that's just a cop-out and a selfish, soft way of dealing with setbacks. They're not the reason you've lost; train harder and take it out on those who you play against next up – that's how I look at it.

Kris Radlinski made his last appearance after coming out of retirement to help Wigan escape relegation, when the Warriors won at Headingley to ease their plight. He was a great servant, with a deserved reputation, although he tended to keep himself to himself even when we'd been together for Great Britain. Around that time, rumours began to surface and appear on message boards that Tony and I had fallen out, which was affecting my play. There were times when we did disagree with each other but having expressed our opinions, we were sweet; we had an excellent working relationship. Any dispute said more about our respective passions to be at our best. As the coach, he has to have the last word but he is one for honesty, which people outside the dressing room have to accept is going to lead to the odd heated debate. Others would see us having one and wrongly assume that we had fallen out but that was never the case. After the Wigan match, we had big words because I wanted to be out there right to the end, helping the team and he substituted me because I wasn't doing the job he wanted and I couldn't see that. We had quite a discussion about it at our usual swimming session straight afterwards and settled our differences but the confrontation – which inevitably got back to the Press – served only to fuel the rumours that we were at loggerheads. We might have agreed to disagree on issues but we worked together really well. One of the things I really admire about him is that he'll call a spade a spade to your face, you are then encouraged to vent your feelings but that's it done with then. He wouldn't duck an issue with any player and that's a very difficult thing for a coach to do – he's very smart at it. It might put a few people's noses out but the stronger characters just get on with it, realise the way it is and that creates a better overall harmony. Disagreements are always going to happen when you've got big personalities, you're losing and it's difficult for everyone to take. It's not always sweetness and light at any sports club, especially when you are under pressure.

We got back to winning games, at home to Warrington at the start of September on a memorable night that saw the new Carnegie Stand opened. It was a special occasion for the club, the first time in over seventy years that new building work at the famous venue had changed its face and we wanted to play our part in the celebration. We understood the significance, especially as so many of the guys came from Leeds. Historically, for quite a few of them, that association was enough and it was certainly evident that year. A lot of lads born in the proud city are just happy to play for the club and everything that goes with it; that was almost enough for them. Winning things while wearing the shirt was seemingly secondary. That attitude changed over time and it was something Tony was very aware of. He wanted to foster the civic pride but never lost sight of the fact that success was why we were all there. We often chatted together about it and that, maybe, the players had been spoilt by the club looking after them so well in every department, which may have lessened the hunger.

Any aspirations for the season we had left were ruthlessly crushed at St Helens. They were electric in the opening twenty minutes – the best team by a mile that year and that encounter emphasised the gulf between us. They continued the devastation, we couldn't hold them and they showed the rest of the competition just how far behind we all were, not so much in playing or skill levels but confidence-wise; we were a shattered bunch by then. The defeats and bitterness from outside had taken their toll on us and that match showed it. The worst moment for me was when Paul Anderson wrapped up his regular-season career by kicking a goal from the touchline to really rub things in. I knew he'd do it as well because I'd seen at Bradford how skilful he could be. It also gave Leon the chance to keep up the banter between us. He realised how pissed off I was about it and I got a message from him not long afterwards where he'd transferred the successful conversion from the match video onto his mobile phone. It showed Baloo putting over the goal and then raising his arm in acclaim. In response, I got an egg, drew a number ten on it, placed it on the kitchen worktop and, while filming it on my phone, smashed it with a hammer. I sent it to Leon with a message saying, 'This is what the humpty-dumpty head can expect next time we play them, he's going to get cracked wide open'. They both appreciated the joke but sadly our paths didn't cross again as we badly slipped out of the play-off picture and Paul retired at the end of the year.

Our Headingley Carnegie loss to Warrington in the elimination play-off ranked alongside the Challenge Cup defeat to Huddersfield when our season was dissected. We were expected to win but as the match unfolded there was a growing sense of inevitability that we wouldn't. When Rob Parker chased back to stop Jamie Thackray's breakaway in sensational style, we knew our game was up. Rob's got a great attitude and willingness to do things like that and his determination won the game as much as Lee Briers dropping the winning last-gasp one-pointer. We were kidding ourselves thinking that we could take the title from third that year; deep down we knew it wasn't going to happen, but my initial dream had turned into a nightmare as I reflected on my first season at Leeds in the dressing room afterwards – it wasn't how it was meant to be. The crashing disbelief at times like that, when no one knows what to say, makes you truly appreciate the good times and successes. When they do come along, they seem to stand out so much more. It was my first season for seven years without a trophy and an incredibly bitter feeling.

Despite all the criticism, rumour and innuendo that had surrounded me from a section of the Leeds fans that season about how I hadn't been the same player they'd seen at Bradford, the Opta statistics for the year ranked me as the best prop in the competition. They aren't the be-all and end-all but they certainly showed the detractors how much work I'd got through, even if I hadn't come up with as much quality as I would have liked. It quantified the effort and commitment I was putting into the shirt and answered those who had the temerity to question it. I'd started the season well, which was quickly forgotten, but I did struggle at the back end and that's what left the impression. Because Leeds hadn't won anything, or made a final, there was immediate speculation about Tony's future which was ridiculous. The club even felt the need to issue a statement confirming that he was staying, which was mindless; he was the best they'd ever had – as was subsequently proved beyond doubt – but no one was taking into account the way the Super League competition had evened up. To make knee-jerk decisions, even though we'd not been at our best would have been a joke; what was needed after such a campaign was resolution and stability but everything has to be judged by results. In that instance, the players need to shoulder more responsibility, rather than just the coach always being hung out to dry.

THIRTEEN

COMPENSATION ABROAD

Warrington's triumph meant my earliest finish to a season since 2000 but that was integral to the way I performed in the Tri-Nations and how I dealt with the disappointment – it was my 'every cloud has a silver lining' moment. I rested for four days to rid myself of the negative vibes surrounding the end of the domestic season, which gave me three weeks to train hard with Jamie Jones-Buchanan, get myself in the best possible physical shape and mentally switched on to go round the world. I channelled the pain of getting knocked out for Leeds into motivation for the biggest challenge in the sport. I knew, as Great Britain captain, that it was probably going to be the toughest six weeks of my rugby life and I didn't want to drag my Leeds form at the end into it. I had to refresh, get ready and front up, not that I could hide with peroxide hair. That was down to Richie Mathers' leaving do. We'd been searching for reasons to create a bit of team spirit at the Rhinos, as things started to go wrong towards the end, when the call came for us to dye our hair for his farewell bash. I'd never done anything like that so I was up for it. The trouble was I had to grow it out gradually because I was starting to lose my locks and couldn't run the risk of having it cut – I was worried that if I shaved it all off it might never grow back!

The preparation for the Tri-Nations included a mid-season international against a New Zealand side made up almost exclusively of British-based Kiwis, held at St Helens. Some considered it a flawed exercise but I felt it had real value. There was a definite benefit to pulling the squad in and it helped us break the ice with each other. It made us a couple of per cent better for when we came to go on tour, irrespective of the strength or otherwise of the opposition. It was good to get another feel for the GB set-up, to run through some structures and analyse how we thought we needed to play. The downside was that again it saw an injury that ultimately ended Paul Sculthorpe's season. He'd finally got to skipper the national side, and on his home ground, but suffered knee damage early on. That match – as well as a number of other get-togethers we had during the year – were the result of our meeting at the end of 2005 about how things needed to be changed and the RFL had responded. I'd prefer to have regular training sessions rather than a game; I think you get to know potential teammates much better that way. One of the series of events we did was held at the Royal Armouries museum in Leeds which was a good link. They gave us some commemorative items to take with us and, as part of a demonstration, Scully and I had to wield a sword at a guy wearing a shield. When it came to my turn, I nearly smashed it in two.

Despite my aversion to flying, I had been ecstatic when I'd heard that the 2006 three-cornered tournament was to be held in Australia and New Zealand. I took the view that an uncomfortable twenty-four hours was worth it for achieving a dream of properly playing out there. I knew the doctor would look after me and give me some tablets to calm me down – like 'Face' to my 'BA' in *The A-Team* – and I couldn't wait. I'd thought about playing well in that series all year; it was a constant incentive. I had a grasp of the lifestyle out there, which made things easier. I knew what I would be in for as the tour skipper; the demands and microscopic scrutiny were not going to come as an unguarded shock. I'd enjoyed my time there whenever I'd been and was relishing going back. What was massively important when the advance party – which set off without the Grand Finalists – arrived was a warm-up match in Newcastle against a Divisional Select outfit. A number of us had and not played for four or five weeks with our clubs and it was really beneficial. We'd trained hard before flying out but we desperately needed the workout. I wanted to get myself into some form, which you can sometimes do against weaker opposition, and took the game really seriously. We knew they'd be a decent challenge but were perfect for breeding confidence rather than trying to find it when confronting the Aussies or Kiwis cold. We got off to a pretty good start, I managed to put Danny McGuire over for the opening try and it was the physical test we expected. They were country boys whose career highlight was to be having a shot at the Poms and they made the most of it. I imagined it was how the old Ashes tours must have been when the Lions rolled into town. It was a big deal for the district and speaking to some of the opposition afterwards, they were absolutely made up to have taken on some of the best Great Britain could offer; it definitely meant something to them and was one of the greatest honours in their rugby life. It's something we need to re-institute next time GB tour; it was valuable for us and good for them.

Towards the end, the game got a bit fiery. They had a dickhead on their team, someone who wanted to come in late either second or third in the tackle but wouldn't carry the ball and show he could take it as well as give it. Sean O'Loughlin managed to get one hit on him but that was it and he was still mouthing off. I was screaming at him for five or ten minutes to show us what he was made of, telling him in my native Bramley tongue that he was a soft cock and next time he took a drive that I was going to crush him. It all kicked off when he went after Mickey Higham, the smallest bloke on the pitch – which summed him up – and deliberately tripped him. I was about ten metres away and immediately flew in. The next thing we were grappling on the floor but he didn't want to know and everyone else came in to break it up. The referee, Shayne Hayne, was taking it all a bit seriously and was looking at sending me off. Their captain was exceptionally good about it, he pleaded that it was only a friendly, which I reiterated, and although the ref would have been right according to NRL disciplinary instructions to dismiss me, the pair of us just got sin-binned. He waved to the crowd as he walked off; milking his moment of fame with his supposed scalp and in the local papers next day he was painted as a national hero. Beforehand they'd run a story about how much I allegedly earned compared to the whole of the district side, it was something akin to when England's footballers take on someone like San Marino. They'd vastly overestimated my wages to make a point and then the next day I'd apparently been smashed. He was okay in the bar afterwards but apart from anything else, it established an important tour principle among us that we weren't going to stand for any crap and would look out for each other, which I'd felt, as captain, I had to set a lead in.

Four players were released after that game and returned home. I wasn't against that on principle but I'm not sure we got the right quartet. Certainly Stuart Reardon could feel himself unlucky not to have stayed, he had a particularly strong game, he was versatile and in the end we were sadly lacking in the three-quarters and could have done with someone of his ability. The GB squad were holed up in a beautiful hotel in Manly and it was important to have a base on a six-week tour. When we first got there we were given four days off to unwind and after a while myself, Andy Coley and Gaz Ellis were becoming bored so we went for a couple of schooners with the locals in the pub next door. The next we knew we'd had about twelve each and spent part of the following day sleeping them off. It was good to have Abi Ekoku on board as the new team manager, I knew him from my Bradford days and he was a high-calibre guy to work with. After the Grand Final, the St Helens and Hull lads hooked up with us and we needed their quality, although a big mistake was made on their arrival. The Saints boys, in particular, after a long and highly successful season said that while they wanted to train they preferred to concentrate on ball skills to get a feel for the structure of the team and increase familiarity of styles. Instead of a light session, walking through roles and positions and aiding decision-making and understanding and then going canoeing, we ended up doing an exhausting fitness session in forty-degree heat. That instantly got a lot of the players' backs up for the rest of the tour. The Saints guys had committed themselves to wanting to do well in the tournament but that was not the way to get them onside; the decision pissed me off so I could imagine how they felt. I was surprised that the coaching staff decided to opt for that and I said to the boys that we'd been ambushed. It wasn't what we needed, especially at that time of year.

We did some of our training at the Australian Institute of Sport which was just full of flies. There were so many of them hovering around that at any moment we expected some of the smaller, lighter lads like Rob Burrow to be carried away by them. It was an adequate set-up but the lingering memory was of trying not to swallow the insects. Although we were about to make our bow, the series had already caught alight with the two clashes between Australia and New Zealand and Willie Mason was at the centre of an ongoing controversy. The one thing about Willie is that he speaks his mind all the time and not many are prepared to do that, so in that respect you've got to admire him. In other ways, he's great for the newspapers because he's the perfect villain for them and a constant headline maker. Sometimes, by playing up to that role, he can become a self-fulfilling prophesy but he has always been a handful to play against. We've had many running arguments on the field since we first came across each other but that's part of the game. He's always been verbal out there and I don't mind that.

In the first Trans-Tasman clash he again gained notoriety, this time for being caught on camera disrespecting the haka by shouting back at the

Kiwis as they did it. He was obviously keyed up waiting to get into the action while he watched it – and I've felt that – but he did something stupid to keep himself on edge and added to his image. The response from the Black and Whites came from David Kidwell who caught him with a massive shot despite not being a particularly big bloke. To put someone like Willie down and out was a real skill; Kidwell didn't miss and the retribution was probably right but it also set the tone for what was to come. Our opening game was in Christchurch and it was my first visit to the 'Shaky Isles'. I'd been constantly told by the New Zealanders at Bradford what a great country it was and the only disappointment flying over it by plane was that we didn't have time to explore the quite stunning, mountainous *Lord of the Rings* scenery. Instead, we were stuck in a crap motel but that's often the way touring goes. The itineraries are more exotic than the actuality. I'd love to see more of the world through rugby league; I've never been to Papua New Guinea, Fiji or the other Pacific Islands and hopefully there is a will to change that now. Playing in strange stadia and exotic locations is what it should be all about. One of the main things that immediately struck me about New Zealand was how clear and beautiful the air was.

There was no margin of error for the Kiwis; the defending champions had to win after two narrow defeats against the Aussies and they were fired up at the start. Moz caught Ruben Wiki high which set off a melee and Brent Webb, being the mouthy type that he is, caught Adrian back with a punch in the face and it kicked off a little – but that's proper Test match rugby. You can't switch on the television at any time of the day over there without such encounters being built up in some way and that transfers to the players. Brent's such a nice, quiet, unassuming guy off the field. On it, he's the sort of player you like in your ranks but when you're up against him you want to rip his head off.

We were on top by some way in the opening exchanges and built up concerted pressure but, yet again internationally, our finishing touch was poor. We clocked off for a second and Webby, who's a fantastic player, scored a magnificent length-of-the-field try. Coming from a kick return, it was a real heartbreaker; you don't mind as much if scores are earned against you and although he showed terrific pace and footwork, we'd given it away. You can't do that at Test level and we were hurt again by a video-refereeing decision, which denied Danny McGuire what should have been a try when he had the ball stolen while scoring. We seemed to struggle for luck when it came to those calls and that one summed up our series with them. We undeservedly went 18-2 down and, as captain, I felt the weight of the country on my shoulders. It was so frustrating because both we and they knew that we had been the better side, the difference was a couple of opportunist tries. Even though I was 12,000 miles away, I imagined hearing people back home saying that we were useless and the commentators having a go and adding that there was no point in the Tri-Nations because it was the same old two-horse race. None of that seemed just given the way we'd played but we gained some measure of our true value with two late tries which were important in shoring up confidence, belief around us and morale.

Back in Manly, preparing for the Aussies, a throwaway line from Leon upped the ante further when he said he'd rather be on Blackpool beach than Bondi. It was a tongue-in-check remark to a BBC reporter and the next thing, the Aussie media had jumped on it and his comment was all over the news bulletins and swamping the papers. We were leaving to go to an ambassadorial, trade reception, and hanging around the hotel car park was a member of the paparazzi hiding in his car, trying to get a photo of Leon. Brian Carney knew what it was all about, having just finished a club season there and he got the bus to edge forward up to the front door so that we could get on without being seen. For an hour the cameraman gave chase across the city until we reached the embassy and when we got off we deliberately shielded Leon so there would be no photo opportunity. The snapper had to get his money's worth anyway and took some shots but all he got was Moz standing in the way which spawned a caption about Leon cowering behind an enforcer. We had a good laugh about that being the best they could do but it was blown up out of all proportion. The constant media stirring turned matters bitter and nasty throughout the week leading up to the game. Some things that Stu Fielden said were taken completely out of context, Leon had people ringing his room at all hours and there was some degrading stuff written about some of boys; Rob Burrow was referred to as a little squirt who the Aussies couldn't possibly lose to – it was all a bit disappointing. Such statements fuelled our resolve, though, and we trained really well, partly down to the shit we were copping from everywhere about how we simply weren't good enough. Analysis like that built intense defiance within us. By the time we got to train at the Sydney Football Stadium in the run-up, we put in the best session we had done by some way, despite the teeming rain; everyone was really on the money and there was very little said throughout it.

After the horrendous defeat there five years before, I'd not imagined going back to the SFS but promised myself that if I ever got the chance I'd do myself justice. I certainly got noticed very early on after Willie Mason again made himself public enemy number one. I didn't really see his initial punch that laid out Stuey but I could sense it. I was jogging up the field but I could tell something was happening behind me, especially as other players started running in the opposite direction. The pair had been mouthing at each other and I don't think Stuart, who had his fist raised, expected Willie to hit him but sometimes that's going to happen if you are perceived to be the aggressor and he was caught clean. I thought, 'Right then you prick, let's have it.' When Willie shoved Sean Long out the way, instinct took over; we grabbed hold of each other and swung a few. I caught him on the jaw and he got me just above the eye but he went down with me on top of him and then others piled in. I'm convinced that Willie had engineered it because he wanted to make a statement and was looking to re-establish his reputation after what David Kidwell had done to him, but in the context of the game we wanted to make a statement too. It showed that we weren't going to have liberties taken; we were drawing a line in the sand and saying: 'If that's how you want to play it, fine.' We had some pretty handy fighters among us and had already pledged to ourselves that we weren't going to be intimidated; we were ready for it going off. The way things had been maliciously built up for a week, it was hardly surprising that the players were going to get embroiled but there were certainly no hard feelings afterwards.

Longy was outstanding, even after becoming Willie's next victim and throwing an intercept for their first try, but I wasn't one who subscribed to the claim that it was his international coming of age. I knew and had seen for the previous seven years in that arena how good he was. He'd always contributed massively but this was the cream on the top. It's easy to blame the half-backs if a side loses; this performance, though, was his pinnacle. My battle was with Petero Civoniceva and I class him and Shane Webke as coming from the same mould and exemplifying the prop's art. The game has gone from being one where you can go around just punching or high-shotting your opposite number; you can't get away with that kind of thing anymore to be a hard man. Teammates respond instead to those who are honest and do the unglamorous toil no one else wants to because of the pain that has to be endured. I was straight into Petero from the off. My aim was to run at their props all night and that meant some early mass collisions with him, in particular. I wasn't concerned if I came off seeing stars and after the first couple of impacts with him there were flashing lights; he was immensely solid. In a show of bravado, because he shook me, I said to him: 'Is that it; is that all you've got? I'm going to be back all day mate.' He just shrugged and walked off. We dominated the early exchanges again and, with the game level at the break, thought that if we could score early in the second half the chance was there for us to make a real mark on the competition. Straight after the interval, we had pressure near their line and I'd run three supporting carries – something that Tony Smith had impressed on me was an extra I needed to add to my game – but had been used as a decoy runner on each occasion. I called for the ball a fourth time but didn't think I'd get it. James Roby somehow managed to slip it away to me and I powered through the defensive line and forced it down for one of the most significant and memorable tries of my career. The only downside was that I wish I could score ones like that later in matches so that I could celebrate more. It was awarded on the video screen as 'benefit of the doubt' but the ball was down; there was a millisecond when there might have been a body under me but it was a try, fair and square.

One of the crucial plays that secured a momentous victory was Gareth Raynor chasing back to deny Ben Hornby, when he looked all-on a scorer, and forcing the ball out of play. We'd spoken about not coming up with any silly offloads to let them back into the game and I'd done one which had given the Aussies the position to launch that attack. I'll be forever grateful to Gareth for cleaning that one up for me; my touchdown would have meant nothing if he hadn't had that attitude and presence of mind and there been a collective sheer determination to win. He's one of the very best at chasing down so-called lost causes either on attack or defence; it's a major facet of his game. His reward was then coming up with the clinching try and watching it unfold felt so good. We were defending our line and a one-score lead late on, when Sean Long came up with a chargedown, which was a massive play. I was almost out on my feet by then and was desperately hoping we could make the most of our last opportunity to seal the contest. The lighter guys started to make inroads on the counter-attack and Gareth was there out wide to finish it in classic winger's style and we knew we'd done it. Longy banged over a drop goal to make sure in the final minute and said to me: 'It's about time we did something like that, they're always rubbing our faces in it.' The euphoria was unbelievable. We'd been totally slated and written off all week, yet come out on top in a big physical battle and performed fantastically well. It was tremendous for all the fans that had travelled halfway round the world to support us and there was nothing better than walking round the ground applauding them as, for once, they had the bragging rights. A couple of my mates, Craig Friend and Ian Sowden, were there and they couldn't believe we'd won and how good the beer was going to taste in the pubs of Sydney. They'd come out with their new wives on a joint honeymoon and victory was an unbelievably special feeling for all of us after waiting so long to make a statement. It was a spectacular achievement that ranked alongside other great one-off Test victories in the modern era but it was a measure of how far Great Britain had moved on that now all that mattered was that we went on and won the Tri-Nations.

Even with a game back in New Zealand a week away, it was important that we briefly enjoyed our Sydney success. I didn't go out on the Saturday night – I was absolutely shattered – but we had a fantastic time in Manly together, as a squad, the following day. We went up to a great pub, the Hilton, which had initially been recommended by Danny and Michelle Gartner. I'd had some meals there with them, took the boys up and they really looked after us. Lee Gilmour got knocked out in the Test, as well as scoring an excellent try, and although he probably still didn't fully know quite where he was, it didn't stop him joining in the celebrations. He'd had a few drinks and was a bit out of it when one of the bouncers asked him if he would mind leaving. Being the captain I took on the job of escorting him from the premises and although Lee was being sweet about it, he made it clear that he didn't want to go. I found him a taxi and it took me about half an hour to get him into it. No sooner had I turned my back and gone inside, then he got the driver to stop and shot into the pub again through another entrance. There was no malice, he was just being a bit of a pest which annoyed some of the boys because we were having a good time, but it was obvious we had to go. The pub staff called a coach for us so we could travel back to the hotel and once we were on it, Gilly started bouncing off a few of the guys. The next I knew, his underpants were pulled up out of his jeans, had been stretched the width of the bus and torn off. Being a top character he was shouting that he wasn't bothered and then, all of a sudden, his top got ripped and his jeans followed suit. Being naked didn't stop him pinballing about but every time he passed someone there was an almighty thwacking sound as he got slapped; it was like he was being assaulted by an octopus. By the time we pulled into the hotel, he was back in his seat but with bright-red hand prints all over his body – as well as taking an unintentional crack across the nose. It would have broken the spirit of any other man but, typically, he rode it all. One or two of us weren't ready to retire and went back to the pub on the corner, which had quite a few locals in it. It wasn't long before me, Paul Wellens and Jon

Wilkin were proudly singing *Rule Britannia* and drowning out or rewording *Waltzing Matilda*. It was such a good buzz being on top for once and because of the sporting nation they are, they copped it in excellent spirit, although they promised to get us next time.

Any tour needs its jokers to keep up morale and I couldn't speak highly enough of Terry Newton. He was the one bloke who constantly had a smile on his face, wound the whole party up – including the coaching staff – and always saw the lighter side of things. We used to call him the terror-ist because that's what he did, tormenting everyone. You could never get a serious answer out of him about anything but that kept everyone's spirits up, which is vital when you are away from home and pretty insular over a long period. Whenever I played against him I was very guarded until such time as I got to know him and could then enjoy some real chat even in the heat of battle. He is a very good player, and if I had learned earlier on that he was signing for Bradford I might have been more tempted to stay. As it was, I had already announced my move away by the time I found out. I really like playing alongside people with a commitment like his and would have looked forward to it. He is the probably the nearest equivalent there is to Jimmy Lowes – they must make hookers that way.

When we landed in Wellington it was snowing and absolutely freez-ing, the wind had come up from the Antarctic and we couldn't believe the change. The second match with the Kiwis was a scrappy affair, neither side played particularly well to start with and we conceded a soft try to Nigel Vagana from close in, which he was renowned for, and for which I was partly responsible. The initial stages also contained a fight between two unlikely protagonists, centres Steve Matai and Keith Senior, which seemed some-thing and nothing – typical handbags amongst the backs – but saw them sin-binned. That certainly hurt us more than them, Keith and his experi-ence was a big temporary loss. We had loads of opportunities and a couple of dubious video-referee decisions go against us while they capitalised on their few chances; it could all have been so different. Going into half-time, Gareth Raynor had a try denied by the official upstairs for not getting suf-ficient downward pressure on a kick through and that looked harsh. In a team sport, you can't rely on decisions like that but sometimes they hurt you. We needed them to go our way; if you are at your best you can ride them, but we weren't. The hosts had an added edge because it could have been Ruben Wiki's last match if they'd lost and coach Brian McClennan cleverly played on that to instil an even greater passion in his men. I had one of my best performances in a Great Britain shirt; I relished the physical challenge and pulled off some last-ditch tackles but it meant so much less because we were beaten. I'd have settled for being crap but on the winning side and in the final. Nothing went for us that night, Reuben scored a try when the ball bounced back off the crossbar, summing it all up. The efforts of the week before had probably taken more out of us than we realised but we didn't deserve a thirty-point scoreline against us. I felt it more as the captain; we were a better group than we'd shown and it was a sombre mood that engulfed us as we prepared for the flight back to Sydney, which became more notorious than the match.

The travelling between matches was never a pain, although I think we made a mistake by not going direct to Brisbane from New Zealand; the hassle is in having to check in two or three hours beforehand and all the subsequent waiting around. By then, the relationship between Brian Noble and Sean Long was hanging by a thread; they were different personalities and just didn't get on with each other. Everyone had stayed in after the game because of the huge disappointment we were shouldering and before catching the plane the next afternoon we had a team meeting at which I said I thought that we'd recovered a little slowly from our drinking after beating the Aussies. We were facing our fourth tough match on the bounce – it was now a game that we couldn't afford to lose – and having canvassed the senior players beforehand we'd all agreed, including Sean, not to have a beer. There is a tacit unwritten code and convention in such an understanding. Those who normally have up to three post-match pints would have none, the ones who might have five or six would cut it down to a couple and guys who unwound on or were accustomed to more – of which, inevitably there were a few – significantly lowered their usual intake. You can't say to such a group 'drink in moderation' because of the different tolerances; to some that might mean drink until you fall asleep in a gutter somewhere. My instigation suggested a level of personal responsibility. Sean had obviously had a few at the airport and I always knew that would happen with some but on the journey back, for me, he was just loud. It was the kind of behaviour you would expect in a pub or if you were out with your mates. Sportsmen swear a bit and in the confined space of a plane, everything was magnified and easily overheard. I was disappointed in him but, partly because members of the Press were on there and witnessed it, the whole episode quickly became grossly exaggerated. Some thought that it was a disgraceful episode and that, understandably, Sean didn't seem to care about the magnitude of the defeat the day before.

What tends not to be considered is that for some it is an emotional response to a loss on the back of very little sleep and exaggerated by alcohol. That is not to excuse his actions, merely to try and understand them. It also made my position as skipper difficult. I felt that Nobby should have said something to him but some were looking at me to tell him to quieten down and behave. In the end, a number of the senior players diffused the situation and offered to swap seats and shield him. When we landed, the coach and player had something of a discussion which resulted in Longy saying that he was going home. That was all we needed with a match against wounded Kangaroos on the horizon, but the following morning Brian and I went to see him in his room to ascertain what his intentions really were. I asked him if he was staying on and he said no but you could tell that he didn't genuinely mean it. I was sure he did want to face the Aussies again because he would be letting all his teammates down if he didn't, but pride got in his way. He had backed himself too far into a corner, despite the fact a number of the squad had tried to talk him out of it when they first heard of his decision the previous evening. Most top professional sportsmen have to have a stubborn streak and as a result of his, he was hurried away to the airport amid ridiculous rumours about gambling.

From a selfish point of view I knew that our chances of reaching the final were seriously damaged with our key pivot gone, especially after Sean's last performance against them. Preparation was disrupted but there were also some strange selection decisions for that do-or-die match. Despite now needing a scrum-half, Nobby was never going to give Rob Burrow a chance. I didn't know why that should be, Rob was a model tourist who was incredibly supportive to those who were in the side and full of his usual cheery good humour, however he might have felt. He showed a year later, when finally handed his opportunity, what we missed and why he should have started that clash. It was the first time I had been to Brisbane and it is my type of place. I've got some great friends in Sydney but the Queensland capital is more laid back; there is less hustle and bustle. It reminds me a bit of Leeds, though admittedly it's miles warmer; it is a big city but feels local. By then, Faye, her mum and Lewis had come out and it was great to meet up with them even though they were staying at a different hotel. We visited Suncorp Stadium a couple of nights before the game for a training session and I was blown away by it. I'd only ever seen it on television but I instantly knew then that I wanted to play there and even whilst empty it didn't disappoint. It is the best Test arena in the sport, especially when packed with some of the most passionate fans in the world who love their league. We met up with the touring British supporters the day before the game, which was great, and they were equally looking forward to it. As well as Rob's exclusion, Leon had to move to the wing where he is always much less effective because we had no cover. We were left with too many props and that's why Stu Reardon should have stayed on. Of those front-rowers, I would have liked to have seen Garreth Carvell given another go. Despite making his bow at that level, he'd already emerged with a lot of credit having twice faced the biggest pack, the Kiwis, but was passed over for the Kangaroos. I greatly enjoyed lining up alongside him; I appreciated and enjoyed the way he played and being another Stanningley lad helped.

We made a terrible start, conceding two tries in as many minutes as the Aussies began magnificently. Ricky Stuart had his boys well and truly fired up and Johnathan Thurston was back for them, which made a huge difference, especially given that he wasn't facing Sean. We were creaking all over as a team but, again, for the next seventy minutes, we were at least their equal. We blew a golden opportunity in the second half, which would have brought us back into it; Darren Lockyer then immediately dropped a goal to lock us out and we knew our chance of making the final had gone, yet again. Even more frustratingly, they blew out the scoreline with a spectacular last-minute try. People were telling me how well I'd played throughout the series but it meant nothing. Looking round at the shattered faces in the dressing room afterwards, what hit home the most was that guys like Gaz Ellis, Adrian Morley and Paul Wellens, who were now in despair, had given their absolute all and just didn't deserve to lose. Their effort could not be faulted and I wanted it to be recognised. Irrespective of the final score, we had only been a couple of per cent off doing it in the most difficult of circumstances. I really felt for them and very close to them for what they had put in.

For the majority of the tour, it had been in back of my mind that these could be my final Great Britain appearances. That might have been one of the reasons why I played so well, thinking every game could be my last. I'd kept it to myself but in the post-match interviews I did hint at possible retirement. I was dejected and I didn't know whether I could do any more in the red, white and blue, especially after what was bound to be another punishing Super League campaign. Because I'd had an unsatisfactory season with Leeds, I was conscious of the need to put that right and my captaincy record with my country wasn't brilliant; we'd won two games out of eight and that was another consideration in possibly calling it a day. I was only in my late twenties but debating whether it was time to step back from representative rugby was indicative of the enormous workload the top players have to put up with. It is an immense task and nigh on impossible to play at the required standard for around thirty-five matches a season. Defeat and disillusionment makes that feeling so much worse but there was one compensation. In the lead-up to the Tri-Nations final, the annual 'Golden Boot' awards were announced and I was named as the 'International Forward of the Year'. It meant a hell of a lot that the selection was made Down Under and it was a massive personal honour, especially as the team hadn't been successful. The stats bore out my efforts and I felt that I'd really earned the recognition. I was dumbfounded when my name was read out at the ceremony; it was in a small room that contained legends of the game like Wally Lewis, Laurie Daley, Brett Kenny, Gary Jack, Brad Fittler, Andrew Jones and all the current Kangaroos; it was a Who's Who of Australian rugby league. When I had to go up and accept it, I was my usual mumbling self on stage, not least because I was overawed and had been out drowning my sorrows the night before. I hoped that my triumph was at least indicative of the efforts put in by those around me. My whole game is based around workload; I can't perform at such high levels without the toil of others and the trophy was reward for all the guys who had dug in on tour. It was meant as much for them. I tried to say that in my speech but I think it came over in the wrong way. I made it sound as though I didn't feel I should really accept the award but what I meant was that it was reflected glory for us all.

Perhaps the saving grace against potential premature retirement was that I genuinely felt that there was a new breed of dynamic, young British players coming through who had enhanced their reputations on the tour. That hadn't been the case in 2004 and 2005 and I'd been worried as to what calibre of talent was available long term. Things had had to change at international level and now the likes of Gaz Ellis, James Roby, Kirk Yeaman, Gareth Raynor and Sean O'Loughlin had, for me, cemented their place on that stage as international players for the future. At last, there was quality and depth in numbers, and that was a redeeming feature of the tour. Those top players should get more opportunities to do proper tours to the southern hemisphere, where conditions would be better suited to rugby than in the autumn over here. Every ambitious player wants to play against the best in their domain and administrators should not lose sight of that. It is something that has been neglected in the summer era, but needs re-addressing.

A further compensation was that Leeds had signed Brent Webb, who was the outstanding performer in the tournament and the most exciting acquisition for Super League XII. As a team, we had struggled in 2006, but Brent's arrival heralded the distinct possibility that 2007 was set to be a good year for the Rhinos. Having watched him at close quarters and seen him give a tremendous all-round performance in a stunning final, he was something else; we'd signed a world-class player.

With rugby commitments over, we spent a few days on the Central Coast at Gosford with Danny and Michelle Gartner and their kids Nathan and Abigail – which is a beautiful area and it was great to see them again – but I was knackered from my exertions and ready for home. It was just good to see and spend time with Faye and Lewis more than anything. On returning, it was announced that Brian Noble's contract would not be renewed as Great Britain coach. It was inevitable and mutual, they wanted someone full-time and Nobby's commitments with a Wigan side that needed regenerating were becoming increasingly onerous. He'd done great things with the national side and been an essential element of the improvements made. He had presided over some famous wins but both parties realised it was time to part ways and to get a fresh perspective on things.

With my profile higher, having now skippered my country abroad, I was invited onto the BBC institution, *A Question of Sport*. All the panellists were excellent and it was a good rush taking part. A lot of the other professional sportsmen have a huge amount of respect for and appreciation of rugby league players and follow the sport. Ally McCoist, Joey Barton and Kevin Nolan all mentioned they couldn't believe what we put ourselves through. Joey said to me: 'You're the one that got sat on his arse against the Aussies!' I quickly put him right and told him that he had got the wrong guy and that it was me who had downed Willie Mason, which seemed to impress him even more. Ally's a funny man who puts you at ease but when you think about it afterwards, you realise that he already knows most of the answers but he lets his teammates have a go. The invitation to appear, though, may not have been quite what it seemed. My friends Si Northfield and Mark Adams had always hammered me, saying that I couldn't say I'd made it until I'd been on the programme and, unbeknown to me, they e-mailed the producers asking why JP hadn't appeared. A couple of days later I got the phone call requesting me to come on and immediately texted the pair to tell them. They rang straight back to tell me they had sorted it out and not to think that I was more powerful than them. To illustrate this point further, they then put the phone down on me.

FOURTEEN

CONFOUNDING THE DOUBTERS

Everyone knew about Brent Webb and the impact he was likely to bring to the Leeds ranks in 2007 but the arrival of prop Kylie Leuluai at Headingley Carnegie was less heralded. Anyone who thought that, because of his name, he would have similar characteristics to an Australian pop icon was in for a rude awakening. His ability in the gym instantly became apparent and deficiencies we'd had in terms of size in the front row looked set to be rectified. We'd all heard rumours ranging from the amount he could lift to what kind of presence he had on the field and, eventually, he became a bit embarrassed about his prowess on the weights; it was unbelievable – I'd certainly never seen anything like it. He was the strongest man I'd ever come across and there are a few of them in league. In the first few days of training, as we started to do contact work, he was so thickset that coming up against him hurt; it was like running into a concrete slab. We first got to notice what an asset he could be on our pre-season trip to Dublin.

The visit there was a bit different to the one I'd previously experienced with Bradford, it was certainly a lot more relaxed and very well organised. As you get older, you get the young guns snapping at your heels and that was the case with me and Nick Scruton on the Emerald Isle. I kept telling him that I was still faster than him and he was constantly disputing it. I reminded him: 'It's alright being able to lift the cow but you've got to catch it first'. We were only there for a couple of days for some light training but we decided to settle matters by having a hundred-metre race. We were about to go on a trip around the Guinness brewery and after that, Gary Hetherington was taking us to the highest-altitude pub in Ireland. The bet became that whoever lost would keep the other supplied with drinks all night. The loser wasn't expected to buy but just go to the bar and fetch them. I knew that if I won, I'd make sure that I'd get everyone in the party asking me for a drink and so I'd be sending him to do the ordering all night. I managed to beat the young pretender by a very convincing five metres. I had to call on all my experience and if it had been the Olympics, I would definitely have been disqualified for wading into his lane and putting him off. We had a great time but Scroots' night got even worse when he accidentally knocked a pint over Gary. However, being the bloke he is, Gary took it in good humour. I don't know if it was because they'd once sponsored Great Britain but Guinness looked after us really well and we were looking forward to the journey home the next day. Unfortunately, the country was hit by gale-force winds and we were confined to Dublin airport for ten hours before finally getting the okay to take off. That was fine, but the landing was the worst ever; we were convinced that the plane was going to get ripped to bits. I'd never been in anything like it but even that experience was a good bonding exercise for the squad.

Not everyone in the squad was a recognised name and Tony Smith deserved tremendous credit for spotting and getting the best out of someone like Ian Kirke. He adapted and thrived in a top-level environment and his confidence grew to the extent that by the back end of the season he was in tremendous form and had really got to grips with the demands of Super League. It was also very important for us that Matt Diskin played well and, although he was out injured for a couple of spells, he did. It wasn't just what he did on the field, though; he was very important to us off it and took over the role of Richie Mathers, getting everything arranged and sorted out for us all.

In the build-up to the season, two of my former Bradford mates agreed to a fight, for the best possible reason. Lee Radford and Stu Fielden faced each other across the boxing ring in Hull, in aid of the Steve Prescott Fund. Steve had been a top full-back who was suffering with a rare form of cancer and, as the game does best, it rallied round one of its own. It was a fine gesture from the pair of them, although asking them to fight was second nature, especially to a street brawler like Radders. We took a table of ten over – Myself, Danny McGuire, Jamie Jones-Buchanan, Moz, Gareth Ellis and Hull's Garreth Carvell together with some of my mates, Si Priest, Gav Fearnley, Jason Spence and Neil Gibbins – and we had a great night. It was fantastic to see Steve taking the applause and a lot of money was raised for his foundation. I couldn't be seen to support either fighter and just hoped to see a decent scrap, which it was.

Our main pre-season match was against Huddersfield as a joint testimonial for Keith Senior and the Giants' Paul Reilly. We were beating them quite easily but towards the end, the game got a bit tasty. I'd already had words with their captain Chris Thorman and when I took the ball in from a tap, after we'd been given another penalty, I thought I felt someone knee me in the back after I'd been tackled. Having subsequently watched the video, that never actually happened, but I got up and pushed my open palm out and shoved it at the nearest opposing player to me, which happened to be Keith Mason. I played the ball and as I was running off, he caught me from the side. I didn't see the punch coming; it was a bit of a cheap shot but he caught me flush on the eye, fracturing the side of my cheekbone, and dazed me for a second. I managed to stay on my feet and slung a few back, in pure annoyance at feeling the blood trickling down my face, but I don't think I landed any! That meant I missed the opening round of Super League, which was annoying but not as much as being selected on the bench for the following week, at home to Hull, when I'd recovered.

I was absolutely fuming with Smithy for that. I thought I deserved better and hoped that we weren't going to be having more mind games again that year. When I look back on it, that was exactly the right thing for him to do but when you are in your own bubble you don't necessarily see the wider picture. He was protecting me because I wasn't at my fittest and it also showed to the rest of the squad that no one's place was safe or could be guaranteed. We probably didn't speak for a couple of days after he'd selected the side, out of sheer frustration on my part, but I channelled all my anger into having a big game and it paid off. I was in the spotlight when we travelled to Perpignan to face Catalans Dragons. I happened to mention in a meeting with the squad that if they all gave me a couple of quid, I could offset the flight by getting our carbon footprint neutralised. It would have made a little bit of difference, was probably the right way to go about things and I felt that by raising awareness of environmental issues, the players would tell someone they knew and word would spread on the subject. I hadn't realised that there was a reporter, Peter Smith, in the room from the *Yorkshire Evening Post*, he picked up on it and ran a story about my ecological stance. I wasn't so keen for it to get into the Press but that's the way it goes sometimes and all of a sudden I was hot media property. I even had BBC Radio Five Live ringing me up about it on a prime-time morning show; maybe we should comment more on wider topics to help raise the overall profile of the sport. My concern is that we should make an effort regarding the environment, watch what we dispose of and how we treat the places we live in. There are detailed arguments for and against global warming but it's more about how we live our daily lives and looking after things a little bit; you don't shit in your own nest.

Out in the south of France, Catalans didn't get enough credit for their second-half performance, when they nilled us and took the spoils. Their passionate crowd got behind them; they got on top and physically really gave it to us. Our one highlight was Jamie Thackray's sensational try, which was so out of the ordinary for a prop. On the last tackle, he chipped over the defence, kicked ahead again over the covering full-back and somehow regathered to go over by the posts. It was a stunning combination of skills. If we had gone on and won that match, we would never have heard the end of it from him. Even in defeat, he must have texted everyone he knew and had previously played with because about half an hour after the game I got one from Lee Radford. Radders had been his teammate at Hull and he asked me if it really was as good as Thacks was making out. Because of the result, he couldn't keep on crowing about it to us; otherwise it would have been the longest journey home ever. The travel arrangements hadn't actually helped us; we flew to Barcelona and then had to endure a three-and-a-half hour bus ride which was pretty disappointing.

We suffered a second successive away defeat at promoted Hull Kingston Rovers, a side many felt that we should have easily beaten. I had a try disallowed but I didn't get the ball down. The main positive for us was the form of youngster Ashley Gibson, who grabbed a hat-trick. When he suffered a bad knee injury not long afterwards, which ended his season, he was sorely missed. He's another from Stanningley and my end in Bramley, and we tend to look out for each other and want one another to do well. He was a shining light for us that evening. Those who were starting to vociferously doubt our credentials – and ultimately ended up with egg on their faces – had not taken account of the overall strength of Super League. Three or four years before, when there was talk that the competition was becoming more competitive and any side could beat another, I thought that was nonsense but in 2007 it was a reality. You could see that from some of the surprise results in the early weeks. There was genuine tightness in the matches and few blow-out scorelines; the landscape had changed.

In the aftermath, amongst the mounting murmurings about our form, it was announced that Tony Smith would be taking over the Great Britain job and relinquishing his Leeds post at the end of the season. I was delighted he'd got it. From the year I'd spent under him, I'd witnessed his thoroughness at first hand and that was exactly what the GB post required. It needed another shake up at RFL headquarters and a new David Waite-type figurehead. The two of them had different personalities but a similar attention to detail and the role needed to be full-time and to encompass the whole rugby department. Tony had shown that he loved, and was up for, a challenge and wasn't frightened of change or upsetting people to ensure that the right things were done. I had spoken to him beforehand when he told me he was going for the interview and actively encouraged and supported him to do so. When he was unveiled, the realisation that he would be relinquishing his Leeds post – at the end of a four-year tenure – may well have further concentrated the minds of those players who owed him. The likes of Jonesy, Matt Diskin, Danny Maggs and Rob Burrow to name a few will be forever grateful for the career that Tony helped build for them. Tony was a massive part in their evolution as players to become the greats they are now. There was an underlying current that we all wanted to perform well for Smithy, for sure.

Over Easter, as if to emphasise how the weekly rounds were becoming closer and less predictable, we were involved in two finishes that went down to the wire; we came out on the right, and then the wrong side of the ledger. I'm always going to be under pressure when I play against my old team; there is an extra personal incentive, especially away at the Grattan Stadium. Bradford had a tendency to spot me and to run a lot of their plays at me – they certainly did that night. In the final, gruelling twenty minutes, I got an increasingly familiar feeling inside that there was no way on earth I was playing in a team that was going to lose that night and I was determined to do everything in my power to make sure we came away with the points. I could see a couple of the Bradford lads were tiring and I knew that if I could get Danny to come with me I might be able to commit them and get the ball away. That's what happened and his smart pass sent Scott Donald over in the corner to wrest the spoils at the death. It was a fantastic feeling, especially because I knew that I'd been targeted defensively. That can take petrol out of you when you do get the ball in your hands but Tony had been teaching me how to push through that. There was massive satisfaction that it had come off in such a match. It was the ultimate sense of winning a personal, gladiatorial battle on the most hostile arena. On the Tuesday, at home to Wigan, the roles were reversed. In the final throes, despite being ahead, we squandered possession when Keith Senior's attempted pass went into touch in our own quarter. We failed to defend the subsequent scrum and the Warriors got over in the corner on an overlap. The Leeds team that finished the year was much smarter than that one. For a while, Brian Noble's men became our bogey side despite their generally indifferent form; Trent Barrett destroyed us three times.

Amends were made somewhat to our fervent home fans when we faced St Helens next up at Headingley Carnegie. There was a lot of pressure on us; the doubters were just starting to come to the fore and saying that we weren't capable of winning anything and it was all, justifiably perhaps, Saints this and Saints that. At the back of our minds was the thought that the last time we'd faced them they'd smashed us at their place but everything fell right for us, helped by the fact that they had three or four top liners missing. That boosted our confidence and, feeling physically fresh, I played a bit more as a second-rower. The first half was nip-and-tuck but we ran away with it after the break, keeping them scoreless. I crashed over for a try early in the second period and that broke their resolve. I've scored some important four-pointers throughout my career, especially when I was younger, but it's not a major part of my game; I'd rather graft for the team. I know my heart rate is about 400 beats a minute, like a gerbil, and often when others are tiring I can make a contribution; that's what means the most. When I played wider out, early in my career, more scoring chances did come my way but now, in the middle, it's rarer and more difficult among the heavy traffic. At Bradford we used to get inside the opposition twenty and power through them whereas most of the Rhinos' scores are from distance, so that rules me out as well. That touchdown against St Helens, though, generated a special feeling because it turned a big game that was in the balance. It matched the rush I got from going over for Great Britain in Sydney. I do admire those players who feed off the confidence gained from scoring and are ruthless finishers, you need that in any successful team but I'm happy being involved in the build-up and letting them take the glory. You have to have that mix, if everyone had my attitude it would be a very boring, low-scoring game. I tried to get up and celebrate my glory moment but Clinton Toopi was on my back trying to ride me like a bucking bronco. There was a period in the game when Gaz Ellis and Jamie Jones-Buchanan, in particular, were creaming them in defence and pinning them in their half but we needed something to show for that dominance and my touchdown was a spark that saw us kick on and post a memorable performance. We won quite comfortably in the end. Those eighty minutes changed a few perceptions about our capabilities and brought home the fact that no side in Super League, or indeed sport, is unbeatable. We'd got sick of hearing that about Saints, although it wasn't coming out of their camp, it was everyone else around the game.

From being on such a high after the magnitude of that victory and my part in it, I lasted little more than a couple of minutes the following week. It seemed serious. I carried the ball in to the Catalans defence, stepped back inside and my ankle gave way beneath me. I felt an immense pain sear up my leg and rolled around on the floor for a bit. I tried to get up but realised I couldn't and the medical boys had to lead me off as my ankle started to balloon up to twice its normal size. I'd torn the ligaments and it had bled into the joint, which normally means six-to-eight weeks on the sidelines. Straight away I set myself a target of being back to face Wigan in the Challenge Cup, which was only a fortnight away, although our physio Meirion Jones humoured me at the thought when I told him. Privately he admitted later that he thought I had absolutely no chance of hitting my goal and wasn't facing up to the severity of the injury. Nevertheless, I looked after myself properly and was there to do battle with the Warriors even though I was still in pain, which was nagging there for the rest of the season.

Part of me getting myself right was not travelling with the squad to Cardiff for the round of Millennium Magic fixtures, which saw all the sides playing in the Welsh capital over one Bank Holiday weekend. It was topped by one of the most controversial matches of the modern era. We downed Bradford in the final play of an end-to-end match and, watching the nail-biting drama unfold on the television, I felt embarrassed. I was delighted the boys had won but knowing some in the opposition ranks so well, I just thought that it wasn't the right way to end such a titanic contest and maybe a draw might have been fairer. At normal speed, you couldn't really tell what was happening and as Kevin Sinfield's penalty came back off the crossbar and Jordan Tansey rushed in to claim the winning try from the rebound I initially just thought, wow. Then they started showing the replays and you could immediately tell that Jordan was a mile offside. I knew he was fast, but not that quick, even though it was great presence of mind from him. As the events unfolded and recriminations started, 'Millenniumgate' became a bit of a debacle. Bradford held the moral high ground immediately afterwards and were rightfully indignant at the officials' combined errors but they lost it when they tried to rewrite the rules of sport by claiming the league points. Sympathy that they had been hard done by was replaced by exasperation at their attitude. Things like that happen in sport; they needed to take it on the chin and get over it, rather than open themselves and the sport to ridicule.

Meirion did a great job to get me back for the Wigan cup game, although it was ultimately to no avail. By then, the Warriors had probably realised that their patchy Super League form wasn't going to see them win the title so – until they met Catalans in the semis – they were geared for a cup run. Trent Barrett pulled the strings and took the plaudits but they also defended like their lives depended on it for huge parts of the game and deserved their success, no matter how much I couldn't believe it. My motivation for desperately wanting to play was that the decider was returning to Wembley; the Challenge Cup was finally going back to its spiritual home. I knew we had a good enough team to get there, but sitting in the dressing room afterwards there was that numb feeling again and all I could keep thinking was: 'How did that happen? It's not supposed to be like this.' I'd had in my mind from the pre-season that, no matter what, I would be running out at the national stadium for the first time. This was the third time in a row I had failed to reach a final and I was still immensely unfulfilled as a Rhino.

What kept spirits up were a series of social bonding events we did as a squad throughout the year to keep us eager and together. They began with a trip to a local indoor karting school. It was like doing a circuit around your house, it was so small. I put my name down as Ricky Bobby from the film *Talladega Nights* and the woman running the session kicked off, so I knew we'd be in for a good time, especially after we'd been given a pep talk regarding the rules. There was to be no bumping or going fast – and this was supposed to be a race among competitive guys! Going paintballing some time after was fantastic. I love doing that – no matter that it's always painful.

At Leeds, there is a massive commitment within the club towards putting something back into the community; it was pointed out recently that there is hardly a day throughout the year when one or other of the squad is not out there doing something to help or promote a local cause. We have a communal table at training where shirts and other memorabilia are left out to be signed by everyone. It wasn't long before my training bag was on it; I put Rob Burrow's personal t-shirt on there and a few of the boys autographed it before they realised and that became normal service. We all get individual promotional sheets handed out by the development staff, via the coaches, and have to attach them into the diary we carry round. They are a standard format on blue paper and give you all your instructions about where to be and when. The community department's office is based in our training set-up at Kirkstall and one morning, when I was in early for physio but had some time to kill before training, I decided to mock a few up. I had a few goes at typing them out until they looked authentic and set about my task. Lee Smith and Jamie Thackray were told that they had to go to Beeston Working Men's Club to judge a chav fancy-dress competition where they would be awarding the prizes. Gareth Ellis had just got a new dog and Kylie Leuluai kept going on non-stop about a programme called *Dog Whisperer*. It was all he watched – and he didn't even have a pooch. I put on their sheet, Harrogate Dog Show and that they would be deciding the winners of the pedigree categories and handing out the rosettes on Wednesday 28 June at 2 p.m. The final work of fiction was for Rob, who was to be sent to the York Garden Festival for a gnome-judging contest and his contact there was Tom Thumb. I gave them to Willie Poching to distribute in the usual manner. He knew what was going on and I stood with him to gauge their reaction and Rob was the first to go off. He glanced down and immediately said: 'They're taking the piss out of me here. I can't believe I've got to do this.' I sidled up and read it over his shoulder and agreed with him that they were wankers. Then Gaz and Kylie read theirs and I heard Kylie say, 'Oh this'll be fun, I'm looking forward to it'. Finally Smithy and Thacks were looking at each other in disbelief, and one of them moaned: 'A chav competition, why us?' One of the other boys dryly commented: 'Because you both look like one.' The game was up when Rob noticed who he should ring and he quickly gathered it was a wind-up. You need stuff like that to keep things going during an arduous season and those kind of antics showed that the squad was a tighter bunch in 2007, and that everyone could take a joke.

Reports started to surface around that time that Brian Noble was set to become the new Leeds coach. My dad had seen him at a Leeds game and told everyone he knew that Nobby was nailed on for the job so it was probably him that began the rumour mill, although there must have been some basis for it. It would have been a strange appointment, especially considering the things he used to say about the Rhinos when he was coach at Bradford. Even so, I wouldn't have been averse to the idea. The vacancy was subsequently filled by Brian McClennan and, although there wasn't any consultation with the players about their preference, I was absolutely certain that Gary Hetherington had got the right man. I'd seen the job he'd done with the Kiwis and that included something no other coach on the planet had achieved: winning the Tri-Nations. I knew we were getting something special.

Mid-season, Tony Smith donned his Great Britain hat for the first time with a Test against France at Headingley Carnegie, for which I was rested. I would have loved to have played, especially on my home turf, but I had to look at the bigger picture and it gave me the chance to get away with the family. We went to Spain with my mate Neil Gibbins, his wife Lindsey and their kids Harrison and Evan. I'd not been away in the summer since turning professional and only been to Spain once before, when I was fourteen. We went to a holiday village near Torremolinos and the week's break and rest was great but I was desperate to see the game over there and there was no Sky Sports at the accommodation so we hailed a taxi to find a sports bar. There were no kids' seats in it and thanks to the erratic driving over there we were involved in a bump. We jumped out and fortunately Lewis and the other kids were alright but we had to leave the drivers to argue among themselves – otherwise we were in danger of missing the kick-off. We wandered through the streets of the town for about half an hour looking for somewhere that had a subscription and eventually found a place called the Wakefield Arms. I put my head round the door and asked if there was any chance that the rugby might be on and it turned out to be owned by a Wildcats fan, so we were in luck. On his wall, he had a big poster of the Wakefield side from the 2000 season that had posed nude for some kind of charity calendar. Gaz Ellis was on it but had kept it quiet and he looked about twelve, though he must have been about five or six years older than that at the time. I took a picture of it on my mobile and sent it through to him, Rob and the other GB lads because I knew they'd get it when they'd finished playing. Adrian Morley was skipper for the day and even with a series against the Kiwis looming in the autumn, I wasn't worried if he took over the role full-time; if that happened, so be it, there would have been a reason for it. I was pleased for Moz, he deserved it for his proud international efforts over ten years and Tony had kept me fully in the loop. Adrian played extremely well and I was really pleased for Sinny who came off the bench and had a massive game to put himself right back in the GB frame.

Our home game with Bradford had a lot riding on it. There was still the simmering fallout from the Millennium Stadium and it was Lesley Vainikolo's final match for the Bulls. He was always going to end with a try and we didn't have to wait too long for his typical blockbusting effort – to which I contributed. I was struggling back as he broke clear on a surging run down the touchline and as I tried to grab hold of him as the last line of cover, he was too strong and spun me off. I could see and feel what all the other wingers had had to put up with over the years. I was pissed off with myself; I hate being beaten one-on-one, even if it is a team game. Afterwards, because it was Les and what it obviously meant to him, I thought maybe it wasn't too bad. Not that I let it happen, there is no way that I would have, though I did suffer quite a lot of abuse from a certain section of the Leeds fans for it. I was pleased that things ended the way they did for Les in rugby league; it was a spectacular, fitting touchdown and one that maybe only he could have scored; he just was not going to be stopped.

I hoped I wouldn't be prevented from attaining untold riches when I was then entered into a prestigious poker tournament. I love the game and it was a £500 buy-in for the night, with the final stages being televised. Gala Casinos in Leeds, who are major sponsors at the Rhinos, were hosting the event and the boss there, David Croft, paid for me, Lee Smith and Danny McGuire to take part. It was part of a Grand Prix-type series and we were among the local 'celebrities' that added spice to it for the members of the public playing and watching. There were some seasoned poker pros on the tables as well, attracted by the six-figure prize money on offer. It took place on a Saturday after a Friday night home game, which wasn't ideal. You always feel like death warmed up, no matter how much sleep you've had or how you look after yourself; it's like your body has gone into shock. I wasn't at my best but was buzzing with the prospect of meeting some of the top guys I'd seen playing, and especially to stepping up a level. We had to get there early to do some interviews and in the end I found it boring, we were in the place for about ten hours and there was a lot of sitting around waiting. We had a bet between the three of us as to who would last the longest, as it was knockout, and I managed to win that particular one. I finished in the top thirty out of 110 entrants, which was a pretty decent effort particularly considering how tired I was. The best part for me was the last couple of hours when I got to sit next to a pro I see on the telly all the time: Willie Tann, 'The Dice Man'. He's in his sixties and a classic bloke, and he just tore our table apart. There was a group of us from Yorkshire who thought we were pretty fair players but he's an international who has won and lost millions of dollars in a true gambler's style. We ended up chatting about his experiences and he was interested in me because I was a sportsman, although it was probably more from a betting side. On the table, he kept stealing my blind, for those who know the game. Every time I limped into a blind hand, he raised me. I pulled an ace on one occasion and decided I was going for it. He re-raised me as usual but I went all-in and forced him to show his cards, which weren't enough to beat me. At least I could claim I'd got one over on him and that suited me. He asked me for tips regarding the next time Leeds played Bradford and I told him to back us. He kept asking me if I was serious, so he must have been a student of form. It was a great diversion and I'd love to do it again.

At Saints, we produced another brilliant second half to nil them again and take the points, which, once more, opened a few people's eyes as to our worth. It was a tremendous defensive display and we knew that we'd have to be absolutely desperate if we were going to beat them, especially at their place. We improved in that respect as the season went on and invested a tremendous amount of energy into it. Rob showed why he should have been 'Man of Steel' in 2007; he was in fantastic form and broke the game with a wonderful solo try up the middle at the beginning of the second half. We had a decent record against the big teams, and they were the ones we knew we would be facing come the end of the year. We took a lot of confidence as a team from that win and the manner of it. What we weren't, however, was consistent and two more defeats of note followed. We just couldn't break down Wigan, yet again, at the JJB Stadium. For the opening fifteen minutes or so we were camped on their line but didn't score. They grew in belief and stature as a result, while we reverted into our shells. They deflated us by holding out our best shots and then kicked on and won. Then came the surprise loss at home to Wakefield and the adoption of a siege mentality as a result, as the critics piled into us. Again, we dominated for long periods but couldn't pull away, confidence began to wane and the Wildcats got on a roll and caught us with a sucker punch. We banked up the booing and vitriol; it was nasty and I was determined that, unlike the losses of the previous year at around the same time that destroyed our belief, we would not crumble into negativity. I really felt for Tony, which was an indication of how much I genuinely liked and admired him, and stressed to him that we all still believed. It's hard sometimes when you live in the city that you play for – not that I'd have it any other way – when people are in your face asking what's going wrong all the time, and the club is constantly major back-page news. The defeat galvanised us, made us tighter as a unit and it was the turning point for the team; we focused solely on what was ahead of us. It was equally responsible for us taking out the title as the victories at places like Knowsley Road and Bradford. After those sorts of high-profile, obvious matches, everyone said we might be champions but after the Wakefield setback, we knew we could be, if we dealt with the issues raised. We were fortunate that having gone out of the cup and having spare weekends, we could prepare for matches in concentrated three-week blocks and then get some proper recovery time.

Harlequins felt the backlash, in my fiftieth game for Leeds, as we posted more than a point a minute in a second-half blitz. It was an early kick-off in extreme heat but we were set. I like going to London; we stay over at a beautiful hotel near Twickenham right on the river and because it was so warm, everyone was outside on the terrace eating breakfast at half-past seven. I turned into 'The Matchstick'; my head goes bright red because I get sunburnt so quickly but the rest of my body is white and skinny. It was evident that day and we caught fire after the break. We lost Webby, twice, to the sin-bin for high tackles, which was strange, but I was pleased to get over for a try. I felt sorry for my mate Brian McDermott, the coach down there, but it was the ruthless attacking performance we needed. Matt Diskin was back, and it always makes such a difference to the shape of a side if you've got a specialist hooker in place. While there was some hysterical debate as to whether Brent should have been sent off for his double misdemeanours, the four-match ban that followed – which was then reduced to three – was just ridiculous. It was a joke and he was made an example of at a time when high tackles were being clamped down on. Then again, his absence only made us stronger mentally as a team. Webby was hugely influential and had a massive year but that was just another hurdle we were willing to overcome and the enforced rest didn't do him any harm either. He came back even stronger for when we needed him the most.

We took the pain of not being involved in the Challenge Cup final onto the training field. On the Friday before the showpiece game, we were back on the gruelling hills of Roundhay – like in pre-season – early in the morn-ing, upsetting the dog walkers and joggers with our retching and gipping. Everyone was into it no matter how much distress it caused; there was an edge, hunger and focus about the session that had been missing the year before. I went to Wembley on the Orient Express, a chartered trip for fans, along with Faye, Garreth Carvell and his missus. They were guests but I had to work that day, going up and down the train entertaining those who had booked corporate packages. It was fun though, and a great occasion. I was having a beer at ten a.m. but then you've got to; it's Wembley, that's the tradition of the pilgrimage. I could see a few people looking at me oddly and them thinking is that really the behaviour of a professional athlete but I raised my glass and toasted them. I told them I was upholding a long-held custom. I thought the stadium was outstanding and felt the tingle that I need to play there before my career is over. The occasion was made even more special when my mate Leon was made joint Man of the Match and was instrumental in his team winning. St Helens' success was also a good result for Leeds; not only would they be more tired because of the effort expended to eventually subdue Catalans Dragons, but capturing the cup does eat away a little at your desire, no matter how professional you are and especially now that the final has moved to later in the season. To me, it was another indication that things were moving in our favour and slowly fitting into place. I got to spend the day and watch the game with Tony and Brian Mac which was very enjoyable and on the way back availed myself of the hospitality available on the plush train to the full.

I shouldn't really have played at Bradford when Super League resumed as I was suffering from a chest infection but it turned out to be probably the best game I'd had for Leeds up to that point. Often, when I'm ill, it comes with a mindset, which is another indication of how important mental prep-aration is for games, especially among elite athletes, and I didn't want to let anyone down. Again, a major part of Bradford's plan was to target me and to run a lot of their plays at me, and they certainly did that night. It was just one of those occasions when you get in the zone and nothing was going to make me tire. It wasn't just that I topped the fifty-tackle mark, more that two or three of them were try-savers where the opposition must have been able to smell the whitewash of our try line. I was succeeding in doing the things Tony had taught me about defensive technique. That sort of improve-ment in my game was why I had thrown in my lot with the Rhinos. The whole team showed a real desire that would be needed to win the com-petition and, even though the Bulls secured a late draw, it was one of my proudest matches; I felt I'd helped keep us in the game.

We went down at home to Hull which cost us the League Leaders' Shield, but it was a match where we felt we had, to use the well-known sporting phrase, snatched defeat from the jaws of victory. Peter Sharp's men were desperate, they needed to win to secure top-four status and rescue their campaign having got to the Grand Final the year before. If there was solace for me, it was that the win took the pressure off my great mate Lee Radford who had kicked on and gone on to become skipper of his home-city club. Whatever my intense personal disappointment, I knew how much flak he had been copping and he was inspirational that night. He played without concern for personal wellbeing, set a proper captain's lead and I felt that they had won because the rest of his side had followed his example.

Tony was still looking at ways to keep the Leeds squad fresh and he arranged a squash session for us. I'd never played the sport before and it was brilliant and refreshing doing something different. At first I couldn't get the hang of it and kept missing the ball but as the games went on, so my coordination improved and I ended with a victory against Rob, although he may have been being a bit sympathetic towards the lumbering big lad. We did some innovative cross-training and probably the most productive work was learning wrestling with a champion, Tony Sykes, at a gym in Huddersfield. It was fantastic, the lads loved it; we're all into Ultimate Fighting Championship and we really got stuck into it. Those sessions were a big part of us staying strong and, ultimately, winning the big prize. Some of them got a bit tasty; there was evidence of gouging and other serious goings-on.

In the last round of the regular season, we had the perfect scenario; Wakefield – who had caused us such introspection – back at Headingley Carnegie. The match gave us the chance to right a wrong on the field, go into the play-offs on a high and restore the confidence of our more fickle fans, who we needed for the run-in to Old Trafford. We put the Wildcats to the sword and my own form was starting to improve significantly; I was getting some big metre gains. Thanks to the coaching staff, we were at our most focused – more ruthless on attack and strong defensively – to go into the post-season matches on a definite roll. It was nice to be included in the 'Dream Team' again, for the sixth time in eight seasons, which was a joint record, and there was widespread recognition for the side, not least Scottie Donald. He'd had a terrific year but didn't receive many mentions; those of us in the dressing room knew the value of his contribution. At the Leeds awards banquet at the Queens Hotel, there was more deserved applause when Jamie Jones-Buchanan, someone who I've got total respect for, was named our Player of the Year runner-up. He was immense and has worked tirelessly to better himself after his career could so easily have come to an end following some terrible injuries. He'd also become a picture editor's dream with his Captain Birdseye beard. It was an outstanding effort that showed the character of the man. We'd all made a pledge at the start of the campaign not to shave until we'd won four consecutive games but he was the only one to stick to it – and some. I tried to keep with up with him but Faye kicked off about it. The best I could get was a moustache; I'd grown one for a little while when I was younger, at Bradford, for some kind of bet but everybody gave me funny looks in the supermarket. The main Rhinos statuette went to another incredibly deserving recipient, Rob Burrow. I was made up for the pair of them; it was such a nice feeling that some good people were being accorded their due.

I was quoted in the run up to our first play-off game at St Helens that I could smell the time of year in the air. The weather was damper, the nights getting darker earlier and your mind and body tell you from past experience that the season's on the line. The mood in the dressing room was good and I was realistic enough to know, having been around a number of successful teams, that it wasn't just bravado. Players were talking about wanting to win with a real conviction. I'd been spoilt; I'd expected on joining Leeds to still be in the major finals and it hadn't materialised and my immense hunger was back. I geared myself up for the biggest domestic games of my life because I could see nothing ahead of me other than making the Grand Final and leaving with the trophy. It wasn't arrogance, just that the collective desire was so strong and we were building up this run to be special. We needed all our resolve when we travelled to Knowsley Road for the match that would provide the first Grand Finalist. It is still talked about as the most physical, if not brutal, game in Super League history. Even though we lost narrowly, the seeds for a fortnight later were sown. I had a big collision early on with Nick Fozzard, who I hit high, but I knew that I had to stand up to him. He'd had a tremendous year for Saints and we needed to make a statement. I took my inspiration from Kylie; he was running into the line with such ferocity and no respect for whether he was going to get hurt or not. That makes everyone else want to do likewise and I was following his lead as he slammed into their defence. The feeling was exactly the same as we'd had in the Bradford team of 2005 when we went on our irresistible surge to glory; it was raw courage. There was a period in the second half when Kylie and Gareth Ellis wrecked about half the St Helens side in one set and we were just clattering them. You have to give them credit for surviving and holding on to win narrowly but it was just the case that they were ahead when the music stopped. Even though it was such a demanding clash and although we felt that we had pushed ourselves as far as we possibly could, I still thought that we had something in reserve, while they didn't. I honestly believe that that game broke them. To win matches like that, you've got to take yourself to places that are scary, where you know there are going to be the highest pain levels and we wanted to be there and in that zone again. We were ready, as a team, to test ourselves to the limit. I'd felt the full force of Kiwi Test prop Jason Cayless, I was taking the ball up into their line with all my might and he absolutely clattered me. I might have been running towards our fans behind the posts but I could feel my teeth disappearing over the scoreboard in the opposite direction. It was revenge for me hitting Fozzard and I was steaming after the game because the two penalties I'd given away against him had cost us the game. There was a bit of psychology behind it, though, I knew that what I'd done would come in handy the next time we played them.

Before we could think about that, we had to come up with a performance to beat the one side that had troubled us all year, Wigan, in the elimination final. In the run-up to that match at Headingley Carnegie, rumours linking me with a move to Hull intensified. According to the websites, I was being measured up for a black-and-white shirt and the deal was done and dusted. It was probably because I speak to Radders a lot and two and two obviously made five, which seems to happen a lot where I'm concerned. It got to the stage that a few of the Leeds lads asked me if there was any truth in it. My reaction was unambiguous: 'I'm here and I'm here for good.' The day before the Warriors encounter, Rhinos Junior Academy coach John Bastian asked me if I would address his lads, who were playing in their Grand Final in the curtain raiser before us, at their last training session. I'd spoken to them at the beginning of the season about what was required to be a professional rugby player. I really wanted to do it, and was grateful to John – who is a smart coach – for the chance. It meant a lot to me, I felt that I'd been fully accepted as part of the Leeds set-up and that with my big-match experience, I could give them some pointers. Almost all of the boys listened intently and I could see that it really meant something to most of them – you are always going to get a couple who think they know it all already – and it seemed to be very well received. I was even more made up when they went on and won their title, especially as they were playing a St Helens side that had totally dominated the competition and had been top of the table all year by some way – except when it mattered the most.

Going into the match-up with Brian Noble's men, I was as nervous as I had been when making my Test debut. For the entire day of the game, I was edgy. During the first round of the play-offs, when we'd had the week off and the elimination ties were staged, I'd gone up to a hotel in Knaresborough with Faye to get away. Just my luck, it was full of Bradford fans at a wedding reception so I watched their match against Wigan with them. During the first half, in particular, they took great delight in giving me grief about what they were going to do to us. Then the Bulls got dramatically beaten in one of the most astonishing comebacks in knockout history. My amusement was tempered with the knowledge that it might be Wigan coming for us and, even though we'd played better than them, they'd beaten us on each of the three previous occasions we'd met them that year. That was why I felt wary and the Warrington match in the play-offs from the year before also played on my mind. If you get to a Grand Final, at least you've made the occasion and anything can happen; the game before is not the one you want to lose. Along with that crushing disappointment against the Wolves in 2006, the Wakefield clash where we had been roundly abused was still raw and upsetting. In the lead-up, I prowled round telling myself over and over again that our plans were not going to be upset and repeating, 'It's not going to be today'. I was nervous but also ultra-determined and I could see that in the others. Before we got changed, Tony had a quiet word and then Sinny stood up at the front and gave us the most inspirational speech I've ever heard or had from any captain in the 300-odd games I've played, and I've played under some of the greatest. The way he came across and the words he used were exceptional. He spoke about the effects if we lost, and especially to all those people around us who we cared for and looked after us. Most importantly, he challenged us as to what it meant to each of us in that room. It was fantastic and the side of things people don't get to see. I was nearly in tears at the end of it and on the perfect emotional edge going into the game.

Although it took a few days to get over the scars of the Saints carnage – I'd struggled to even lift Lewis three days afterwards – my body was battle hardened and I knew that I still had two huge efforts within me. I was pushing the boundaries of how many times I could carry the ball, setting new personal standards and I was ready to do it again against Wigan. That was manifested in the first meaningful move. I pride myself running round the middle and our game plan was set up for testing them out in that area. It suited me down to the ground and I wasn't going to die for lack of trying; I wanted the ball in my hands as often as possible. A quarter of an hour in, after they'd kicked deep to us, I got back to try and make quick ground. I split them through the centre, Webby was at the side of me and the rest was history; his try was a fantastic feeling. We knew that we were going to win but sometimes things that should go your way don't and that small percentage of doubt drove us on. Our completion rate in the first half showed just how focused we were – it was an unprecedented hundred per cent. The concentration was total and even the little things like awkward offloads were caught. We weren't far off repeating that stat in the second period and we put the final piece to our jigsaw with a confidence-infusing attacking performance that yielded seven tries to go with our defensive steel. The coaching staff had led us the right way and our belief in each other, and what we could do, was total by that stage. To win the ultimate, you have to essentially become brothers and that transformation had happened over an eight-week period.

I was excited at the press conference on the Monday at Old Trafford to build up the Grand Final. I'd not been there the year before and there was a renewed spring in my step because up until then it had become second nature. I was back being the kid in the sweet shop, thinking this is the place to be and wanting to make it special again. One of the reasons Leeds wanted me was for my experience of those sorts of occasions and the ground had become something of a second home. I'd played there a lot and understood what it took to win there, so I was comfortable with the set-up. One of the reasons we fulfilled our aim was changing our routine to make the occasion feel unique and that much more special. On the day before the game, on the way to what was to become our never-to-be-forgotten team meeting, we called in at Manchester United's ground so that everyone could experience it. I didn't particularly want another trip but I knew how important that was to the team. After that it took a while to get to the Worsley Marriott but it was well worth it; they always look after rugby league players and teams. There was a confident manner to the boys and an electric feeling in the air. If we needed a further gee-up, it came with the announcement that Sinny had signed a new four-year deal on the eve of the game.

For me, channelled emotion is a vital ingredient for being successful in the highest-profile games. I was speaking to some of the lads in the run-up saying that they shouldn't be thinking about the game all the time but they needed to spend five or ten minutes concentrating on being out there, what they would be doing in that arena and building up the emotional reasons as to why they wanted to win. You can't just block off emotion and pretend it doesn't affect sport; you have to use it instead to your best advantage. That was the basis behind Tony calling us together on the night before the action, to bring us even closer. He'd told us on the Thursday, and advised us that we had to bring to the table what winning the Grand Final would mean to each of us, so the rest would know our innermost motivations. Tony started the discussion off by saying: 'I want to win it for you guys. I've seen how much you've improved, what shit you've taken and I want it to be special for you because of the amount of effort you've put in.' His remarks were particularly aimed at Gaz Ellis, he told him that he'd promised, when he signed him in 2005, that one of the reasons for coming to Leeds was so he could win things. Gaz couldn't have done any more to help that process but had so far come up empty handed and this was their last chance together. I was on the cusp of welling up, which was heightened as Carl Ablett related how his career looked in jeopardy but in the space of ten games he was set to play in his greatest match. Likewise, Ian Kirke said that he couldn't believe that a couple of years before he was trying to make his way in a York side that was struggling to win a game and now here he was on the edge of glory. It got worse as Keith Senior spoke passionately and lovingly about his daughter and Sinny said he wanted to do it for his son and those very close to him. When it came round to me towards the end, I was trying not to choke up. I knew I couldn't break down, not there.

My reason was a different one again. I always feel that you take a little bit of the spirit of all the blokes you've played with out on to the field. I had the essence of those I'd been with at Bradford and who had then retired as part of my composite make-up. There were some special people among them and I like to think that while I'm out there, I'm also doing it for those who have guided and influenced me. My thoughts and motivations went back to 2002 when I was in a side that was beaten by St Helens, by a drop goal. Some of the people who meant the most to me never got to put that right against Saints in a final. They were Bradford's nemesis when it came to silverware. I told the assembled gang that I wanted to win for myself and what it meant to me to be representing Leeds; for those blokes in the room with me but also for the ones who had always lost out to the men from Merseyside. I was now lucky enough to have the chance to right their wrong, having waited five years to play in a team that I knew was good enough to finally put that to rest on the biggest stage. I went on to explain how that current Leeds squad was similarly part of my spirit now, something I hadn't felt the previous year when I had taken the field with them, and that I knew we could do it.

Jonesy was one of the last to speak and his deep-seated desire was down to his ultra-competitive nature. He could have been picked on and a target as a youngster but went the other way and victory in a Grand Final was, again, his way of making a statement about standing up for yourself. When we broke the meeting up, my immediate thought was: 'Fuck me, Saints are going to have dig incredibly deep to beat us.'

The announcement of the death of Leeds great Jeff Stevenson on the morning of the match brought home my notions of transferring history. Although the Leeds shirt was mine for the day, he had honoured and graced it in the 1950s – it was almost exactly fifty years since he'd become the first Loiner to win a Man of the Match award in a final – and wearing a black armband to remember him really meant something to the class of 2007. What was not so appreciated were the predictions of another former Leeds great, Garry Schofield, who reckoned in the papers on the morning of the game that Saints would win by eighteen points. He'd spent a fair amount of the campaign bagging the players and coach; that's what he's paid to do unfortunately, but things like that – and any other criticism from the outside – was not going to have the slightest effect. Teams that win Grand Finals are those that feel as one.

We were on the up and Saints were coming off the back of a long season, which now saw them having fitness doubts over two key players, Sean Long and Maurie Fa'asavalu, in the lead-up to the game. Our dressing room was tight and we warmed up sharp and well, everyone fired into it and by then our drills were of shorter duration anyway. Another key battle was won in the tunnel. You line up alongside your opponents for around three minutes while the pre-match show ends and the military personnel symbolically parade out the trophy for the teams to run past. It's pretty quiet while you're waiting in there although you can feel the mounting energy and intensity. I was standing second in line behind Kev and with Nick Fozzard at the side of me. I could feel him looking at me and wanting to say something but my focus was straight ahead; I wasn't going to engage him and bearing in mind we were at the head of our respective teams it was vital to set the correct example. After a while of not responding, he tapped me on the shoulder and said: 'You're going to give a penalty away for head-tackling me tonight.' My only reply, without looking over, was to say: 'We'll see mate, we'll see.' I knew from that moment on that we were going to win. Fozz is a bit of a strange character anyway, but the fact that he had broken the silence said everything.

Although he wasn't fully fit, Longy showed in the early stages what a class player he is and was stringing us about with his kicks and orchestrating the game. Surprisingly though, he missed an early penalty shot. Psychologically, that might have been important to them but we felt that our resolve was the greater. Sinny didn't miss with his first shot and both sides defied the usual Grand Final fare by coming up with tries of stunning quality. They showed why we were the best two teams in the competition. There was nothing between us in a quality first period but there were significant differences as the hooter went to end it. Normally, as Tony likes us to do, we get together and run into the dressing room and I was shouting at the boys to get in there. Then I changed my mind and said: 'Forget that, let's just look at them.' Leon and Paul Wellens – who, for me, are their two warriors – were trying to pump the Saints boys up but we could see that they'd gone; the season and that first forty had taken its toll. The way they'd played in the first half-hour showed why they'd been on such a terrific trophy run and would have overwhelmed most other sides, a fact that was largely forgotten in the aftermath when analysts just looked at the final score. It needed Leeds' greatest ever performance in a final to beat them.

Two exceptional tries in as many minutes at the start of the second half were the basis of it. Ali Lauitiiti started playing like he knew he should towards the end of the season and was sensational for us. I'd always thought he was the most difficult second-rower I'd ever had to play against and he was clearly enjoying his rugby in the last two months of the campaign. He's a world-class player and the try he came up with, holding off Matt Gidley, no one else in the world could have scored. Scott's touchdown showed just how good a side we were. We won by a huge collective effort; we were prepared to go to the darkest places, which are the most enjoyable to return from when you get to the end of the game – we also had the moments of genius. Ali and Scott came up with two truly inspirational plays and Lee Smith's leap later on wasn't far behind; it was sensational execution. We knew we'd won when Rob dropped a goal straight after Scott's effort with twenty-five minutes left and we had the perfect swansong when Jonesy crossed. I was so made up for him. He is 'Mister Leeds', he lives and breathes the club and the city. For him to top it off in such a manner was unbelievable and so apt.

I played for the full eighty minutes. Tony built up the game time I was allowed to play throughout the year and for the last three matches he left me out there for the entire match. I pride myself on working hard and even I couldn't believe my stats afterwards. If that is an accepted measure, then it was my greatest performance, although that's hard for me to judge. It was just so satisfying to test myself in the middle, in an emotionally draining Grand Final against such a fantastic side and come up with that kind of effort. It was the pinnacle of my domestic career, a performance that had been ten years in the making. When the match ended it felt truly amazing; there was a rush of competing thoughts: it was my home club; we'd proved countless people wrong and come up with an almost surreal display to beat a fantastic team. I was asked to go up first to collect my winner's ring, which is always a pleasure, although I was absolutely exhausted by the realisation of the achievement and what it had taken to get it. Our joy was summed up by Gaz Ellis, who had to go up twice to get his reward. The best feeling at the end is hugging your teammates and he was so excited by it all that he went up, shook hands, forgot to collect his box and had to run round and be presented again. He was incredibly emotional and deservedly so. It's always a bit disappointing that they don't allow you to take your kids on the lap of honour with you, I'd have loved Lewis to have been out there but it was just such a fantastic feeling anyway. It should never be forgotten how the Rhinos fans had been absolutely magnificent and to see their unrestrained joy added to ours. I'd broken the Saints hoodoo and, bizarrely, maintained my winning run in odd years at Old Trafford going back to 2001, which was weird.

I'd not had a drink for six weeks and the celebrations were unbelievable. We had a few beers on the Saturday night and met up again at Trio's in Headingley the next day before going to the ground for the official photo shoot and homecoming. That was amazing to be among thousands of jubilant fans and with my family there. Lewis was out on the stage in the middle of the field for that and I gave him my winner's ring as a belated third birthday present. We were back in the pubs of Headingley afterwards but had to keep something in reserve for 'Mad Monday'. I'd arranged it would be fancy dress and we settled on parading round as chavs. It was a tremendous day, even though they didn't seem too keen to let us in to a few places. We ended up at Woodies on Otley Road and they were fantastic, really looked after us and we had a fitting celebration. Jamie Thackray was unbelievable on the karaoke. I tried to get hold of Garry Schofield to tell him that the boys were about and, if he hadn't heard, we'd won the title. Fortunately, for him, the phone number I was given didn't work.

The curtain came down on Tony Smith's Leeds career, which was a card that neither he nor the squad had played on in the run-up to the Grand Final, although it was mentioned a lot and tributes were paid in the aftermath. He left Leeds as their greatest-ever coach and one of the most influential in Super League; he was a trailblazer. To go out at the top at club level the way he did spoke volumes. Having got to know him I now regard him as a genius both in and out of a tracksuit. All you can ask of someone is honesty and he was straight down the line, all the time. It was a fitting end to his Leeds career and, for all those who spat at him, you often don't know how good something is until it's gone.

FIFTEEN

A FITTING CLIMAX

Tony Smith had no time to really commemorate his achievements with the Rhinos, he was straight onto his new job as the national coach and a match that commemorated a hundred years of touring. A re-creation of the 'Northern Union' made up of predominantly fringe Great Britain players played the 'All Golds' who were New Zealand's equivalent, in a prelude to the Gillette Fusion Tests. I was rested and Adrian Morley again given the captaincy. Tony hadn't said anything about who his international skipper was going to be for the three-match series and I wasn't sure which way it was going to go. I felt my form was good but Moz did a really good job and, for me, he was the best on the field for the home side. The day after, on the Sunday, Tony rang me to tell me I'd got the nod. I was in church, at Lewis' christening at the time, and my phone was on silent. I went outside to call him back and was absolutely elated by the news. I spoke to Moz, who was named as vice-captain, and he had no problems about me resuming my duties. By then, I'd featured in the merchandising brochure for replica kit and souvenirs and on the promotional posters, although one of the first shots I'd posed for wasn't used. The design agency decided that my head should be morphed into that of a lion so I had to scream, shout and roar in front of them which was excruciatingly embarrassing. I called on all my dramatic experience from Intake High but I don't think that Robert De Niro or Sean Bean would have been too worried.

The British squad contained some new names, two in particular receiving the bulk of the attention. Teenager Sam Burgess was pretty awesome on his 'Northern Union' debut; you can tell the sign of a classy player when they step up a level and look comfortable doing so. He'd been good all year for Bradford, in numerous positions, and in camp he was confident and adapted quickly to the Great Britain mentality. His call-up was less controversial than that of Samoan Maurie Fa'asavalu. I'd heard rumours throughout the year that he might be included and was pleased. Sometimes we can be too traditionalist and inward-looking and the truth is that this country has changed and is continuing to do so. Rugby league has to move with it, like every other sport has. In our code, Australia and New Zealand have welcomed whatever talent is available to them under the qualification strictures. We are a multicultural society and speaking to Maurie sportingly, at least, he has totally pledged himself to Great Britain ahead of any other nation. Pertinently, he has played all of his rugby league over here. He wants to perform at the highest level open to him and I was glad that I would have his explosive power alongside me rather than having to worry about how to stop him. He'd shown throughout the year what a devastating player he could be coming off the bench for St Helens and that was going to enhance our stock. The same debate had been thrown up over Tony's appointment and sometimes the arguments against can border on racism. The fact of the matter is that they both have access to British passports. I don't think than anyone can really question Tony's commitment now he has applied for British nationality.

Going into camp is vital for breaking down barriers and that was important for the new coaching staff which also included Steve McNamara and Jimmy Lowes, who I was particularly keen to link up with again. Getting together initially is a bit like going to a friend's party; you might know a few people to start with but often it's a bit quiet and those who are normally the more extrovert need time to find an audience. Having come off such an impassioned run to the Super League crown, I had the extra edge and incentive I needed for the Kiwis because I knew that the series was likely to be my last in a Great Britain shirt. With a World Cup on the horizon for the home nations and the encounters here from now on being under the guise of England, the GB name was only going to be resurrected every four years for genuine Lions tours. We wanted to end the season well, impress the new coach and, for those of us who had yet to take a series in the red, white and blue, to pass on the shirt in the best possible way. It was about time to come up with some better results to match the pride. The senior players were consulted by a marketing agency working on behalf of the RFL about the restructuring and we were all adamant that there still had to be a place for the British jersey. It was a very good meeting with them and we certainly got our points across that it shouldn't be retired. Now that it is there specifically for touring, it's going to be extra special to wear it and that is exactly how it should be.

Interest in the series was sparked before the First Test when Adrian Morley was cited for a head-high tackle in the Northern Union game but not given a ban when the judiciary met. NZRL chairman Andrew Chalmers added to the fire by calling Moz a maniac but that only applied to the poker table where he raises and bluffs too much. It was a foolish thing to say and I know Moz noted it. In the build-up to each match, and after such an arduous campaign, Tony made sure that our interest levels were maintained by introducing some innovative training sessions. Before the first Test we trained with the GB women's netball team at a school in Leeds, which was good. It was set up through Tony's wife, Lisa, who plays the sport and it was great to try something different as part of some smart preparation in limited time. Smithy also changed the camp arrangements. Normally, with Tests in this country, we were together Monday to Thursday and then sent back to our own beds but with the World Cup looming he reversed that to get us more familiar with not having our usual comforts before the day of the game.

We were a bit rusty in the opening Test at Huddersfield but that was not helped by Kevin Sinfield's late, enforced withdrawal. I'd had word, as captain, on the Saturday morning that he'd pulled up sick and when I spoke to him he said he was going to try and get through it. Mid-morning we went for a team stroll and when I turned round he was a hundred yards behind us spewing into the gutter. He'd had such a good season, now had someone at the helm internationally who really valued his contribution and had been selected in his proper position at loose-forward. Missing out was incredibly disappointing; I really felt for him that his opportunity had been taken away, through no fault of his own. Sean O'Loughlin came in and I'd enjoyed playing alongside him in Oz the year before. He's a quiet lad but a special talent and he took his chance well. The Kiwis arrived on the back of a massive home loss to the Kangaroos but I felt that only made them more dangerous first up. When I saw the margin I knew it would make our job harder because of their inherent pride. There was also the fact that we would be less prepared than them.

One of the big battles was between Sam, on his debut, and Fui Fui Moi Moi. He was supposedly the Kiwis' hardman although he spent a lot of his time stood behind the ruck with his hands on his hips looking for breath.

Sam fronted him up and the man with one of the best names in the game quickly found out how hard the young Bull could hit. Maurie came on and made a huge impression. His first carry was massive and then he came up with the try that we needed. It was a big moment for us and it was what he came into the team to do alongside his two colleagues from Saints, James Roby and James Graham. They'd all perfected the art of changing games from the bench. I was looking forward to that being a new aspect and tactic for us and wasn't disappointed. In the second half, Gareth Raynor produced his speciality by chasing down a seemingly lost cause to turn Rob Burrow's inch-perfect kick into a try. It's something of a speciality of his. We'd been denied a couple of opportunities and I was starting to feel that things might not be going our way when Gareth struck. It was unfortunate for Sam Perrett who misjudged it, and had had a good game up to that point, but Gareth's spirit is what it's all about and he saved our arse again with a great effort. Although we'd scored three touchdowns each, goal kicking won the day for us. In another innovation from the coaching staff, Tony allowed the Press into the dressing room straight after the game, which we were in agreement with. We should have a closer working relationship with them and that's something which happens in Australia and in American Football. It helps them see another side of us.

Kev's illness struck me in the build-up to the Second Test a week later. I'd felt poorly on the morning of the opening game but kept it to myself. After it, we played a few hands of cards in the hotel for a bit but when I retired to my room, it was my turn to test the plumbing to the full. I tried to sleep but couldn't and drove home at about three in the morning. I spent the next couple of days properly throwing my guts up so missed out on the next team-building exercise in the Yorkshire Dales. Things improved from midweek and I reverted back to prop from second-row for the match at Hull, to give Sam Burgess a break. Going into it, I knew that I'd have to focus really hard to make up for the missed days' training and not to give in to inevitable, mounting fatigue. Tony again stamped his mark on the side by dropping Terry Newton, which was not something other British coaches might have done. He said he would pick solely on form and not reputation, and that's one of the things that endears him to his players. You need to perform to play and that decision set a marker for the World Cup. I felt for Tez but Jon Clarke came in and was excellent on his debut. He'd been outstanding during the season as Warrington struggled and had got one of my votes for the Players'

Association 'Player of the Year'. I felt increasingly comfortable in the Great Britain set-up, I'd known everyone in it for a while and with six Rhinos in the side – including Sinny, who was back – things were a lot tighter. There was more of a club atmosphere and that showed in our performance at the KC Stadium.

We got off to a terrific start and I managed to get over for the first score before the New Zealanders had even touched the ball. Moz did what all props are aiming for; took a great carry up and got a quick play-the-ball away which, for once, I got on the back of. I beat a couple of markers and then thought: 'Right, I'm having a go here.' I managed to bump off a couple more Kiwis as I went wider before taking two others over with me for the try. It was one of the greatest touchdowns I've scored. We knew the Kiwis would come out really big and, as captain, you've got to set the right lead in response. All the New Zealanders had a go but we were just too good for them. We were clinical, patient and Leon and Rob at half-back totally dictated matters. It was a fantastic performance from everyone and was summed up by Paul Wellens' try-saving tackle on the huge winger Taniela Tuiaki. He made it when we were already over thirty points ahead. He didn't have to do that; Wello's not that big and the guy he was facing was over eighteen stone but there was no hint of self-preservation. Total courage saw Wello hit him with everything he had, which jarred the ball loose and that's the kind of commitment we'll need if we are to do well in the World Cup. The seven tries illustrated our flair but to nil the Kiwis was exceptional, especially to win a series. To stop any side from scoring is near-impossible but they had a varied array of attacking options and to keep them out was special.

I'd never been in that position with Great Britain in the dressing room afterwards and it was a magnificent feeling. We said before the game that we had the perfect chance to prevent the series going to a decider and that we knew we could put in a better performance than the week before, and we did it. Everyone rose to the occasion superbly and to play well personally in the midst of that team performance and combine it with doing something the national side hadn't for fourteen years was just incredible. Some tried to detract from the success by claiming that the opposition had been understrength but games are not played on paper. All of their squad were acknowledged performers in either the NRL or Super League and what was forgotten was that we had lost a host of top-line combatants, either through injury or retirement. Not enough credit was paid to the fact that we'd transformed ourselves without the likes of Andy Farrell, Keiron

Cunningham, Iestyn Harris, Sean Long, Kris Radlinski, Brian Carney, Paul Sculthorpe and Stu Fielden. All of these guys were senior caps who were missing and we'd had to rely on them in the past to pull out big performances. We'd filled those gaps and got on with playing. No one moaned about it, we just proved the quality of the talent coming through in Super League. For the Kiwis to focus on their missing troops was damage limitation. The last time we'd played them in a must-win game, over there a year before, they'd beaten us by a similarly convincing scoreline, which made the victory even sweeter.

Moving into the third week, we were in unchartered territory. We had a great trip to British Aerospace to see the Eurojet Fighter and I got to meet pilot Damian Clayton who was instrumental in setting up rugby league in the RAF and Combined Services, after it had initially been banned. Psychologically, for once, we weren't chasing a series or trying to come to terms with one that had already passed us by and we were relaxed as a result, knowing that we could arrange a genuine celebration with the wives and partners afterwards. There was still a major goal to achieve; we were desperate to send the shirt into temporary retirement with a whitewash. Tony had been round a few of us who'd played the most throughout the year and asked if we wanted to be rested. The answer he got was a resolute no. We'd suffered some bad times wearing the colours and been involved with them a long time. I wanted to put it to bed in an appropriate manner for what it meant to us. Maybe that was a bit selfish but we'd earned the right. I was desperate to accept the Baskiville Shield in the sweat and muck of having been out there rather than in a nice, clean suit, no matter how punishing the overall schedule. The body was definitely creaking but sometimes you can get your heart and mind to take it to places it doesn't want to go.

We had to win in a different style in the Third Test at Wigan, coming from behind, which will stand us in good stead for what's ahead in Australia come the autumn of 2008. I tried to get the message over to a number of the younger lads just what the occasion meant to some of us out there. I was desperate to make the previous legends who had represented their country proud of our achievements. I spoke again about how we were just borrowing history and that in my position at prop, I was conscious that the likes of Andy Platt and Kevin Ward had been my predecessors and heroes of mine as a kid. I stressed that whoever they'd looked up to, the same applied and that there was a new, young generation out there looking at them now in the same light. We had to treat what that signified in the right way. I wanted to capture the sense of legacy and make the point a win was vital because of it. It obviously had the desired effect because after twelve minutes we were as many points down. We were taking some calculated risks but they weren't coming off. I thought I'd got Martin Gleeson away because Tony wants me to pass more often, but it was ruled forward. We gave them two tries to start with but ground our way back into the game and defended a lot better in the second half. Two scores just before the break to snatch the lead showed our desire, with James Graham coming off the bench to play a crucial part with a superb, belligerent score. The Kiwis dominated possession for the opening twenty minutes, the referee seemed to want to penalise us to death for the opening thirty-five, but then Jammer came on and turned it round with his barnstorming charge. I was pleased for him because he'd missed out the year before through an unfortunate injury. Rob Burrow was again sensational and fully justified his George Smith Medal for Man of the Series to go with his Grand Final and club haul. There's so much more to him than just his stature. He is a remarkably good half-back who can score tries out of nowhere; a sensational tackler who is has no respect of size; has learned how to organise a team to get them effectively around the park and he can kick. His heart is bigger than his head and he has no fear whatsoever. Off the field, he's such a nice guy and I'm just so glad he got his opportunity with Great Britain. The same was true for Jonesy who made his debut in the last match. For me that was really important. Three years previously he was seriously thinking about having to give up the game because of a run of serious groin injuries but he'd shown remarkable perseverance to get where he was. It was another member of the Stanningley mafia who'd now represented Great Britain at the highest level.

The series whitewash meant that we'd achieved another of our targets, of overtaking the Kiwis to become the second-ranked nation. We were also collecting silverware on the back of a victory which made it even more special. Knowing that I would have the supreme honour of going up there to collect the shield on behalf of a near-generation, it was a moment that needed to be truly savoured and shared. Moz had been an international since 1996 and was unbelievably passionate about playing for his country. The fact that he'd done so well over in the Australian domestic game was a catalyst for our international improvement. He blew the myth open that the Aussies were invincible and had been captain before. I asked him as we lined up awaiting the presentations if he'd like to come up with me to collect the trophy and he bit my hand off. I think it was the right thing to do and showed the rest of the world that we were together, and that the success, after so long, wasn't just about one person. We'd had some bad memories together and now deserved to share the good ones. To me lifting trophies is just the icing on the cake, the nice stuff; I enjoy the other responsibilities that go with being a captain in a team sport. I wouldn't have been up there if Adrian hadn't supported me, especially after leading the side in the first two representative matches of the year when I hadn't played. The subsequent way he took my return to the duties on the chin was the mark of a top man. In an ideal world, if you could, you'd have everybody lifting the reward up there together because they all contribute. I almost asked Keith Senior to come up with us as well; he'd been around the international ranks as long as Moz but three's a crowd.

Among the previous GB skippers of the modern era were genuine icons of the sport: Ellery Hanley, Garry Schofield, Mike Gregory, Andy Farrell and Paul Sculthorpe. Every one of them had carried with them the expectation from the age of fifteen or sixteen that they would lead their country. I'm different from them because I never had that. At that age, I wasn't even playing the game and I hadn't even made the Bradford first team by the time they were leading out the national side. I'm just thankful for the input of everybody who helped me achieve such a status; hopefully, lifting that trophy was recognition for their hard work and help along the way. It's never a solo journey.

SIXTEEN

NO END IN SIGHT

In the middle of December 2007, after the end of my best and most satisfy-ing season, I turned thirty. For the first time, at the end of a professional campaign, there was no bitter taste that might have tainted the sweetness. The grin that was etched on my face at the end of the Gillette Fusion series success lasted a full week. It was topped up by again being voted the 'International Forward of the Year' for the second successive season and runner-up in the 'Golden Boot' for the world's best player. They were both massive honours that indicate consistency, that I'm playing as well as I can and relishing and responding to the new demands put in front of me. Over the final three months of the season, the family understands how much of my concentration is on matters rugby league. It's not to the same extent that it was in 2005 but it was good to get back to a sense of normality with them and we enjoyed a week abroad in the sun followed by a weekend at Center Parcs with friends. It was a contrasting relief, away from the on-field pressures and ceaseless round of interviews. It would be easy to draw a line under the achievements and landmark age and feel self-satisfied but there are new challenges on the horizon that look as though they will be equally, if not more, exciting. Being the kind of person I am, 2007 is not a year to dwell on despite the glory; it is just a stepping stone to another level of achievement. Chronologically, I've turned into a new decade but biologi-cally I feel a lot younger than that, especially after resting up.

Meeting Russell Crowe and the side he part owns, South Sydney, in Jacksonville Florida, and then playing the Rabbitohs in a full-on trial game whetted the early appetite for 2008. The link-up between the clubs is another innovative idea from Leeds and holds great potential for swapping techniques and methods and staying at the forefront of innovation in the sport. Then, there's Melbourne Storm in the World Club Challenge at a packed Elland Road; so the season will begin with club competition at international level and end with a World Cup for England. Hopefully, I can maintain my form and lead the guys Down Under, which will see my wheel come full circle. I went into the last global tournament in 2000 as a virtual unknown and finished it with a bit of a reputation that really started this story. Now, if selected, I'll be one of the leaders in the squad and it's a measure of how the sport is progressing that for the first time for thirty years it will be staged in the southern hemisphere. There is a renewed confidence in the competitiveness of the fare on the field and with the ever-increasing numbers watching it at grounds and on the television on both sides of the world. The profile of rugby league is high, witnessed by the northern hemisphere World Cup launch at the prestigious Hilton hotel in Leeds while the Test series with the Kiwis was on. I was fortunate enough to be asked to represent England at the opulent gathering and there was a massive sense that things were being taken very seriously. The Aussies can organise an event – witness the Olympics in 2000 – and perhaps we've been forced into holding a global contest by the success of those in other sports but nonetheless it should be a career pinnacle for everyone selected. It's going to be a tough six weeks out there playing the leading nations, but I just can't wait and it will be like a light on in the background throughout Super League XIII. The harder the task, the sweeter the success.

At the Rhinos we enter a new era with Brian McClennan at the helm. I've been fortunate in my career that at Bradford all my coaches were people that I knew – promotions were internal – and when I came to Leeds, Tony Smith was from the same school and background where the primary influence is his elder brother. This is the first time I'm going to be working under someone who has come from outside that circle and is a disciple of an alternative system. All those who have been under him say only good things. Such differences of style, approach and what is expected from you keep you fresh and eager to impress, no matter what your perceived status in the game.

Once back from holiday, before I was required to get to work in the tortuous Leeds pre-season regime, I began a course that started me on the road to the next phase of my life, in the code I so passionately love. I might be the skipper of my country, but I'm not going to earn enough money through playing rugby league to live a life of leisure when I hang up the boots and I want, and need, to work when the playing days do eventually come to an end. Maybe my reputation will get me a job in sport but it is knowledge and qualifications that will help keep me in one. I've set the next ball rolling through Premier Training's 'Conversion to Learning' scheme which was fixed up by the players' union. Fitness and conditioning is a side of rugby I enjoy and the study of it has been particularly interesting. The tutor, Alan Smith, has been good and the course, a three-level diploma in physical training, has already shown me some great theories and insights. It's been different and highly stimulating exercising the brain again in the classroom environment, with students outside of the league fraternity.

I've been pretty lucky, despite the high-impact nature of rugby, to play around thirty matches every season since going full-time but there is a genetic factor behind that. Some players have innate hand-eye coordination and vision but my body just seems to be programmed to put up with discomfort. I've played injured a lot of times and a physio once told me I had a very high pain threshold. Rarely do you take the field fully fit; you probably aim for between ninety and ninety-five per cent, which is why rest is so important and there is a constant debate about how the fixture list should be structured to take that into account. No one likes to lose in the Challenge Cup but, because it takes up to two weeks to properly recover from a match, if you do go out in the earlier rounds then the benefit is that you get a better chance to refresh. When I speak to footballers, they claim that they don't take the field unless they are totally fit, which I guess is understandable. It is so hard to get to their top level because of the numbers who play the game that you don't want to jeopardise your position when you finally get there by underperforming. In rugby league, you've just got to get on with it and work through it.

I grew up as a rugby and football fan; Leeds is that kind of a city, although I have become somewhat disillusioned with soccer players as potential role models. The game is everywhere, and kids, like my own young son, can't fail to be drawn to it. One of the main strengths of rugby league is that it hasn't lost touch with the close-knit communities that formed it, and it never should – that is its core strength, which cannot be said for the round-ball game. Although it's not the players' fault, the money involved has detached them from the general public, the reality and normality of everyday life. For me, what's more important is that some of their behaviour on the field is not honest. It may have come from abroad but trying to cheat to win penalties, for example, sends out the wrong message about value systems and doing right by your fellow professionals. The behaviour of some high-profile players legitimises diving, play acting and trying to get your opponents sent off by underhand means and teaches kids that lying is a fair part of society. The likes of John Terry, Wayne Rooney and Ryan Giggs don't seem to subscribe to that and they're the ones I admire rather than, say, Cristiano Ronaldo, whose disgusting gamesmanship made me sick in the last soccer World Cup. Nevertheless, children still wear the named shirts and think that it's the right way to win. It starts with the governing body of the game; they've got to have a real will to stamp such behaviour out. League players have more in common with boxers and, now, the Ultimate Fighting Champions, not just in terms of collisions but in the laying down of physical challenges to try and overcome the guy in front of you, rather than backing away from them.

I've got an enthusiasm, willingness to learn and to do the right thing, and a determination not to be beaten. If you are doing those things well, I reckon the other good stuff will come, in life as well as rugby. I'm fortunate that the way I've been brought up by my parents and the genes I've inherited have enabled me to come through setbacks – many of which I've inflicted on myself – shining. I'm also forever indebted to the senior players and coaching staffs that have been around, educated and protected me. My story is a tribute to their selflessness.

CAREER STATISTICS

Born: 14 December 1977

Junior club: Stanningley ARL

Professional clubs: Bradford Bulls 1996–2005; Featherstone Rovers (on loan) 1998; Leeds Rhinos 2006–present

Senior debut: Substitute for Featherstone Rovers *v.* Widnes (H) 26 July 1998

Year	Club	App	Sub	Tries	Goals	DG	Points
1998	Featherstone Rovers	2	2	1	0	0	4
1999	Bradford Bulls	2	16	6	0	0	24
2000		23	12	9	0	0	36
2001		31	0	8	0	0	32
2002		30	0	1	0	0	4
2003		28	0	4	0	0	16
2004		32	0	4	0	0	16
2005		33	0	10	0	0	40
2006	Leeds Rhinos	29	0	3	0	0	12
2007		28	1	2	0	0	8

Totals

Team	App	Sub	Tries	Goals	DG	Points
Featherstone Rovers	2	2	1	0	0	4
Bradford Bulls	179	28	42	0	0	168
Leeds Rhinos	57	1	5	0	0	20
Great Britain	23	3	4	0	0	16
England	3	2	7	0	0	28
Yorkshire	4	0	0	0	0	0
Grand totals	268	36	59	0	0	236

Honours

Challenge Cup: Winner 2000, 2003; Runner-up 2001

Super League Grand Final: Winner 2001, 2003, 2005, 2007; Runner-up 2002, 2004

World Club Challenge: Winner 2002, 2004

Baskiville Trophy: Winner 2002, 2007

Great Britain captain (2005–2007) on eleven occasions; joint-seventh highest in history (with Jonty Parkin)

Super League 'Man of Steel', 2003

Rugby League Professional Players' Association Player of the Year, 2003

World XIII: 2005, 2006, 2007

International Forward of the Year: 2006, 2007

Super League Dream Team: 2000, 2001, 2002, 2003, 2005, 2007

Opta Stats Super League Team of the Year: 2001, 2002, 2003, 2005, 2006, 2007

Rugby League Writers' Association Player of the Year: 2003

Parliamentary All-Party Rugby League Group Player of the Year: 2007

(To the end of the 2007 season)